THE LOYALTY OF FREE MEN

ALAN BARTH

The Loyalty of Free Men

FOREWORD BY

ZECHARIAH CHAFEE, Jr.

1951

THE VIKING PRESS · NEW YORK

For

Adrienne

CONTENTS

FOREWORD

By Zechariah Chafee, Jr.

Mr. Barth's book is important for at least two reasons.

First, he gives us (especially in Chapters I and X) a fresh and persuasive presentation of the strongest arguments for the determined maintenance of freedom of thought and speech in a self-governing country like ours. Milton and Mill were great in their time, but our age badly needs to learn anew the indispensable values of liberty of opinion by hearing them stated in its own language and in the context of familiar facts. That is what Mr. Barth does. These pages are full of wise and quotable sentences: "The government of a free people must take certain chances for the sake of maintaining freedom which the government of a police state avoids because it holds freedom to be of no value." "Tolerance of diversity is imperative, because without it life would lose its savor. . . . The totalitarian . . . society . . . is stultifying and degrading to the human beings who live in it. Freedom gives a release to the human spirit, provides the indispensable condition for the realization of its limitless possibilities."

Second, Mr. Barth tells us what has been going on. A sort of war correspondent at the heart of the battle in Washington, he recounts the outstanding events in the rapid retreat of Jefferson's ideal that the only right way to combat bad opinions is by good opinions and not by punishments. "Tolerance of diversity and faith in the democratic process are giving way to the reliance on the quarantine of hostile doctrines." "The techniques of freedom have kept us safe and made us strong. To forsake them now is to forsake the most vital element of national defense." But we are forsaking them, and doing so much faster than citizens can realize from their ordinary sources of information. To understand what has been happening, one needed to run hither and thither, and read scores of scattered materials—press accounts of legislative hearings, reports of committees, minutes of university trustees, unpublished records of loyalty hearings, debates in Congress. This is a prodigious and exhausting job. Even scholars in the field of free speech could not spare the time and effort necessary to sift the wheat out of these many bushels of chaff. Mr. Barth has now done the job for all of us. Except for events which came too late for him, he supplies us with the basic facts about what has been happening. And they are very disturbing.

Perhaps some readers agree with a good deal of what has been done to suppress objectionable doctrines, but they ought to be disturbed too. They should be worried by the probability of further suppressions ahead. There is no escape from what Justice Black says:

Centuries of experience testify that laws aimed at one political or religious group, however rational these laws may be in their beginnings, generate hatreds and prejudices which spread rapidly beyond control. . . . Restrictions imposed on proscribed groups are seldom static.[1]

We are drawing the American party line and questioning all deviations from it. Then we are punishing these deviations more and more. In the author's words, "Nothing that the agents of communism have done or can do in this country is so dangerous to the United States as what they have induced us . . . to do to ourselves."

Mr. Barth is well aware of the objectionable nature of American Communists (Chapter II). But, instead of treating them like Gorgons who must not be looked at, he tries to understand what Communists are really like. His proof of a constant flow of men

[1] 339 U.S. 448-49 (1950).

out of the Communist Party of America encourages the belief that many Communists can be converted to American ideals, if we only use wise methods. The central portion of his book then discusses the three main ways in which the nation has lately been throwing overboard large parcels of freedom in a wild panic to escape from this one-thirtieth of one per cent of our population. First, he takes up congressional investigations (Chapter IV); then the loyalty and security-risk programs, and other methods for controlling government employees, including scientists (Chapters V-VIII); and last, the question of insuring the loyalty of teachers (Chapter IX).

The following reflections were evoked by the author's admirable treatment of each of these three problems.

I

Congressional Committees—Investigation or Invective?

The special problems presented by the Un-American Activities Committee of the House are only part of much broader problems raised by the whole subject of congressional investigations. Their extensive use is rather recent. Such committees were comparatively powerless to compel witnesses to answer questions until the Supreme Court, during the Teapot Dome affair, upheld the right of Congress to range widely while collecting evidence in order to ascertain what is best for the national welfare. Consequently, even though the First Amendment is involved, the Supreme Court is not likely to do much interfering with the kind of legislative investigations with which this book deals. Judges are naturally reluctant to tell Congress how to do its own job.

Yet this does not mean that Congress ought to do whatever it can do. If the courts refuse to impose constitutional limitations on probes into men's opinions and intellectual associations, then the responsibility is put on Congress to work out wise limitations for itself and put an end to abuses and unfairness on the part of its own committees. Justice Holmes said that "legislatures are ultimate guardians of the liberties and welfare of the people in quite as great a degree as the courts." [2] Usually Holmes' words are taken as a directive to judges to keep hands off, but they are also an exhortation to Congress and the state legislatures to resume their great traditional task of protecting the ordinary man from governmental oppression.

Congress has the obligation of reshaping the procedure of investigating committees so as to give a citizen rights approximating those which the Constitution gives him in a criminal trial. And when senators or representatives baselessly slander decent citizens on the floor and in committee rooms, the fact that the Constitution exempts them from paying damages in court ought to make the Senate or the House alert to punish such baseless statements itself. The constitutional provision that "for any Speech or Debate in either House, they shall not be questioned in any other Place" ought to be read, as it rarely is, in connection with the preceding words of the Constitution, "Each House may . . . punish its members for disorderly Behaviour . . ."

The two outstanding points about legislative investigating committees are that they are well suited to pass on general questions and badly suited for the decision of individual cases. By general questions I mean the collection of large masses of information which may show the need for new statutes and how new laws ought to be wisely drafted. And I mean more than preparation for legislation. These committees enable Congress to review the past expenditure of vast sums of taxpayers' money and to keep a constant watch upon the conduct of public officials. This last matter is especially important today because of the great number of federal employees and the wide range of their activities. The people whose lives are affected by these multitudes of unelected officials have no control over them except through the chosen representatives in the Senate and the House. Such far-flung functions as I have been describing could easily be hampered by judicial interference. Congress should be free to choose

[2] 194 U.S. 270 (1903).

the ways for carrying out these important tasks. That is what Congress is for.

On the other hand, Congress was not designed to determine whether an individual is innocent or guilty of crime or other misconduct. That is what courts are for. Hence the constitutional prohibition of bills of attainder. And a congressional committee is just as unfit for this task as the whole House. In certain special situations a court may be replaced by an administrative tribunal equipped as far as possible with the impartiality of a judge, but that is the sole proper alternative way of trying citizens for offenses. Senators and representatives cannot be expected to display impartiality. Everything they do in the day's work runs in just the opposite direction. The Constitution does allow them to conduct one kind of trial—an impeachment, and what happens then is very significant. President Johnson escaped removal by one vote, but today the evidence against him seems utterly flimsy. This is a striking proof of the unavoidable influence of purely political considerations on congressional determinations of the guilt of an individual. Party policies and the desire for re-election cannot be excluded from the minds of senators and representatives. "We have been unearthing your New Dealers . . . ," said the Republican chairman of the Un-American Activities Committee. Judges are kept impartial by professional training, the customary safeguards of the courtroom, and the ingrained traditions of the bench. No such factors operate on the men who sit in the Capitol. They are sent there by the people to do a very different job from that of judges, a job that demands very different qualities. Consequently congressmen and senators should, as far as possible, keep away from the judges' job of passing on the guilt of individuals.

If we apply these two points to a committee investigating the possibility of disloyal government officials, for instance, in the State Department, the proper work of the committee is to look at the loyalty program as a whole and furnish Congress and the public with a set of general conclusions about the way that program is actually administered. Are the methods used efficient to detect really bad people and do they furnish adequate protection to the innocent? What better methods can be suggested? Such a general survey is peculiarly within the capacity of Congress, which is concerned with both the welfare of the nation and the liberties of all the citizens. But when the congressmen on a committee get away from a general review of methods and undertake to reverse or affirm the decision of a loyalty board in a single case, as if the committee were an appellate court, then questions of innocence or guilt are submerged in partisan battles. Moreover, the committee's disagreement with the outcome of an individual case is not good proof that this case was wrongly decided. Every student of law knows that two different judges or juries frequently disagree about close issues. The purpose of the double-jeopardy clause in the Constitution is to protect a released prisoner from this very fact. When an acquitted man cannot be forced to undergo a second trial before a jury, his second trial before a congressional committee is surely abhorrent to American traditions.

Of course there cannot be a rigid rule wholly excluding individual cases from consideration by an investigating committee. Sometimes elaborate examination of particular actions is indispensable to establishing a general conclusion. The Teapot Dome investigations showed this. But this task, if it has to be undertaken, calls for special caution and restraint on the part of the committee. When individual cases do have to be brought in, they should be regarded as incidental to the review of a general situation and not as ends in themselves. Congress sits to make laws for everybody and to supervise administrative methods for everybody. It is not its business to pass judgment on one man, except by impeachment.

Matters are still worse when the committee undertakes to investigate thought and speech in private life, as in the notorious hearings to discover objectionable features in motion pictures. Congressmen are even less fitted to be dramatic critics than they are to be judges.

When a congressional committee does find itself obliged to examine an individual charged with disloyalty, for the sake of settling some general policy or procedure, then the first thing to remember is that the committee is, for the time being, charged with the same responsibilities as a court. Although it has not the same power as a judge and jury to send men to jail, it is able to impose different and very severe punishments. It can smear a man's reputation grievously, and to many men a good name is as important as merely being out of jail. The committee can also do a good deal toward depriving the men whom it condemns of their jobs, whether they be government officials or Hollywood writers. Nor does the committee completely lack the power to imprison men. It can send them to jail for refusing to answer questions, even those which decent people would not ask.

A committee which possesses so much of the power of a court ought to behave like a court. When its members see fit to be judges of a particular individual, they should try as hard as they can to overcome the political partialities which (as I have pointed out) differentiate congressmen from real judges. At least their proceedings should have the formality prevailing on the floor of the House and of the Senate. It is high time to throw out the klieg lights, the cameras and television. They hinder calm determination of the fate of the accused person just as much as they would in a courtroom, and they destroy the dignity which ought to be displayed by the chosen representatives of the American people, sitting to discharge a grave public duty.

It is not enough, moreover, to imitate the outward qualities of a court. Still more important, the procedure for deciding an individual's guilt or innocence in a committee should seek to approximate the safeguards against bias and error which prevail in criminal trials.

Here is a problem for statesmen. The history of criminal trials brings out the nature of their task. Go back three or four hundred years, say, to the trial of Sir Walter Raleigh or the Earl of Essex, and you find a startling lack of our commonplace decencies for determining guilt. The prisoner was browbeaten by judges as well as prosecutors. He had no lawyer. He was not allowed to call any witnesses, much less compel them to appear. He could not testify on his own behalf. It took centuries of struggle and hard thinking to obtain impartial judges and to work out the civilized procedure for trials in a courtroom embodied in our Sixth Amendment:

> In all criminal prosecutions the accused shall enjoy the right to a speedy and public trial, . . . and to be informed of the nature and cause of the accusation; to be confronted with the witnesses against him; to have compulsory process for obtaining witnesses in his favor, and to have the assistance of counsel for his defense.

Now, the nation is starting a new kind of tribunal—congressional committees. Nobody has really thought about working out a civilized procedure for them. So sometimes their investigations have a good deal of resemblance to criminal trials in 1600. Harlow Shapley was questioned in secrecy by the Un-American Activities Committee, his lawyer was forcibly ejected from the room, he could call no witnesses, his written statement was torn from his hands by the presiding member of the committee. On other occasions there has been far too much publicity, amounting to a mob in a courtroom. Mr. Barth supplies many further details of the rudimentary nature of committee procedure. Congress should be ashamed to let this go on any longer. Perhaps a committee hearing which can ruin or clear a man's reputation ought not to be an exact counterpart of a criminal trial. All the more need for Congress to get to work and plan what different safeguards should be provided for the innocent man. The First Congress formulated decent procedure for criminal trials in federal courtrooms. The Eighty-second Congress ought to give us a decent procedure for this new device for punishing an individual in its committee rooms.

Just how far it is wise for a congressional inquiry to imitate a criminal trial cannot be stated offhand, but the person summoned for questioning should surely be allowed to bring in his own lawyer. He needs him badly, to advise him about improper questions and perhaps about his right to refuse to incriminate himself. The Un-American Activities Committee has defended its occasional denials of the right to counsel by comparing itself to a grand jury, into which the witness goes unaccompanied. Yet the situation is obviously different—the grand jury insists on secrecy in order to protect innocent persons, whereas, even when committee proceedings are held in secret, some member issues a statement to the press relating the smears of the day. The right to cross-examine hostile witnesses raises more difficulties. Perhaps the way out is to allow the lawyer of the accused to suggest questions to be asked by the chairman, and for the chairman to have the honesty to disclose discreditable facts in the past careers of the witnesses on whom the committee relies. At least the defense should be able to bring in witnesses in order to attack the credibility of the man who has been telling damaging stories about the accused. The situation now is what Mr. Barth calls an "open-house invitation extended by legislative investigators to every renegade Communist and stool pigeon . . ." And common decency should allow the accused to produce other testimony in his own defense, within reasonable limits. Moreover, he is fairly entitled to some sort of specification of the lines of inquiry well ahead of the hearing, so that he may prepare an adequate defense. He ought not to be obliged to come into the committee room knowing nothing of what it is all about, and then be forced to answer questions roving over his whole life, or else go to jail if he prefers to preserve his privacy.

So much for the rights of the person actually before the committee. Serious harm can be done, as well, to a man who is not in the room at all. Suppose a former Communist takes the stand in Washington and accuses Mr. Jones, a reputable citizen in New York City, of having been an active member of the Communist Party. The afternoon newspapers spread the charge on their front pages. Mr. Jones is helpless. Weeks later he may have a chance to appear himself and reply, but by that time the matter is cold. Some war scare or another political scandal is on the front pages. Most of the readers who saw the charge do not see the reply. The mud sticks, and there is nothing he can do about it. Surely there must be some remedy for this gross unfairness. The committee's counsel knows what the ex-Communist is going to say long before the hearing. So there is time for him to give Mr. Jones advance information of the general nature of the future testimony against him. Then, Mr. Jones should be allowed to appear before the committee on the same day as his accuser, or at least to file a brief reply to his accuser; and the committee should do its best to make sure that the reply is printed by the newspapers in the same issue as the damaging charges against Mr. Jones.

Finally, the members of the investigating committee might try to behave like judges after the committee session is over. No self-respecting judge expresses opinions about a pending case, either to the press or in public addresses. Contrast the uncontrolled revelations by the Un-American Activities Committee while evidence is going in.

Some people may think it makes no difference what methods are employed by this committee—the sufferers are "Communists" anyway. But public opinion is capable of rapid shifts to fresh objects of excited detestation. Instead of radicals, businessmen may easily become the target of investigation, as has frequently happened in the past. Suppose the methods now employed by the Un-American Activities Committee were taken over by a congressional committee investigating monopolistic practices or high prices of the necessities of life. Suppose a prominent manufacturer is grilled about all his private economic and political opinions. Suppose he is ordered, like the Anti-Fascist Refugee Committee, to bring all the ledgers and all the correspondence files of his organization several hundred miles to Washington. Suppose he is given no lawyer, no chance to cross-examine the psychopaths who accuse him of nefarious schemes to starve the poor, no opportunity to present testimony of his own to discredit these witnesses and establish his own innocence.

The only real remedy for abuses by investigating committees lies, not in the courts, but on the floor of Congress.

II

Loyalty and Security Risks in Federal Employees

A shrewd insurance man in Providence remarked, "I can insure you against everything and take all the money you've got." The price for perfect protection of governmental activities may be too high to pay. If every paper in the State Department had to pass through the hands of a dozen separate checkers before it was released for study and then sent back through the same dozen checkers every evening, Whittaker Chambers and Henry J. Wadleigh would have been blocked in their rotten plans—but fewer papers would have been sent for. Rather than wait for all this time and trouble, officials would have gone ahead and made policies without examining all the documents they ought to have read first.

Apart from the question of a military attack from abroad, which the military people seem to be handling pretty well, internal communism (as Chapter II shows) is not a serious threat to the United States. Only a thorough demoralization due to inflation or widespread unemployment would lay us open to a philosophy wholly at odds with our traditions and aspirations. Incipient fascism (under other names) is much stronger among us—many more citizens long to use illegal force to defend vested economic or racial interests than to imitate the Soviet Union. However, there is no need to worry much about fascism either. The biggest danger to the United States is from stuffed shirts— stuffed shirts in positions of authority who seek to fill every government office and every teaching position with stuffed shirts.

The loyalty and security-risk programs, like the teachers' oaths, have detected very few Communists, as Mr. Barth shows, but they have greatly increased the power of stuffed shirts over American life. The two main arguments for these programs are as follows:

In the first place, any employer wishes a considerable amount of freedom in the selection of his subordinates in high positions and those who require special trust. Even after a man has been hired, his employer wants the power to dismiss him if found unworthy of confidence. Plainly, the law should not compel a private employer to retain a subordinate who has already engaged in a plan to betray the secrets of the business. The federal government has, in general, less freedom than a businessman to discharge employees, because of Civil Service regulations designed to combat the spoils system, but it is urged that these should not operate to protect unfaithful officials.

Second, conditions for the past two decades have subjected the natural loyalty of employees to an unusual strain. Whether or not it be true of all American Communists, there is no doubt that some Communists in Western countries like ours are enlisted heart and soul in promoting the interests of the Soviet Union, even ignoring their plain duties to their own nation. If they be outside the government, they are ready to extort information from babbling officials and pass it on to Moscow. If they be officials themselves, they have been willing to go the limit for the sake of helping the USSR. The report of the Canadian Royal Commission which investigated the betrayal of atomic energy secrets to Soviet agents established the guilt of Boyer, a distinguished scientist, and recent disquieting revelations show that Fuchs, a British official, engaged in espionage on both sides of the Atlantic.

To sum up these two arguments, there has been a clear and present danger that there might be Communists and other men of bad character in the employ of our government who would become the channel for conveying valuable information to the Soviet Union and otherwise serve its interests. However, the weight of these arguments diminishes for officials who do not have access to important secrets and could do little to help a foreign power.

The chief arguments on the other side are as follows:

First, it is very important to attract into government service and retain there for life men with strong and vigorous minds who are capable of independent thinking. Some men of the caliber required are sure to be critical of features of our existing economic and political situation. Without being in any way disloyal, they have ideas which are unpopular in certain conservative quarters. Such men may easily become the targets of unwise or intolerant investigators. Among Mr. Barth's many examples of this trend, we find a loyalty board condemning an official because his views on free speech for Communists in private life coincided with the judicial opinions of Holmes and Charles Evans Hughes. Such an attitude on the part of investigators will lead men of independent minds to refuse to enter government service or to resign as quickly as they can find work elsewhere, in order to avoid becoming targets. What is very important to remember is that the harm to the higher Civil Service extends far beyond officials with actual Leftist sympathies. Many middle-of-the-road people with sensitive and able minds will be lost to the government because of their disgust over the way some loyal radical has been treated by a review board or a congressional committee.

Under Franklin D. Roosevelt the federal government became a prized place of employment for many of our ablest young men. We were at last getting something like the British Civil Service, where the higher positions have the attractiveness and prestige of professorships in leading universities. This was very fortunate because governmental problems were getting to be more far-reaching and difficult than ever before, and they have not become less so since V-J Day. The spirit the government needs in its servants is shown by Paul Appleby's story of the expert who, in retiring after long service, wrote, "I have been only a small part of the Department of Agriculture, but the Department of Agriculture has been a great part of me."

This dream of harnessing intelligence in the service of the American people has now been shattered—at the very time when its realization was essential to our welfare. The attainment of "security by achievement" has been sacrificed to the craze for "security by secrecy." An atmosphere of perpetual distrust and eavesdropping is abhorrent to "quiet and sensitive and gifted people," and yet their help is indispensable for the formulation of information and ideas so as to make possible wise policies.

Dismissal of a man from a government job on a disloyalty charge is a very severe punishment. This was pointed out in a letter to the *New York Times* from Milton Katz and other professors at Harvard Law School, which urged the importance of proper rules of procedure in the administration of the loyalty program:

> Consider the case of one who, for twenty or thirty years—his entire mature life—has worked in the Forestry Service, or the Bureau of Animal Industry of the Department of Agriculture, or the Postal Service, or the Bureau of Standards, or the Tennessee Valley Authority. To deny him all opportunity for employment in governmental service, federal, state, or municipal, is to deprive him of the only means of livelihood for which he has any training or experience.[3]

Thus men are being punished, not for any offense they have done, but because of what they might conceivably do someday. Imagine the effect of this hurly-burly on a young official who is eager to master the problems of his particular agency, reads widely, and thinks for himself. If he has formed some private opinions which happen to be out of favor, the prospect that his wife and children will face starvation is always in front of him. Consequently he must shape his studies and friendships and little humanitarian gifts so as to avoid that terrible disaster. He must constantly ask himself, not "What is true and right—how can I best develop the powers that lie in me?" but "What is safe—what will keep me out of trouble?"

Second, the best way to combat communism is to stand by our own institutions and our own way of life. Spies and informers have always been hated among us. As Mr. Barth writes, "Secret dossiers are paraphernalia of a police state." He mentions the alarming possibility that some former members of the Federal Bureau of Investigation will use their memories of FBI files for

[3] Sunday, April 13, 1947, editorial page.

blackmail or for political pressure. Among the most cherished American principles are freedom of thought, which is guaranteed by the First Amendment, and a fair trial, which is assured by the Sixth Amendment.[4]

Mr. Barth demonstrates how far loyalty investigations have sacrificed the rights in the Sixth Amendment to have your alleged offenses specified and meet your accusers face to face. The inquiries ramble beyond the listed charges into a man's general outlook. "What causes us concern," said one loyalty investigator, "is your basic philosophy." The official put on the carpet is obliged to grope blindly in a desperate attempt to discover what part of his past has brought him under suspicion—a process "galling and degrading to self-respecting human beings." "A hearing before a loyalty board is not an agreeable experience for an innocent man." "There is literally no way for a defendant to refute such [anonymous] charges." He cannot cross-examine an unseen and unknown informant or produce evidence to demonstrate the accuser's bias or psychopathic lying. Mr. Barth's accounts of some of these inquiries read uncomfortably like the transcripts of Soviet purge trials, except that the punishment is not death but loss of the means to live.

This grave departure from our basic traditions disturbs many conscientious men serving on loyalty boards and the Loyalty Review Board, but they see no way out of the present practice of concealing the stooges and other informants from whom the FBI gets the material laid before the boards. If the boards insisted on the normal principle that facts must not be reported at second or third hand, but actual eyewitnesses must appear in person and face cross-examination, the operations of the FBI would be crippled. Congress, outraged by this interference with a favorite agency, would then replace the President's loyalty program by something far more destructive of the traditional requirements of a fair trial. Therefore, excellent members of the Loyalty Review Board, though worried by the predicaments of accused men which the author describes, believe it impracticable

[4] Quoted on p. xvi.

to bring a loyalty hearing closer to the constitutional form of a criminal trial.

I have always found it difficult to get away from this reasoning, but the author meets it head-on. The boards' position is, "You cannot improve the practice if you are going to have a loyalty program at all. It is either this or something worse." Mr. Barth's reply is, "You ought not to have a loyalty program at all—the whole business was a mistake." One of the most interesting parts of his book is the forceful exposition (in Chapter VI) of the failure of the program to attain its two chief objectives: (1) it has not removed public anxiety about "the infiltration of disloyal persons into the ranks of [government] employees"—the McCarthy affair revealed wilder fears than ever; and (2) it has not afforded "protection from unfounded accusations of disloyalty [to] the loyal employees of the government," as the McCarthy affair showed *ad nauseam*. Perhaps both Mr. Barth's points would hold good even if the boards felt able to adopt all the procedural improvements suggested in Mr. Katz's letter to the *Times*.

Then the book makes a constructive proposal for assuring loyalty without a loyalty program. We should trust the superior officials in the department and agencies to pick and keep the right men to work with them, just as we did for a century and a half, from Washington's inauguration until the spring of 1947:

It is not unreasonable to assume that persons who . . . have won the confidence of their colleagues in previous governmental service, in private business, or in their professions are neither traitors nor fools. It is on this basis that private industry chooses its most trusted and responsible employees. . . . There is no need to suppose that administrators will hire the worst among competing applicants . . . or be heedless of security considerations. They want able and trustworthy subordinates and can be counted upon to exercise ordinary prudence in selecting them.

This is wise counsel, but it is not likely to be heeded. Congress, which is eager to set up worse loyalty hearings, will prevent a policy of no loyalty hearings at all. Thoughtful Americans will

simply have to wait, and have faith that a democracy eventually
gets over a bad fit of tantrums and returns to common sense.

III

Academic Freedom

Political leaders who are constantly invoking the name of
Thomas Jefferson would do well to read him occasionally. They
might then stop undermining the magnificent ideal which he
held out to prospective teachers at the University of Virginia:

> This institution will be based on the illimitable freedom of the human
> mind. For here we are not afraid to follow truth wherever it may lead,
> nor to tolerate error so long as reason is free to combat it.

It is not easy to add anything to Mr. Barth's thoughtful application of Jefferson's principle to current academic problems (in
Chapter IX). I can only reinforce some of his points by stating
propositions which seem particularly important. Because my
experience with public schools was only from 1898 till 1903,
these observations will be pretty much confined to the somewhat
different problem of teaching reasonably mature students.

First, the fitness of any man to be chosen for a teaching position in a higher educational institution should be decided on the
basis of his individual intellectual qualities, general behavior,
and other personal factors which conduce to good or bad teaching and scholarship. There should be no blanket disqualifications
beyond a few rules which were well recognized long before the
Russian Revolution. Of these general rules, the one most pertinent to the present situation is that men who have been convicted of serious crimes in the regular criminal courts are not
appropriate members of college and university faculties.

Even here there might be occasional exceptions for political
crimes, as to which public opinion often changes. For example,
Thomas Cooper, who spent six months in prison under the

Sedition Act of 1798, later served the University of South Carolina as president for fourteen years and "added greatly to its distinction."[5] He was a pioneer in teaching political economy in America, and a prime factor in the establishment of the first school of medicine and the first insane asylum in South Carolina. What a loss if conviction for crime had automatically made Cooper ineligible! At any rate, this particular matter is not likely to raise acute problems, because all the critical cases of academic freedom will probably involve men who have never been convicted or even indicted. And certainly there should be no general rule barring men whom the authorities have not thought worth prosecuting, even if congressional or state investigating committees have stigmatized such men as guilty of political crimes.

Second, the important principle that each case should be judged on its own merits applies even more strongly to the dismissal of professors with academic tenure. When a new man is to be hired or a young man is to be promoted, the decision for or against him is necessarily governed by a great many different factors. It is a question of predicting the quality of his service to the institution, and prediction about human beings is unavoidably entangled with the general likes and dislikes of those who do the deciding. But it is different when it comes to cutting short a scholar's career in a university which promised him lifelong security. Such a proceeding resembles a criminal trial and should be similarly conducted for the purpose of determining the truth of specific charges against him. These charges should usually be based upon his personal misconduct in the performance of his duties. External affairs should normally be considered irrelevant unless they involve convictions of serious crimes or perhaps grave moral delinquencies which unfit him for contact with young men and women. The fact that he holds unpopular opinions on political matters or associates with outsiders who hold such opinions is a very dangerous basis for dismissal, because it opens the way to purges whose scope can be fixed to meet the passions of the moment and by the selfish interests of

[5] *Dictionary of American Biography*, Vol. IV, p. 415.

influential groups outside the institution. Here, as always, the issue ought to be whether this man is derelict in his duty as a teacher. The usual principles and considerations governing the dismissal of professors which long have been recognized as wise by leading educational institutions should remain applicable. Dismissal of professors for new kinds of political and economic heresy are open to the same objections as the discharge of persons a century ago for unorthodox religious opinions and the attempted ouster of E. Benjamin Andrews from the presidency of my own college, Brown, because he was a free-trader and supported Bryan in 1896.

Third, the effort to concentrate the current problems on the question whether a Communist is automatically ineligible to become or remain a professor is unrealistic. Such a case will arise very infrequently. My point is that if you once recognize a blanket disqualification for Communists, advantage is sure to be taken of this concession to try to bar a considerable number of teachers who are not Communists. If you start with Communists, you won't stop there.

To begin with, the attack will extend to persons who were once Communists. No doubt there are exceptional cases like Professor Budenz at Fordham, but an ex-Communist is likely to be in the same box as a Communist for academic positions, just as he is in the same box for purposes of deportation under act of Congress. Next, people will insist that the ineligibility should extend to teachers who are thought to behave like Communists although they never held a party card. It will be urged against them that they deliberately abstain from enrolling themselves in order better to carry on the nefarious purposes of the party. From there on, the alleged evidence of relationship to the Communist Party will become increasingly remote. Teachers will be declared ineligible because they belong to organizations which play along with the Communists or have been listed as subversive by some official or because they are as good as Communists or because they backed Henry Wallace, who was supported by Communists. In short, the main object of controversy will not be enrolled Communists but teachers of more or less Leftish views. For example, as Mr. Barth relates, the president of Harvard was lately asked to dismiss two non-Communist professors for actions said to be helpful to Communists, and the regents at the University of California expressly stated that the numerous professors they discharged were not Communists.

Consequently the present problem can most profitably be considered as a problem of radicalism among teachers.

Fourth, professors are different from the general run of people. They ought to be different. Most people think in order to take action; but professors ought to think for the sake of thinking. Ease of mind is an almost indispensable requisite for fruitful thinking.

This principle, at any rate, applies with equal force to teachers in schools. At all levels of education, teachers are faced by one of the most baffling tasks in the world—how best to shape growing minds, not to suit the passing passions of the moment, but so as to enable these present children and youths to live happily and effectively in the unpredictable community of ten or twenty years hence. Such a task demands every ounce of energy a teacher possesses, and nothing is better calculated to sap that energy than the poisonous atmosphere of vague fears and telltale rumors which inevitably accompanies loyalty investigations.

Instead of beginning the consideration of problems of radical teachers by stressing the dangers of radicalism, it is very important to start with the harm which is done to all the teachers in an institution by the policy of keeping out objectionable ideas. The comparatively few men who will be denied appointment or dismissed will suffer from such a policy, but the harmful effect embraces almost all the teachers in the particular institution. While the affair is going on as to a particular radical, everybody takes sides. The institution is in an uproar and the ordinary work of teaching and scholarship are demoralized. Professors of fairly moderate political views begin to wonder if they are running risks. Intellectual activities come to be shaped with reference to the danger of dismissal and not to the pursuit of truth. The

dean of the College of Chemistry at the University of California
hit the nail on the head:

> No conceivable damage to the university at the hands of the hypo-
> thetical Communists among us could have equaled the damage resulting
> from the unrest, ill-will, and suspicion engendered by this series of
> events.

On the other hand, speaking from my own experience after
having been, thirty years ago, on the receiving end of an academic investigation for heterodox writing, I know what a great
encouragement it has been to feel absolutely assured that the
authorities of Harvard will never dismiss a professor because of
his honestly held opinions, whether expressed in or out of the
classroom. For the sake of having a university do its special and
essential work well, it is worth while to run the risk of whatever
injuries may come from a few men with objectionable ideas on
its faculty.

Finally, the rapidly increasing practice of singling out teachers
for oaths and declarations of loyalty is an insult to law-abiding
and hard-working men and women. Teachers were once esteemed
in American communities, but now they are treated *en masse* as
if they were peculiarly inclined to betray their country. Nothing
could better demonstrate the depths into which self-styled patriots have sunk than their enraged clamor for test oaths which,
as Justice Black warns, "were an abomination to the founders of
this nation." [6] And Alexander Hamilton, whom nobody would
call a radical, denounced the expurgatory oath which was designed to root out Tories in New York:

> It was to excite scruples in the honest and conscientious, and to hold
> out a bribe to perjury. . . . Nothing can be more repugnant to the true
> genius of the common law than such an inquisition . . . into the con-
> sciences of men.[7]

The Massachusetts Loyalty Oath, enacted in 1935 in response
to assertions that the schools and colleges of the Commonwealth

[6] 325 U.S. 577 (1944).
[7] 4 Wallace 331.

were riddled with Communists and traitors, has not ferreted out a single teacher with the slightest taint of disloyalty. Only three teachers in fifteen years failed to take the oath. What is especially significant is that these three had served in the public schools for years with unquestioned devotion. They stopped their lifework because they were sensitive men and women who thought it wrong to be forced to swear that they possessed the common virtues of decent citizens.

Mr. Barth wisely observes, "The proponents of special loyalty oaths for teachers commonly ask the question, 'Why not?' . . . But a prior and more apposite question is 'Why?' Why should teachers be singled out as a special class and be asked to profess their innocence of an attitude which there is no good reason to suspect them of holding?"

Supporters of the California regents express surprise that a score of professors, all found not to be Communists by both the faculty and the regents who fired them, should refuse to sign a statement that "I am not a member of the Communist Party or any other organization which advocates the overthrow of the government by force or violence, and I have no commitments in conflict with my responsibilities with respect to impartial scholarship and free pursuit of truth."

The first part states plain facts, and the last part acknowledges compliance with the ideals of all professors. Then why not put down their names and end the fuss?

In order to understand the attitude of these scholars toward this demand of their beloved university for a public avowal of their allegiance to impartial scholarship and the pursuit of truth, which ought never to have been doubted for a moment, let us picture the parallel situation of a loyal wife whose chastity is similarly doubted by a suspicious husband. He too demands a public assertion—at a dinner party in their home. He insists that his wife tell all their guests that she has never been unfaithful to him, and particularly not with a person he names. It is all true—why not say so?

If we are going to revive the abomination of expurgatory oaths, why stop at one profession and one kind of objectionable behavior? Why not extend the device to other occupations and other offenses? Let us require every legislator to swear that there were no illegal practices at his election and that he has never taken a bribe or purchased land knowing of a contemplated public improvement nearby. Let us require every lawyer to swear that he has never solicited clients by ambulance-chasing or otherwise, every doctor that he has never performed an abortion, and every businessman that he has never violated the antitrust laws and the Robinson-Patman Act. Imagine the indignation which these proposals would raise from men who see no harm in teachers' oath laws. Yet these offenses are far more frequent in the respective occupations than disloyalty among teachers, and they are at least as injurious to society.

It is high time to stop this persistent probing of the patriotism of professors and schoolteachers. We teachers have a difficult job, and perhaps we are not doing it very successfully, but we shall surely do it worse when misguided people are constantly tearing us out of the ground to see whether we are growing straight or crooked.

You can have perfectly sterilized minds in schools and universities, or you can have good teaching, but you can't have both. The American people should heed the warning of Justice Jackson:

Only in the darkest periods of human history has any Western government concerned itself with mere belief, however eccentric or mischievous, when it has not matured into overt action; and if that practice survives anywhere, it is in the Communist countries whose philosophies we loathe. . . . Communists are not the only faction which will put us all in mental strait-jackets.[8]

[8] 339 U.S. 437 (1950).

THE LOYALTY OF FREE MEN

CHAPTER I

THE CULT OF LOYALTY

Behind the dozens of sedition bills in Congress last session, behind teachers' oaths and compulsory flag salutes, is a desire to make our citizens loyal to their government. Loyalty is a beautiful idea, but you cannot create it by compulsion and force. A government is at bottom the officials who carry it on: legislators and prosecutors, school superintendents and police. If it is composed of legislators who pass shortsighted sedition laws by overwhelming majorities, of narrowminded school superintendents who oust thoughtful teachers of American history and eight-year-old children whose rooted religious convictions prevent them from sharing in a brief ceremony—a government of snoopers and spies and secret police—how can you expect love and loyalty? You make men love their government and their country by giving them the kind of government and the kind of country that inspire respect and love: a country that is free and unafraid, that lets the discontented talk in order to learn the causes for their discontent and end those causes, that refuses to impel men to spy on their neighbors, that protects its citizens vigorously from harmful acts while it leaves the remedies for objectionable ideas to counter-argument and time.[1]

T HE RELATION of the individual to the State—or of individual liberty to national security—is the crucial issue of our time. The emphasis in this relation marks the essential distinction between a totalitarian society and a free society. A totalitarian so-

[1] Zechariah Chafee, Jr., *Free Speech in the United States* (Cambridge: Harvard University Press, 1942), pp. 564-65.

ciety emphasizes the supremacy of the State, seeking national security through rigid governmental control of individual activity and expression. A free society emphasizes the supremacy of the individual, relying for its national security upon a democratic adjustment of diverse views and interests and upon the freely accorded devotion of its constituents.

The function of national security in a totalitarian society is to preserve the State, while the function of national security in a free society is to preserve freedom. Those who established the American Republic counted freedom among man's "unalienable" or "natural" rights and believed that it was in order to secure these rights that governments are instituted among men. But there is a looseness about freedom that makes it seem hazardous to security. It involves an inescapable element of risk. There have always been men everywhere who viewed it skeptically as a luxury to be enjoyed only within prescribed limits and when the nation is not subject to any external threat. It is commonly in the name of national security that individual liberty is lost.

The purpose of this book is to show: (1) that we have accepted, without full awareness of their meaning, piecemeal encroachments on personal freedom that threaten to corrupt our richest inheritance; (2) that these encroachments have been accepted as the result of what are in large part groundless and neurotic fears; (3) that, although accepted in the name of national security, they operate, in fact, to impair the security they are intended to protect; and (4) that whether or not individual liberty is, as the founders of the United States believed it to be, an "unalienable" or "natural" right, it serves vital practical purposes and is an affirmative source of national strength.

This is by no means to suggest that national security can be neglected. The institutions of liberty are under attack. They are threatened by an aggressive totalitarianism abroad, and they need the protection of a strong and resolute government. If that government should fall, the institutions of liberty would fall with it. In some measure, too, the institutions are threatened in novel ways by agents of that totalitarianism at home. They are threatened most of all, however, by well-meaning and patriotic but frightened Americans, who have come to think of liberty as a liability rather than an asset.

The error of these men is that they confuse loyalty with orthodoxy. Acting upon this confusion, they tend to suppress diversity and to insist upon a rigid conformity. But loyalty may take as many forms as religious worship. This much about it seems indisputable: like love, it must be freely given. It can be evoked but it cannot be commanded or coerced. Members of a family are loyal to one another, not through any oath or compulsion, but as a result of shared experiences, community of interest, and long mutual dependence. A great aggregation of individuals and families becomes and remains a nation, not through geographical propinquity alone, but rather through much this same process of shared experiences—which is to say, a common history—and, above all, through common acceptance of certain fundamental values. The national loyalty of free men is not so much to their government as to the purposes for which their government was created.

The United States, which is the supreme example of national union by voluntary compact, is peculiarly illustrative of the point. Founded by men committed to the idea that the just powers of government are derived from the consent of the governed, it began as an experiment. The vast American wilderness was populated by men and women who came to it voluntarily from a more settled world, desiring to participate in the experiment. Thus, a pledge of allegiance to the United States was essentially a pledge of allegiance to a political ideal. This ideal is, to be sure, very difficult of expression and susceptible of varying interpretations. But its kernel may fairly be said to lie in the concept of a society affording the widest possible scope for the realization of individual potentialities.

"The American compact," Walt Whitman wrote, "is altogether with individuals." Certainly respect for the individual personality is among the most settled and generally extolled of American principles. This is a respect necessarily rooted in the recognition, tolerance, and even encouragement of diversity. This country has grown to greatness on the premise that wide diversity of interest and opinion is not only consistent with loyalty but essential to the generation of it. The only genuine loyalty is the loyalty of free men.

The United States was established as a nation by men whose national loyalty was rooted elsewhere. Most of them had been born and bred in allegiance to the English crown. They were divorced from this allegiance and from divisive sectional loyalties only by common adherence to certain overriding ideas and values. There were no national traditions, no national heroes, no national history to unite them. When they dissolved the political bands that connected them with the British people and affixed their names to the Declaration of Independence, there was no nation to which they could pledge devotion; for the support of this Declaration, they said, "we mutually pledge *to each other* our Lives, our Fortunes, and our sacred Honor."

The new nation they created became an embodiment of the ideas they shared. It drew devotion not because of its past but because of its promise. The Constitution which made it a Federal Union guaranteed freedom of expression and of conscience. The constitutions of its constituent states had already provided similar guarantees. Freedom and opportunity were its dynamic elements. They were the elements that evoked loyalty and cemented union and afforded the matrix of growth.

The tolerance on which freedom and opportunity must rest was a necessity of early life in America. Conquest of a continental wilderness fostered a tradition of individualism. The opening of successive frontiers widely different in physical conditions and in the problems of settlement encouraged a variety of political forms. Differences of religion, of social background, of economic interest among the settlers required tolerance of diversity. Out of this necessity the early Americans made a virtue. The idea that they had raised a standard to which the lovers of liberty could repair became a source of tremendous pride to them. "This new world," Thomas Paine boasted in *Common Sense,* "hath been the asylum for the persecuted lovers of civil and religious liberty from *every part* of Europe." [2]

It was tolerance of diversity that made possible the union of thirteen disparate colonies. It was tolerance of wide differences in religious faith and cultural background that enabled America to absorb and gain enrichment from the great variety of immigrants seeking opportunity and freedom here. Opportunity and freedom were sufficient to make loyal Americans of the newcomers. There was never, until very recently, much fear that those who came to this country, let alone those who were its native sons, could grow up in American homes, attend American schools, play American games, join in the robust rivalry of American life, and turn out disloyal to America. "It is nothing to us," Congressman Page of Virginia contended in 1790 in support of a liberal naturalization policy, "whether Jews or Roman Catholics settle among us; whether subjects of Kings, or citizens of free States wish to reside in the United States, they will find it in their interest to be good citizens, and neither their religious nor political opinion can injure us, if we have good laws, well executed." [3] Whatever may have been the vices and weaknesses of this country in the past, want of confidence in itself was not among them. The nation knew that the American dream would inspire all who had a chance to dream it.

But that sublime self-confidence has now disappeared. Aliens are suspect; there is no longer the old certainty that they will be swept into the mainstream of American life. Prospective immigrants must prove that they are not the bearers of contagious opinions, and even transient visitors are feared. In 1950 the State Department denied visas to the Dean of Canterbury and later to twelve members of the Communist-sponsored World Congress of Partisans for Peace, Pablo Picasso among them, because of their political and economic views. The faith of Americans in their

---

[2] Quoted by Merle Curti, *The Roots of American Loyalty* (New York: Columbia University Press, 1946), p. 69.

[3] Ibid., p. 73.

own institutions is apparently no longer considered strong enough to withstand Communist propaganda. Eminent artists have been barred merely because their political sympathies were suspect. The German conductor Wilhelm Furtwängler was kept out because he had collaborated with the Nazis. Later Joseph Krips, the conductor of the Vienna State Opera, was forbidden to fill a summer engagement with the Chicago Symphony Orchestra because he had previously conducted performances at Moscow and Leningrad. Tolerance of diversity and faith in the democratic process are giving way to reliance on the quarantine of hostile doctrines.

Indeed, even those born into the American heritage are now only tentatively trusted; they are obliged to affirm and reaffirm their allegiance. And beyond this ritual of affirmation, in the potency of which there is no longer any confidence, they are commonly required before entering upon any post affecting the national interest to deny disloyalty. Anyone who goes to work for the government of the United States today must swear that he does not advocate its overthrow. In point of fact, Congress thought it necessary in 1940 to make it a penal offense for any citizen to teach or advocate the duty or necessity of overthrowing "any government in the United States by force or violence."

A terrible distrust lies behind this shift to negativism. The country's doubts about the loyalty of its citizens are not unlike the doubts of a husband about the fidelity of his wife. The protestations that answer his doubts are never convincing and are likely to dissipate the mutual confidence that is the essence of a marriage. When men lose faith in one another, they lose the substance of what constitutes a community among them. Thus, to a national community, there is nothing that so dangerously corrupts its integrity as such a loss of faith. As in the case of the suspicious husband, this distrust is the expression of a neurotic insecurity.

Such insecurity is perhaps the most pervasive characteristic of our time. The fear of freedom and the difficulties of realizing its potentialities have been illuminatingly treated by the psychiatrists and the social psychologists. They have contributed invaluable insights of which political theorists have as yet made too little use. The forces that have led great numbers of Europeans and Asiatics to seek the fellowship of disciplined submission to authority as an escape from the responsibilities and isolation of freedom are at work here too. They exhibit themselves in the exertion of powerful pressures, cultural as well as political, toward conformity and in an attitude novel among Americans that they can neither comprehend nor change the awful tides in which they feel themselves engulfed. The consequence is a stultifying tendency to seek unity through uniformity.

"Loyalty" has become a cult, an obsession, in the United States. But even loyalty itself is now defined negatively. It is thought of not so much in terms of an affirmative faith in the great purposes for which the American nation was created as in terms of stereotypes the mere questioning of which is deemed "disloyal." The whole postwar accent is on something called "un-Americanism"—a hyphenated synonym for unorthodoxy. Deviations to the Left are regarded as more suspicious or criminal than deviations to the Right; but the tendency is to question all deviations. "Loyalty" consists today in not being un-American, which is to say, in not being different or individualistic. The very diversity which was the wellspring of loyalty in the past is now distrusted.

The term "disloyalty" as it is commonly used today is nothing more or less than a circumlocution for treason. The authors of the Constitution went to a great deal of trouble in dealing with the subject of treason because they knew from experience how readily the term can be twisted to make discontent or dissent, or mere criticism of the government, a major crime. They took care, therefore, to define treason in the narrowest terms. "Treason against the United States," they declared in Article III, Section 3, of the Constitution, "shall consist only in levying war against them or in adhering to their enemies, giving them aid and comfort." No acts other than those specified in the Constitution can be made treasonable by legislation. Congress can neither extend, nor restrict, nor define the crime. Its power over the subject is limited to prescribing the punishment.

The Constitution is no less exacting as to the means by which conviction of treason may be obtained. "No person shall be convicted of treason," Section 3 continues, "unless on the testimony of two witnesses to the same overt act, or on confession in open court."

James Madison explained in Number 43 of *The Federalist*—that brilliant exegesis of the Constitution characterized by Thomas Jefferson as "the best commentary on the principles of government which ever was written"—the reasons that prompted the Constitutional Convention to define treason so narrowly and to make conviction of it so difficult:

> As treason may be committed against the United States, the authority of the United States ought to be enabled to punish it. But as new-fangled and artificial treasons have been the great engines by which violent factions, the natural offspring of free government, have usually wreaked their alternate malignity on each other, the convention have, with great judgment, opposed a barrier to this peculiar danger, by inserting a constitutional definition of the crime, fixing the proof necessary for conviction of it, and restraining the Congress, even in punishing it, from extending the consequences of guilt beyond the person of its author.

There is a whole lesson in political science in this paragraph—a lesson peculiarly applicable today. The use of "disloyalty" as a "new-fangled and artificial" form of treason has indeed promoted the rise of violent factions and led to a wreaking of "their alternate malignity on each other." There is no way to measure the impairment of national security that has resulted from this disruption of the sense of national community.

Disloyalty, to be sure, has not officially been held to constitute treason. But when a congressional committee or a quasi-judicial government board says that an individual is disloyal—or that he is un-American, or subversive, or a security risk, or ineligible for employment by the United States, or any of the other circumlocutions of the circumlocution—it is saying in not very euphemistic terms, or at least is encouraging the public to believe, that he is a traitor. The difference is that disloyalty is nowhere to be found detailed as a crime upon the statute books, that nowhere has it been defined, that nowhere has a punishment been prescribed for it by law. This ambiguity merely makes the charge more difficult to avoid and a condemnation less difficult to obtain.

Real disloyalty presents a threat to national security. It might find expression in betrayal of the nation—even in espionage or sabotage. Of course these are statutory crimes, clearly defined and punishable through the normal processes of indictment and trial by jury. The law can easily be used to punish any actual spy or saboteur. But the law can no more be used to punish a potential spy or a potential saboteur than it can be used to punish a potential pickpocket or a potential embezzler. The law punishes specifically prohibited antisocial acts. It does not prohibit and cannot punish antisocial ideas or intentions. The distinction has always been considered basic to a free society.

In a period of international tension, however, a potential spy or saboteur is likely to seem very dangerous—so dangerous that there is enormous temptation to deal with him outside the law. The United States, engaged in a world-wide struggle that has led to armed conflict in Asia, has yielded to this temptation to an alarming degree. It has devised an elaborate system and ritual for punishing men—and punishing them most cruelly—for crimes they have not committed but are suspected of desiring to commit. It punishes them by stigmatizing them as disloyal.

Anyone so stigmatized becomes to some degree an outcast. If he retains any friends, he knows himself to be a menace to them. Any association with them may result in their stigmatization too. Wherever he goes he is marked as a man who would be willing to betray his country. He remains at large but is regarded as a menace to society. He is expatriated without being exiled and denied the opportunity to gain a livelihood without the compensation of being maintained in prison at the community's expense. He and his fellows might come, in time, to constitute something new in American life—a caste of untouchables.

The punishment in such cases is something like that in the old story about the Quaker and his dog Tray. " 'Go to,' said the Quaker to poor Tray, 'I will not kill thee, but I will give thee a bad name,' as he turned him into the streets with the cry of 'mad dog,' and somebody else did kill Tray." [4]

Perhaps the punishments meted out on the ground of disloyalty are not too severe for anyone who clearly and demonstrably intends to serve the interest of a foreign government to the detriment of his own countrymen. The fact is, however, that these penalties are meted out without any of the safeguards embodied in the Anglo-American system of justice for the protection of innocent persons against unjust conviction. They are inflicted on the loyal and the disloyal almost without discrimination.

By the simple stratagem of charging a man with disloyalty, instead of with treason or espionage or sabotage, it is possible to evade the constitutional requirements that he be indicted by a

---

[4] Quoted from the Argument by Whittelsey, counsel for appellant Glover, in the Murphy and Glover Test Oath Cases, Supreme Court of Missouri, 41 Mo. 340, 360 (1867). Glover had been indicted and found guilty of having practiced as an attorney at law without first having taken and filed the oath of loyalty prescribed by Missouri's post-Civil War Constitution. This required practitioners of the professions to swear that they had neither committed treason nor sympathized with it. In behalf of Glover, Whittelsey said: ". . . No crime is laid to his charge, no wrong done to the State is preferred against him; but in the utterance of his free thoughts he has dared to say those who administered the public affairs were not entirely in the right, nor those in rebellion wholly in the wrong; that those who had risen in insurrection from following out erroneous political principles were not traitors of the character of those who betrayed their country from lust of gold, or wreaked vengeance for their disappointed ambition by consigning their native land to the horrors and fury of civil strife. And yet for expressing his opinions merely, he is to stand and be adjudged, attainted, and is to forfeit his franchises and liberties. No chains are placed upon his body, but the bonds are fixed upon his soul— he is taught that the lessons of his past life were falsehoods—he had thought himself a free man; he finds himself a slave who may not speak but as his masters please—he had thought that he could be punished for no act which a previously enacted law had not forbidden him to do; he finds that innocence is treated and punished as crime—he had thought that he might study to learn and to know the truth, and that to what he believed to be the truth he might give utterance; he finds that he must believe and speak what the majority choose to believe and give permission to say . . ." (Pp. 356-57.)

grand jury, that he enjoy a speedy and public trial by an impartial petit jury, that he be informed of the nature and cause of the accusation and confronted with the witnesses against him, that he be accorded the benefit of compulsory process to obtain witnesses in his favor. He is indicted and tried and sentenced by congressional committee or administrative tribunal, with the same men acting as prosecutors, judges, and jury. The presumption of innocence supposed to surround him is ignored. The mere charge of disloyalty is treated as evidence of guilt.

The part played by the press in this process of extra-legal punishment falls, because of its complexity, outside the scope of this book. It can only be noted here that it is the press which executes, so to speak, the sentences passed by congressional committees or by mere individuals speaking under the immunity from suits for slander or libel afforded by Congress. Newspapers especially tend to make headlines out of accusations and to treat denials less prominently. This stems in large measure from the concept of news as sensation and is scarcely less true of those newspapers that strive for objectivity than of those that deliberately use their news pages to serve editorial biases.

The tradition of objectivity, which is the great virtue of the American press, has operated in this context to make the press an instrument of those seeking to inflict punishment by publicity. Allegations which would otherwise be ignored because they would be recognized as groundless and libelous are blown up on front pages and given a significance out of all relation to their intrinsic merit after they have been made before a committee of Congress. Thus, what is one day properly regarded as unpublishable gossip is treated the next day as news of great moment because it has been uttered under official auspices. Refutation, no matter how compelling, never catches up with charges of disloyalty and never erases their imprint. In addition, of course, many newspapers welcome such charges and inflate them for political reasons or for their commercial value in stimulating street sales.

The cost of this system of punishment by publicity is worth reckoning. It entails sacrifices not only for the individuals who become involved in it, but also, on a wider scale, for the society as a whole. If all the elements of due process can be thus evaded, the personal security of individuals in the United States from arbitrary and summary punishment becomes a fiction. One result is to heighten the general insecurity of which this evasion of constitutional safeguards is a symptom.

The short-cut to punishment has an effect on society in other ways as well. The knowledge that men may be accused and found guilty of disloyalty in so summary a manner becomes a restraint on the exercise of constitutional rights. It is no longer safe to talk recklessly or foolishly. If the effect of this were no more than to silence recklessness and folly, perhaps the loss would not be great. But the discouragement of reckless and foolish talk tends inescapably to suppress sound and sensible dissent which may seem unpatriotic because it happens to be unpopular.

The trouble with putting any halter upon individual freedom to talk nonsense—even subversive or seditious nonsense—is that it tends to frustrate the democratic process. That process is one in which nonsense cannot be silenced by authority; it can be silenced, or overcome, only by sense. Since it is often not altogether easy to distinguish between the two, silencing of the one cannot help but result in silencing of the other. What happens, of course, is that unorthodox ideas, whether sensible or not, are suppressed in favor of orthodoxy. And consequently the attention of the society is diverted from its real problems, which call for adaptation and change, and focused instead upon a preservation of things as they are.[5]

[5] "The imagined insecurity of the strongest democracy in the world in the face of the cold war with communism has created an atmosphere in which fear makes the maintenance of civil liberties precarious. Not only the liberties of real or suspected Communists are at stake. Far beyond them, the measures to protect our institutions from Communist infiltration have set up an unprecedented array of barriers to free association, of forced declarations of loyalty, of blacklists and purges, and, most menacing to the spirit of liberty, of taboos on those progressive programs and principles which are the heart of any expanding democracy."—"In the Shadow of Fear," Report of the American Civil Liberties Union, 1948–49.

The situation should not be overstated. There has been, as yet, no formal or statutory suppression of speech in the United States beyond the prohibition of advocacy of violent overthrow of the government and the punitive restrictions of the McCarran Act. Men may, and fortunately a number of them still do, express noncomformist views liable to be termed treasonable. But, as Senator Margaret Chase Smith observed in a speech expressing her revulsion against the name-calling tactics of Senator Joseph McCarthy, "Freedom of speech is not what it used to be in America. It has been so abused by some that it is not exercised by others." Freedom of speech does not mean, to be sure, that a man who says what is unpopular should be protected from the penalties of unpopularity. Heretics and reformers must expect denunciation. The alarming characteristic about what is happening today lies partly in the official source of the denunciation, partly in the easy identification of dissent with disloyalty, partly in the punishment of it by the government itself through extra-legal mechanisms.

The cult of loyalty, and its attendant hunt for heresy as a symptom of disloyalty, has generated an intellectually shackled feeling for which terror is too strong a term, but which is marked nevertheless by widespread anxiety. The feeling is most acute, naturally, in Washington, and among government employees. Their situation under the Federal Employee-Loyalty Program will be discussed in a later chapter. But outside the capital, the pressures for conformity are mounting to a degree never before experienced by the American people. The Committee on Un-American Activities in the national House of Representatives has spawned imitators in state legislatures; some of them, such as the Tenney Committee in California, the Canwell Committee in Washington, the Broyles Commission in Illinois, have rivaled the tactics of the congressional body. In their role of investigators and with the stated object of protecting national security, they have had the effect of penalizing Americans for exercising the fundamental rights of advocacy and association.

Similarly, the Federal Employee-Loyalty Program has been aped and embellished in states and municipalities—where there is far less warrant for such restrictions. Protective measures designed to keep disloyal persons out of jobs that directly affect the national security become merely punitive when applied indiscriminately to all forms of public employment. In many states extremely repressive legislation, of doubtful constitutionality, has been adopted. These laws are aimed at Communists, but their result is to penalize all forms of heterodoxy. Some of the laws deny a place on the ballot to Communists, thereby revealing a distrust of the democratic process. Some, like the Ober Law in Maryland, drastically restrict the right of citizens to join in voluntary associations if the purpose of these associations is officially regarded as subversive. A number of municipalities, especially in the South, have adopted ordinances banning Communists and Communist *sympathizers* from the city limits. Birmingham, Alabama, for instance, announced that it would jail anyone found guilty of "voluntary association" with a Communist. Other cities have undertaken to require the registration of all Communists. The patent invalidity of such edicts from a constitutional point of view has given no apparent pause to local legislative and law-enforcement bodies. In a number of places, police chiefs have intimated that they mean to apply virtual lynch law to political undesirables. Behind all these measures is a fear of freedom and a panicky willingness to disregard the great procedural safeguards that distinguish a free from a totalitarian society.

The hounding of heterodoxy in the name of loyalty takes an especially ugly and mischievous form in connection with schools and universities. The proliferation of loyalty tests and oaths required of teachers inhibits discussion precisely where it should be most free. But perhaps the gravest consequence of the official cult of loyalty is the inflammation of public opinion to a sometimes hysterical pitch. When political disagreement is branded as disloyalty, when neighbor is invited to look with suspicion on neighbor, the bonds of national unity are strained in a way that is directly injurious to national security. Tragic incidents such

as the Peekskill riots in the summer of 1949—when war veterans
expressed their devotion to American ideals by behaving like
Nazi stormtroopers—flow inevitably from official stimulation of
intolerance. No matter how wrong-headed Paul Robeson may be,
nothing that he might have said or sung at Peekskill could have
injured the credit and the peace of the United States as grievously
as the silencing of his voice by violence.

The war in Korea gave a tremendous impetus to this intolerance. In the grip of its excitement, many normally rational and
gentle people tended to look upon any association with communism, no matter how remote or tenuous, as evidence of disloyalty
and to regard a mere charge of such association as incontroverti-
ble proof of guilt. A pathetic instance of this tendency occurred
in connection with the cancellation of a talk scheduled to be
given at a New Hampshire resort hotel by Professor Owen Lattimore in the summer of 1950. A woman who had been active in
having Professor Lattimore's appearance cancelled gave this explanation of her attitude: "Just now with the critical condition
of this country, anyone about whom there is any question should
not be allowed to speak." This extraordinary patriotism came
well after the Senate subcommittee appointed to investigate
Senator McCarthy's charges had given Professor Lattimore the
most complete exoneration of which it was capable and had
called the charges "a fraud and a hoax" perpetrated on the
United States Senate.

Apparently exoneration is impossible today for anyone who
has ever expressed unorthodox opinions, unless he is willing to
profess the most extreme anti-communism and denounce everyone
who shared his past beliefs. One is reminded a little bit of a letter
written about 112 A.D. by the younger Pliny to the emperor
Trajan:

I am also very uncertain . . . whether repentance should earn a pardon,
or if, when a man has once been a Christian, he gains nothing by leaving the sect; whether nominal Christianity without crime deserves
punishment or only when crime is coupled with it. In the meantime
this is the procedure I have adopted when any so-called Christians

have been brought before me. I asked them if they were Christians. If they admitted it, I asked them a second and again a third time, adding threats of death. If they still claimed to be Christians, I gave orders for their execution. . . . Soon in the usual way the investigation itself led to further accusations, covering several types of charge. An anonymous accusation appeared, containing many names. Some of those named denied that they were Christians or ever had been. As they joined with me in invocations to the gods and offered supplications with incense and wine to your Majesty's ikon, which I had brought in with the divine images for this purpose, and finally cursed Christ, I thought they could be discharged, as it is said that genuine Christians cannot be forced into these acts. Others whose names were quoted by the informer said they were Christians but soon withdrew their plea; to be sure, they had once been Christians but they had ceased, some three years before, some for a longer time and a few even for twenty-five years. All these worshipped your Majesty's ikon and the images of the gods; and cursed Christ.

The emperor commended Pliny's conduct but added this warning:

There should be no search made for Christians; though, if they are summoned and convicted, they must be punished. But the method should be that anyone who denies that he is a Christian and proves it by his actions, namely by worshipping our gods, whatever suspicion he may previously have incurred, should earn pardon by repentance. Public accusations by anonymous persons should have no place in criminal practice. Such a procedure would be thoroughly bad and out of keeping with the spirit of our age.[6]

Intolerance has taken its most extravagant form in relation to entertainment and the arts. Self-appointed censors have aimed, like Soviet commissars, to dictate the forms and observances of what they consider patriotism and to purge from the stage, screen, and radio any performer whose private associations or opinions cross the frontiers of conformity they have delineated. Paul Draper and Larry Adler were their most notable victims in 1949; their procedure has since been put on a mass-production basis. A

[6] Quoted in *The Rise of Christianity* by E. W. Barnes (New York: Longmans, Green & Company, 1947), pp. 307-309.

formal index for their purge from radio and television was published in June 1950 under the title *Red Channels;* this interesting brochure, issued under the auspices of *Counterattack,* a newsletter founded in May 1947 by a group of former FBI men, contains the names of writers, actors, dancers, and directors, together with a listing of the committees and organizations with which they are alleged to have had some affiliation. The listing is based in most instances on statements made by or before the House Committee on Un-American Activities or its California counterpart, or on newspaper references, generally from the *Daily Worker;* in some cases it is based on nothing more than information contained in *Counterattack* itself, and often the alleged affiliation is so tenuous as to involve no more than an appearance as an entertainer before some group supposed to be subversive. *Red Channels* makes no charges; its technique is accusation by innuendo. It could perhaps be considered as negligible as Elizabeth Dilling's *Red Network* of a decade ago were it not for the fact that it has been made effective by an organized program of pressure and intimidation brought to bear upon the advertisers and broadcasters who employ the performers it blacklists.

Advertisers appealing to a mass market are obviously vulnerable to this kind of pressure. *Red Channels* scored its outstanding triumph shortly after its publication in the dismissal of Miss Jean Muir, a television actress, from the leading role in a network program. Her name appeared in the book, and a few telephone protests led the sponsor of the program to drop her from the program as a "controversial personality." It is clear that, if this sort of vigilantism is permitted to flourish, the American public will be able to see and hear only those entertainers who can pass the censorship of the vigilantes.

Censorship in the name of patriotism occurs on an unorganized basis too. Perhaps the most sensitive example of it was provided by a Hollywood motion-picture studio which, after six months of work, shelved plans to produce a film dealing with the life and exploits of Hiawatha, the Onondaga Indian chief immortalized by Longfellow. Hiawatha had succeeded in establishing peace among the warring Five Nations; and it was felt, according to a studio spokesman, that this might cause the film to be regarded as a message for peace and thus as Communist propaganda.[7]

Political discussion has been debased to a species of fishwifery by shrill and redundant accusations of disloyalty. The immunity from suit for slander afforded by the floor of Congress has been abused over and over again to launch extravagant attacks on the good faith of opponents in every issue of policy. Demagogic exploitation of popular anxiety, such as Senator McCarthy's blanket indictment of the State Department early in 1950, can have no other than a shattering effect on the confidence of the American people in their government. The prestige of the United States abroad suffers incalculably from such attacks. And the formulation of foreign policy is paralyzed at home by the fear that restraint and reason will be characterized as traitorous. In such an atmosphere only the most extreme chauvinism can pass for patriotism.

The point is patently illustrated in connection with events in the Far East. The readiness of the China Lobby to impute disloyalty to every realistic appraisal of the collapse of the Chinese Nationalist government has made a rational China policy impossible. The State Department has been forced to cling to a transparent fiction. In other areas as well, mere anti-communism has taken the place of a reasoned evaluation of American interests, allying this country with discredited regimes abroad. Those who dared to protest or dissent were liable to vilification as Communist sympathizers.

George Kennan, the former counselor of the State Department, expressed the nature of the danger:

The atmosphere of public life in Washington does not have to deteriorate much further to produce a situation in which very few of our more quiet and sensitive and gifted people will be able to continue in government. . . . The margin of safety with which our country moves

7 *The New York Times*, September 13, 1950.

in the world today is not great enough to permit us to be reckless and wasteful with the talents and the idealism of those people we depend on for the generalship of our peacetime battles.

This is not an atmosphere conducive to national security. The men responsible for creating it may be credited with good intentions. They will be referred to in this book, for the sake of convenience and to avoid imputing to them any impropriety of motive, as Americanists. But they are guilty nonetheless of the gravest and most dangerous form of disloyalty to the United States. They are disloyal to the principles and purposes that are the genius of the American society.

In the aftermath of World War I, when there was a similar fear that America might be subverted by enemies from within, the late Senator William E. Borah observed:

The safeguards of our liberty are not so much in danger from those who openly oppose them as from those who, professing to believe in them, are willing to ignore them when found inconvenient for their purposes; the former we can deal with, but the latter, professing loyalty, either by precept or example undermine the very first principles of our government and are far the more dangerous.

The disloyalty of the Americanists impairs national security more seriously than the comparable disloyalty of the Communists —which will be discussed in the succeeding chapter. It is more deeply subversive, strikes more injuriously at the real roots of loyalty and of American strength. It would, in fact, meet the threat of communism by the substitution of Communist techniques for the techniques of freedom. If the relatively impotent Communists aim at overthrowing the government of the United States, the Americanists, whether they are aware of it or not, aim at overthrowing the essential values which that government was instituted to secure.

CHAPTER II

THE COMMUNIST PROBLEM

Those who won our independence by revolution were not cowards. They did not fear political change. They did not exalt order at the cost of liberty. To courageous, self-reliant men, with confidence in the power of free and fearless reasoning applied through the processes of popular government, no danger flowing from speech can be deemed clear and present, unless the incidence of the evil apprehended is so imminent that it may befall before there is opportunity for full discussion. If there be time to expose through discussion the falsehood and fallacies, to avert the evil by the processes of education, the remedy to be applied is more speech, not enforced silence. Only an emergency can justify repression. Such must be the rule if authority is to be reconciled with freedom. Such, in my opinion, is the command of the Constitution.[1]

T HE COMMUNISTS present a perplexing problem to the American people. Those who gloss over the problem distort reality no less than those who are obsessed by it to the point of seeing no other dangers in the world today. It needs to be faced in its true dimensions and to be dealt with pragmatically. Two tough facts require recognition at the outset.

One is that the Soviet Union is today pursuing expansionist and aggressive policies. Americans would be fatally shortsighted to pretend, as many of them did about Italy, Germany, and

[1] Louis D. Brandeis: Concurring opinion in *Whitney* v. *California*, 274 U.S. 357 (1927).

Japan in the 1930s, that these policies do not imperil them. Totalitarianism endowed with power—whether totalitarianism of the so-called Right or the so-called Left—is made aggressive by its inner compulsions and for that reason is always a menace to free societies.

The second fact is that the Communist Party of the United States (CPUSA) is an instrument of Russian foreign policy. Judged by its conduct, it is not a native political party in the accepted American sense of the term. Rather it is an organization which, if not directly controlled by orders from the Kremlin, is at any rate so responsive to the aims and changing directions of the Russian Politburo as to make the distinction academic.

There has been nothing in the previous history of the United States quite like this organization which consistently serves a foreign power. In earlier times of international tension the United States has had to cope with clusters of foreign-born individuals whose fidelity to this country was colored by old-world ties and sympathies. The Communist Party is by no means to be confused with these. It is made up of men and women who wish to transform America in the image, real or idealized, of the Soviet Union and who believe that non-democratic means will be justified and necessary to effect that change. When the Supreme Court ruled on the constitutionality of the Taft-Hartley Act, with its provisions that labor unions shall be denied access to the facilities of the National Labor Relations Board unless their officers sign affidavits that they are not members of the Communist Party, Mr. Justice Jackson offered a concurring opinion that was remarkable for the sweep of its dicta and its judicial notice of data not in evidence before the Court. "Congress could rationally conclude," he said, that:

1. The goal of the Communist Party is to seize powers of government by and for a minority rather than to acquire power through the vote of a free electorate. . . .

2. The Communist Party alone among American parties past or present is dominated and controlled by a foreign government. . . .

3. Violent and undemocratic means are the calculated and indispensable methods to attain the Communist Party's goal. . . .

4. The Communist Party has sought to gain this leverage and hold on the American population by acquiring control of the labor movement. . . .

Although unsupported by the kind of evidence that would usually be required in a court of law, this broad indictment comports with the common sense of the subject. But Mr. Justice Jackson added a fifth generalization, the validity of which is much more open to question. "Every member of the Communist Party," he said, "is an agent to execute the Communist program." It is true that every member has undertaken to obey party orders and has been admitted to membership only after he has been certified as reliable; and most of the political innocents who joined the party in the 1930s have by now withdrawn or been purged, so that today only the self-deluded and the extreme zealots remain. Even among these, however, there are important differences in motivation and purpose and depth of devotion to the party. They are not equally irredeemable; many could be brought back into society if a way were left open to them. There is certainly not nearly as much uniformity among them as the party's discipline aims to impose.

The generalization remains true that Communists are people who have rejected the American system of government. The system they espouse is called radical because it embraces an element of economic novelty. In its political arrangements it is reactionary. Russian Communist political philosophy represents a reversion to authoritarian rule from which the American colonies led in the emancipation of mankind nearly two centuries ago. Arthur M. Schlesinger, Jr.,[2] is among those who have shown the fallacy of looking at communism and fascism as though they were at opposite ends of a linear political spectrum. They are in point of fact a great deal closer to each other than either of them is to

[2] Arthur M. Schlesinger, Jr., *The Vital Center* (Boston: Houghton Mifflin, 1949), p. 144.

the more moderate philosophies supposed to lie between the extremes of the spectrum. Their relationship might be more illuminatingly represented by a broken circle or a horseshoe, with the fascist and communist systems almost joined.

In their political arrangements fascism and communism both subordinate the individual to the State. Both control the media of public information, vest power in a single disciplined party, suppress all opposition, and presume the infallibility of an appointed or self-appointed leader. These have always been the characteristics of a dictatorship. Thus, to speak of present-day communism as a radical innovation is to ignore history.

The radicalism of the communist system lies in its substitution of public for private ownership of the means of production and in its introduction of comprehensive economic planning. These have, to be sure, important political implications. But a socialization of industry, as Socialist and Labor parties have demonstrated in Britain and elsewhere, need not entail the destruction of civil liberties; and a good deal of experience in the United States as well as abroad has shown that it is possible to undertake many kinds of economic planning without suppressing political opposition. Whether political totalitarianism will inevitably result from economic totalitarianism—or, to put it in different terms, whether political freedom is necessarily dependent on free enterprise—is a matter about which reasonable men may differ.

It can scarcely be disputed, however, that in Russia totalitarianism has ruled by terror, and individual liberty as we conceive it has been extinguished. The real guilt of the American Communists—a guilt they share as individuals in varying degrees—has been their willingness to close their eyes to this reality and to regard the suffering and degradation of millions of human beings as incidents in the journey to their classless Nirvana. If loyalty to the United States means loyalty to American principles and to the American experiment, the Communists cannot claim any share in it. Their devotion, however sincere it may be, is to values antithetical to those that inspired the formation of the American Union and have guided its development. They have renounced self-government and individual responsibility.

The Communists, then, are enemies of the United States because they are enemies of American values, no less than because they are tools of a foreign government. To recognize them as enemies, however, is not to acknowledge that they gravely imperil the nation. The beginning of common sense in the situation is to gauge the strength of the CPUSA as based on its present membership and its history during the last two decades. Only then will we be in a position to judge its real potentialities for mischief.

When the stock market crashed in 1929 the party had been established in this country for ten years, but according to the testimony of Benjamin Gitlow, twice its candidate for the vice-presidency, its membership had never risen to more than sixteen thousand. Sympathizers with the party were more numerous and could fill Madison Square Garden whenever a protest meeting was called; but without bringing all their children along they could hardly have filled the Yale Bowl. Two presidential elections had given a partial tally of their numbers. In 1924 the Communists had received 33,361 votes and in 1928, when they made a vigorous campaign, they had received 48,770, as against more than twenty-one million for the Republican candidate. The party had a fair amount of financial support (about half of which, Gitlow says in a book about his experiences,[3] was supplied from Russia); its members worked for it devotedly, planning, speaking, and traveling about, so that each man counted for ten or a dozen; yet for all its talk about the "broad masses," it had so far made no impression on them.

Nor did it win their support during the years that followed, in spite of crises at home and abroad and its own frantic efforts. Its highest voting strength was achieved in 1932, a few months before the bank holiday, when its candidate for the presidency, William

[3] Benjamin Gitlow, *I Confess* (New York: E. P. Dutton, 1940).

Z. Foster, received 102,991 ballots at the polls.[4] That was far from being enough to win him a single electoral vote; and neither in that campaign nor in any other has anyone achieved election to Congress as a Communist Party candidate.

In 1936, when the party supported Earl Browder for the presidency, its popular support dropped to 80,159 votes. Browder was again the nominee in 1940, and his popular support dropped farther to 46,251 votes. In that year, however, the voting was not an accurate index of the party's strength, since it was off the ballot in many states and its members had received a sort of dispensation to vote for Roosevelt. There were no Communist candidates and in theory there was no Communist Party in 1944; it had become at that time the Communist Political Association. In 1948 it threw its support to Henry A. Wallace, running as leader of the Progressive Party. How largely the Communists contributed to his total of slightly more than a million votes is necessarily a matter of guesswork. With their dogged industry they performed a great deal of organizational work and doorbell ringing for the Progressives, although it was the general opinion among political commentators that they alienated more voters than they won over. It cannot be doubted that the great bulk of Wallace support came from pacifists, disillusioned Democrats, and others who supposed that they could thus register a more impressive protest against the inevitable Republican landslide than they could by voting for Harry S Truman, who, as everybody knew, had no chance of being elected.

At the height of its numerical strength, about 1940, the CPUSA boasted of having a hundred thousand dues-paying members, in a nation with a population of a hundred and thirty-one millions. New members were being recruited continually, but old ones were dropping away with each shift in the party line; and meanwhile the "broad masses" remained untouched and hostile. The question is why this little party, torn apart by doctrinal disputes and personal rivalries and directed from Moscow without

[4] The figures on the Communist vote in different elections are from the *Information Please Almanac, 1949.*

much knowledge of the American mind, nevertheless won the temporary support of many American intellectuals, so that its influence during the 1930s was far greater than its numerical strength.

The answer has to do with the emotional atmosphere of the depression years. Throughout the country there was a profound sense of bewilderment and dislocation. The young intellectuals, including those who would for a time be Communist sympathizers, were more articulate than the rest of the population; but they shared with the public at large a loss of confidence in the business and political leaders who had been in power when the crisis was in the making and an undefined, generalized demand for reform—or at least for change—that manifested itself in the presidential election of 1932. Sherwood Anderson expressed it in these words:

> We are people who passed through the World War and its aftermath. We saw the upflaring of prosperity, lived through the Harding and Coolidge times. We got the hard-boiled boys and the wise-crackers. We got, oh, so many new millionaires. As a people now we are fed up on it all.
>
> We do not want cynicism. We want belief. . . .
>
> There is at least a chance to set up the framework of a new thing. Be quiet. Wait! Don't push. Those who have had a stranglehold upon America have been served long enough.[5]

Whatever the American people were looking for, they were through with "normalcy" as Warren G. Harding had intended the term when he used it in 1920. They were not prepared to insist upon any fundamental change in the capitalist system, but they were quite prepared to demand that the system should serve the general welfare a great deal more effectively. They were ready to embrace a moderate change in the relationship of the individual to the State, by which the federal government would maintain the economic well-being of the American people, as well as guarding their lives and liberties. Franklin D. Roosevelt,

---

[5] Sherwood Anderson, *Puzzled America* (New York: Charles Scribner's Sons, 1935).

an astute interpreter of the public mind, was ready to give them the degree of change they desired.

But before the New Deal could demonstrate by various measures, not always consistent with one another, its responsiveness to popular hopes, there was a frantic search for simple and magic remedies. A sick society listens to political medicine men. The United States listened for a while to Howard Scott with his streamlined, erg-powered technocracy. It listened to Huey Long and his glittering proposals for sharing the wealth and making every man a king. It listened to Father Coughlin's pieties about a system of social justice in which "Jewish money-lenders" would be scapegoats for all the wrongs of the past. It listened to Father Townsend's appealing plan to convert the country into a rest haven for grandparents. In the Middle West it listened to William Lemke's ideas for a revived agrarian revolt. In California it listened to Upton Sinclair's EPIC program for Ending Poverty, at least In California.

Liberal intellectuals listened more seriously to the socialist plea for a planned, classless society to which every man would contribute according to his ability and by which he would be sustained according to his needs. Socialist theory appealed to the liberals because its approach to the problem of the times was not a hastily concocted nostrum but a program which had long been in the minds of men, comprehensive, carefully thought through, and ready with answers to most of the criticisms leveled at it. The socialists, moreover, were the only physicians whose diagnosis of the ills of capitalism had preceded and predicted the disease.

The socialist movement had the force of a tremendous idealism. The kind of society envisaged for America by Edward Bellamy, at the end of the nineteenth century, was in far greater conformity with Christian ethics than was the ruthless competition of capitalism. The kind of society advocated by Norman Thomas was one in which all the libertarian tenets of the United States would be retained and economic changes would be carried through by peaceful and constitutional means. Mr. Thomas polled 884,781 votes—about nine times as many as William Z. Foster—when he campaigned for the presidency on the Socialist ticket in 1932. Many felt, however, that his idealism, his moderation, and his personal integrity were the qualities of a philosopher rather than those of a practical politician. Besides, much of his program was quietly incorporated into the New Deal.

The one place in the world where socialist ideas had been in some measure tested by operation and experience was the Soviet Union. There, of course, they had suffered gross distortion; but it was possible to believe, at least in the early 1930s, that the distortion was temporary and that the ideal might still be realized. Socialist economics, as put into practice by the Russian Communists, seemed to promise a vast improvement in the material welfare of the Russian people. Moreover, the hope that liberty would develop out of the party dictatorship in Russia was fostered by the professions of the Soviet leaders. Theirs at least was not a system which, like that of fascism and nazism, glorified authority for its own sake. A dictatorship that called itself "proletarian" was disarming; it tempted Americans to feel that in this case despotism was the necessary means to a utopian end. The end could enlist the fervor of men devoted to freedom even though the means seemed abhorrent—and should have been recognized at the time as inevitably destructive of the end.

The illusion that freedom would grow out of despotism in Russia was encouraged by the publication of the Soviet Constitution in 1936. Being word men, the intellectuals put too much weight on Russian words. Their impulse was to take the constitution literally, as the expression of ideals that were already being put into practice. In the same way their imaginations were fired by the Five Year Plans, which seemed to be the scenarios for great dramas of collective effort. Taught to believe that the American press printed lies about Russia, the intellectuals refused to credit one story that was documented more fully with each passing year. It was the story of the 1932–33 famine in the Ukraine that resulted from one feature of the first Five Year

Plan: the forced collectivization of the peasants. For hundreds of thousands or millions of Ukrainians the collective drama had ended in a mass tragedy.

Industrial production was rising in spite of the famine; it was marching ahead with seven-league boots along roads surveyed by the planners in Moscow. That was what impressed the intellectuals: the progress at all costs of a huge planned and collective effort in Russia, at a time when free enterprise seemed to be leading this country into economic chaos. Many Americans were beginning to believe that our own problems would have to be solved by planning on a similar nation-wide scale and by the use of government for the achievement of collective purposes.

The Soviet policy toward racial minorities also evoked enthusiasm among all those who were opposed to racial discrimination. Negroes were told that Russia was genuinely free from color prejudice and the restrictive regulations that kept them from being first-class citizens of the United States. During the early depression years the Communists made special efforts to win them over, even promising that, after the inevitable revolution in this country, the Black Belt in the Southern states would become an autonomous Negro republic. They also tried to win over the Jews, by telling them that the Russian revolution had put an end to pogroms and persecutions. The Communists made surprisingly little progress with either of these minorities, but their pretensions made some impression on American liberals. Devoted to the principle of human equality, the liberals came to regard the Soviet policy toward racial and religious minorities as something of a model for a bigoted world, an actual putting into practice of American principles.

All during the middle 1930s the Russian government was seeking to win the support of liberals and the labor movement in Europe and America. The party line had changed, and faithful members made a point of being kind even to socialists, whom they temporarily stopped abusing as "social fascists." It was the time of the "People's Front" against war and fascism. The Communists invented the phrase; and in Spain and France they helped to form People's Front governments under Socialist prime ministers. Liberals were favorably impressed by the foreign policy of the Soviet Union, which seemed to be guided by liberal ideals.

The USSR had joined the League of Nations and was trying to convince the Western Powers that they should unitedly oppose the rise of fascism. The Soviet Foreign Commissar was Maxim Litvinov, an old revolutionist who felt at home in Western Europe. In this country the heirs of Wilsonian idealism were full of admiration for Litvinov, since he was trying harder than any other statesman to revive the authority of the League and since that authority seemed to offer the best hope for the preservation of peace. It was Litvinov alone, except for Haile Selassie, who sought to have the League impose sanctions on Mussolini when he launched his attack on Ethiopia. Litvinov said what American liberals desperately wanted to hear from their own Secretary of State; and he said it once more in connection with the Japanese invasion of China in 1937. At the same time he was assailing Mussolini and Hitler for having plotted with Franco and the other Spanish generals to overthrow the popularly elected government of Spain. In this last instance the Soviet Union supported his words with deeds. While the Western democracies were pretending to believe that the assault on the Spanish republic, with German planes and Italian troops, was merely a civil war, Russia was doing its best within the limits of international law to help the Loyalists.

The part played by Russia in the Spanish tragedy ended ignobly. One can see from the vantage point of a later decade that the Loyalist cause, after being aided by Communist support, was eventually corrupted by it. We cannot, however, be altogether sure that the role played by Russia was a more ignoble one than that played by Britain and the United States, and the Russian policy was in any case much less shortsighted. The Russians understood how much the Spanish war meant in the growth of Nazi and Fascist power. They foresaw the terrible consequences that

might have been avoided if the conquest of Spain by German and
Italian arms had been forbidden by the democracies.

Capitalizing on the powerful anti-fascist sentiments stirred by
Hitler's persecution of minorities and later by the Spanish war,
the American Communists organized the League against War and
Fascism as an instrument for money-raising and propaganda. A
great number of non-Communists joined the League, not because
they were followers of the Politburo, but because they shared the
aversion it proclaimed for war and fascism. In the hope of achieving a broader popular base the League was suddenly transformed,
in October 1937, into the League for Peace and Democracy. An
even greater number of non-Communists joined it then, because
they were heartily in favor of peace and democracy.

Soon there were developments in the world that made peace
and democracy seem less effective as Communist catchwords.
After the surrender of the Western democracies at Munich (September 1938) and the fall of Madrid in March 1939, it was evident that there would be a sharp change in Russian policy. If
the Western liberals were unable to determine the foreign policy
of their own governments, why should the Russians bother to
keep them as allies? Litvinov with his Western sympathies was
replaced at the Foreign Commissariat by V. M. Molotov, who was
no friend of the liberals. The Russians were getting ready to
reveal that their liberal policies, admired by Western journalists,
were policies only and not principles to be followed at all costs.
The real principle was power and still more power for the Soviet
government.

The American Communists fell into line, at the cost of thousands of resignations from the party and the weakening or destruction of its united-front organizations. They ceased to be in
favor of peace and democracy on August 23, 1939, when Molotov
and Ribbentrop negotiated their short-lived non-aggression pact.
After that the Communists were in favor of peace (except for
Poland and Finland) and became the rather embarrassed apolo-
gists for German and Italian fascism. Nearly all the liberals with-

drew from the League for Peace and Democracy after the announcement of the Russo-German Pact; but a small band of incorrigible innocents joined its successor "front," American Peace Mobilization, which lasted until it was caught picketing the White House, in protest against American aid to the Allies, when Hitler began his invasion of the Soviet Union on June 22, 1941.

The League against War and Fascism, with the two other leagues that grew out of it, was the most prominent of the united- or popular-front organizations that flourished during the 1930s, but there were scores and hundreds of much the same nature— leagues, committees, clubs, alliances, and associations; national, international, or local in scope; formed ostensibly for purposes of defense, relief, aid, or friendship. Their real purposes, if they were controlled by the Communists, were propaganda and money-raising. The propaganda was carried on through public meetings and newspaper publicity for usually quite worthy causes, with the implied lesson that Communists took the lead in supporting them. The money-raising was persistent, ingenious, and also uncontrolled, in the sense that very few of the "front" organizations published a yearly audit of the funds they collected. Later there was abundant testimony by ex-Communists that money donated for one cause, such as the defense of some prisoner convicted after an unfair trial, was often diverted to another, less popular cause, or simply went to defray the current expenses of Communist headquarters.

If the organization had a large membership, like the League against War and Fascism, it was composed in the majority of people who were not even Communist sympathizers, but who merely supported some of the same popular causes. In the real Communist "front" organizations, however (and it must be remembered that there were many organizations improperly accused of being "fronts"), there was always an executive board which was dominated by Communist sympathizers; and there was also an "executive secretary" who was the effective head of the organization and was under party orders. Some of the smaller "front" committees consisted essentially of the executive secretary and a letterhead. The letterhead carried an imposing list of names: those of the president, two or three vice-presidents, the treasurer, the secretary (not "executive"), and twenty or thirty "sponsors." All the names would be those of more or less prominent liberals, although there might be two or three party members sprinkled among them. The actual work of the committee—raising money by appeals typed below the imposing letterhead —would be performed by the executive secretary. Very seldom did the sponsors know just how the money was spent.

It is an interesting question why intelligent persons lent their names to organizations in which they had no power and about which they had not even much effective knowledge. "I wanted to help," one of them said long afterward, "but I had no time and very little money; all I had was a reputation for being honest and public-minded. When a new organization asked me to be a member or a sponsor or a director, I'd ask them to tell me what they proposed to do. Then, if I approved of their aims, I'd say, 'Look, I can't speak for you or write letters or come to meetings, but if you want to use my name you can have it as a donation.' They would take my name and go away as if I had given them a hundred-dollar bill, and that would be the last I heard from them." It wasn't quite the last, because the same man was offered a wartime job by the government and was forced to resign it in the face of attacks by the House Committee on Un-American Activities, which had always made a point of collecting letterheads. The committee accused him of having belonged to more than fifty subversive organizations. "They couldn't prove that I was disloyal or unpatriotic," he said, "but they certainly made me question my good sense."

Lack of good sense or judgment or experience, not lack of loyalty, is the worst charge that can be brought against most of the men and women who, by the hundreds of thousands, joined various "front" organizations during the 1930s. They didn't want to overthrow the government; they wanted to help in good causes, as a civic duty. It is important to remember, moreover, that for the most part these were genuinely good causes at the time these men and women joined them. Some of them subsequently came under Communist domination; and sooner or later the non-Communists, after an attempt to recapture control, left them in disgust. In the main, their participation, while it lasted, was not only innocent but altogether praiseworthy. But the Committee on Un-American Activities has always been prone to judge the character of an organization in the 1930s by what it became in the 1940s—and in the climate of still later anti-Communist emotion.

It cannot be denied that some of the organizations they joined served as recruiting grounds for the Communist Party. There were always enthusiasts who wanted to do more for the cause, whatever it might be, than merely lending their names to it or collecting money or shouting slogans in unison. The Communists told them—and succeeded in convincing some—that the best way to make their help effective was to join the party and work under its leadership. The opportunity to work hard for a fixed purpose and assist in changing the world was among the strongest inducements that the Communists offered to their proselytes.

From memoirs and confessions published since that time we learn that intellectuals, during the 1930s, temporarily joined the party for other reasons as well. They felt lonely, isolated, and the party offered them a sense of comradeship or communion, of working together toward common goals. They were morally confused, and the party offered them what seemed to be a fixed standard of conduct: anything that brought the revolution nearer was morally justified. They were propelled by a need to defy the world—perhaps because they had never been able to defy their parents—or a need for self-punishment which found satisfaction in affiliation with an outcast group. They felt a sense of personal guilt, and perhaps this was the strongest of the circumstances that tempted them into the party. The intellectuals had struggled too little, surrendered too easily, been entirely too fortunate; and now in the midst of a world-wide depression they felt a wish to change everything, not only in the world outside but in their hearts. They wanted to bury the dead past and be reborn into a new life. That, after all, is one of the oldest human desires, expressed in the rituals of almost every religion.

At other times a mood like this might have led to a widespread religious revival. Most of the churches, however, had let themselves be cut off from the main current of American ideas. It is true that the Catholics gained a few distinguished converts among the intellectuals, and would gain many more at the end of the decade; but the Communists gained hundreds or even thousands. Communism is most certainly not a church in the ordinary sense of the term. It proclaims its opposition to all existing religions, asserting that they are allied with the ruling class and that their principal function is to make people patiently bear their present sorrows. On the other hand, the party has performed for its members the social and institutional functions of a church, providing them with a creed, a code of conduct, and even a sort of ritual, while the more zealous party members have acted as a priesthood. There is a simple reason why Communism gained converts in the 1930s: it was almost the only crusading religion.

On the record it has not been a religion that has permanently satisfied the needs of human beings. Except in countries under Communist domination (and perhaps even there, if we could look into people's hearts), it has lost its converts even more rapidly than it gained them. In this country thousands of pilgrims boarded, so to speak, the Moscow Express, clustering thickly on the steps and in the baggage car; but at every sharp turn in the party line they were jolted from the train. The rapid turnover in party membership during the 1930s is a historical fact that has never been sufficiently discussed; of course the party tried to keep it secret. With the announcement of the Russo-German Pact and after the Finnish war, cars on the Moscow Express were running empty.

The most authoritative estimate of the numerical strength of the Communist Party in 1950 was offered by J. Edgar Hoover, director of the Federal Bureau of Investigation, in the course of testimony before a Senate Appropriations Subcommittee:

According to our best information, there is a total of 54,174 members of the Communist Party in the United States at the present time. . . . Most of the members of the Communist Party in the United States are in the concentrated sections of population of the country. For example, New York State has 25,000 members; California, 6977; Illinois, 3361; Pennsylvania, 2876; Ohio, 2834; Michigan, 1250; Massachusetts, 1022; Nevada, 23; Wyoming, 10; Tennessee, 27; Alabama, 141; New Hampshire, 43; and so on.[6]

The simile most in fashion regarding the Communist Party is that it is like an iceberg, only a fraction of which is visible above the surface of the sea; the real menace is said to be represented by the major portion that remains submerged. Mr. Hoover observed in his testimony before the Appropriations subcommittee:

Even though there are only 54,174 members of the party, the fact remains that the party leaders themselves boast that for every party member there are ten others who follow the party line and who are ready, willing, and able to do the party's work. In other words, there is a potential fifth column of 540,000 people dedicated to this philosophy.

One might expect Mr. Hoover to be among the last to regard the boast of party leaders as authoritative. It is impossible to accept their claim that "for every party member there are ten others . . . ready, willing, and able to do the party's work" unless one also accepts their public description of the party's work. Undoubtedly a great many persons are ready, willing, and able to work, for example, against racial discrimination or for abolition of the poll tax or for a tax-supported system of health insurance. But although the party professes to support these purposes, it would be as naive to suppose that all others who support them

[6] In its issue of October 4, 1949, the *Daily Worker* published, in accordance with the act of Congress requiring such information from daily, weekly, semiweekly, and tri-weekly newspapers, a sworn declaration that "the average number of copies of each issue of this publication sold or distributed, through the mails or otherwise, to paid subscribers during the twelve months preceding the date shown above is 23,400." The figure is a rather pitiful one, whether looked at from a commercial or from a political point of view.

are Communist fellow-travelers as it would be to suppose that these efforts constitute the real work of the party.

Certainly the party has concealed sympathizers; but there is no good reason to believe that the number is nearly so great as that claimed by the Communists. When Mr. Hoover talked about "a potential fifth column of 540,000 people," he was confusing the Communist problem with the ex-Communist problem, which is quite a different matter.

In appraising the real strength of the CPUSA and its hidden supporters, it is essential to distinguish between their aims and their potentialities. Their capacity for evil is not necessarily commensurate with their evil design. It is a fundamental misapprehension to suppose that they are powerful simply because they are abhorrent.

Let us look at the ambitions of the Communists in terms of the means and the forces available to them. They are generally said to aim at the overthrow of the United States government by force and violence. Merely to state this aim is to make it ludicrous. To suppose that in peacetime 54,000 or 540,000 Communists, however disciplined, however enthusiastic, could overthrow the United States government and make the American people accept them as masters is as rational as a belief in sea serpents or dragons. Americans are not docile; our country is not in a state of chaos; we have law-enforcement agencies, not counting the Army, the Navy, the Air Force, and the Marines, quite capable of putting down any uprising so fantastic.

Revolutions are the offspring of wretchedness, despair, and the frustration of all orderly efforts to accomplish needed reforms. Governments are not overthrown by citizens they serve; they are overthrown only by subjects they oppress or by the pressure of armed force from outside the country. There is not a single instance since the establishment of the Soviet Union in which a duly constituted government was overturned by a native Communist uprising. The case of Czechoslovakia is sometimes cited as an exception; but the Czechoslovak people succumbed to the threat of a Red Army massed on their borders; Soviet officers were actually in Prague. They were not subverted by Communist propaganda or overcome by an internal coup; and they did not, in the majority, welcome Communist rule. In a sense they were as much the victims of external military aggression as if their country had been invaded. In France and Italy, where the Red Army was not an immediate threat and where ECA funds aided the process of postwar reconstruction, the strength of the Communist Parties has declined significantly.

In the United States the conditions that give birth to revolution do not exist, no matter how Communist propaganda may strive to magnify the shortcomings of American life. There is no widespread discontent or disaffection; nor will there be so long as orderly avenues for the redress of grievances are kept open, so long as dissent may expend itself in free expression—so long, that is, as the government itself remains loyal to the purposes for which it was established.

The real menace of communism, as Mr. Hoover sees it, lies in infiltration which may make possible espionage or sabotage in behalf of the Soviet Union. It may be taken as a matter of course that the Russian government has trained secret agents working in the United States. So have other governments, and it is to be hoped that American agents are inside the USSR, and elsewhere, discovering and reporting as much as they can about military strengths and weaknesses. Doubtless American agents in Russia derive as much assistance as possible from such dissident elements as they can find there. Doubtless, too, the American agents take pains to avoid having themselves identified as Americans or as members of any group suspected of being anti-Communist. Similarly it may be presumed that the professional Russian agents in America have at least enough wit to try to avoid identification as Russians or as affiliates of the CPUSA.

The Communist Party, or rather its concealed members and hangers-on, give Russian agents here a peculiar advantage. The lesson taught by the detailed and careful report of a Canadian Royal Commission on Russian espionage activities in Canada is that Communists and some Communist sympathizers are susceptible of exploitation for espionage purposes. It would seem that they form a natural pool from which professional Soviet agents tend to draw recruits for their espionage activities. But it scarcely follows from this that all Communists, let alone all Communist sympathizers, are spies or even potential spies. Espionage requires a kind of skill and hardihood that not many possess; and the opportunities to practice it are rare. Nevertheless, the danger is a serious one; and as the case of Dr. Klaus Fuchs and his American accomplices made plain, incalculable damage can be done by concealed Communists serving the Soviet Union. Extreme care needs to be exercised to keep such persons from access to information affecting national defense. It is, however, a danger that calls for caution, not panic. It can be averted by rational security measures that neither violate civil rights nor resort to extra-legal sanctions. It is essentially a counterintelligence problem, not a political problem.

A more serious danger might arise from Communist infiltration of labor unions. Testifying in 1947 before the House Committee on Un-American Activities, Mr. Hoover said:

Now, so far as the danger in this country is concerned in case of any conflict with a foreign country, there is no question but that any divided loyalty of any kind to any other country is a serious menace to the security of this country.

I think it was clearly shown in the early days of the war. We had two very serious strikes, one in Los Angeles and one in Wisconsin, which were largely instituted by Communist groups.

As soon as the shift in alliance of great powers came about and Hitler was separated from the alliance with Stalin, those strikes faded out and were discontinued.

Now, you well know from the investigations that this committee have already made that there are officers in charge of certain great unions in this country dealing with transportation, communications, and other various phases that are very vital to our structure, who are Communists, and could therefore bring about a general strike, if they so desired. That is the danger.

The danger is not lightly to be dismissed, since it could produce serious slowdowns or shutdowns in vital industries; but it should not be exaggerated. The strikes at the North American Aviation Company and at the Allis-Chalmers plants, to which Mr. Hoover presumably referred, were called by unions whose principal officers were said to be Communists or under Communist influence. Behind these two strikes, however, were real grievances over wages and working conditions, and it is important to remember that they occurred at a time when the United States was not yet directly involved in the war. Even after Pearl Harbor there were, of course, strikes by both management and labor, and they were not instigated by Communist groups. Those were the years when Russia was fighting on our side, and the Communists were promoting labor-management cooperation.

Today they are again preaching the class struggle, but they have lost most of their strength in labor unions. Even if they were ten times as powerful, it is very much to be doubted that Communist labor leaders could persuade American workers to engage in any strike, let alone a general strike, the purpose of which was to injure the United States and assist an enemy country in time of war. Men with a strong sense of loyalty to leaders who have served their union effectively may obey them blindly so far as their relations with their employers are concerned; but they will not necessarily obey them blindly in other matters. John Lewis's mine workers, who follow his orders in most instances when he negotiates in their behalf with the coal operators, respectfully declined to follow him into the Republican Party in 1940. The longshoremen of the West Coast have shown great faith in Harry Bridges as their agent in dealing with the stevedoring companies; but they did not let him lead them into obstructing shipments for the support of American intervention in Korea, and there is nothing to indicate that they voted in state or national elections as Harry Bridges presumably would have liked them to vote.

It is easy to exaggerate the extent of Communist infiltration in the American labor movement. Probably none of the vital industrial unions in which Communists or their sympathizers have won key positions has any large number of Communists in its rank and file. They are virtually nonexistent in the AFL and in the railway brotherhoods. In the CIO they have recently been reduced to insignificance. Labor unions are probably the most sophisticated element of American life with respect to the tactics of Communists, having been most intimately subjected to them. They can be confidently counted on to keep their Communists under control so long as outside attacks on the Communists are not made a pretext for attacks on the unions themselves.

There is no valid substitute for the democratic process in dealing with the problem of communism in the labor movement. In union after union where Communist influence had grown at one time to serious dimensions—the Automobile Workers, the American Newspaper Guild, the National Maritime Union, to name but a few at random—non-Communist opposition recaptured control and relegated the Communists to impotence. The CIO cleaned its own house early in 1950 of affiliated unions which remained under Communist domination. This is the only way in which the disease can be destroyed without destroying the patient in the process.

The provision of the Taft-Hartley Act denying unions access to the facilities of the National Labor Relations Board unless their officers swear that they are not Communists may be, as the Supreme Court said it was in May 1950, a legitimate exercise of the congressional power to regulate interstate commerce. But under its terms, as the Chief Justice acknowledged, "Congress has undeniably discouraged the lawful exercise of political freedoms." One may reasonably doubt whether, as a matter of expediency, the anticipated gains were worth so heavy a cost. Anti-Communist labor leaders such as Philip Murray refused to sign the affidavit because of an objection on principle to test oaths. Some unions whose officers did sign the affidavit remained under disguised Communist domination nonetheless. Organized labor as a whole tended to look on the affidavit requirement as a hostile attempt to circumscribe its freedom in choosing leaders. The non-

Communist provision of the Taft-Hartley Act accomplished little
that could not and would not have been accomplished by voluntary democratic action within the American labor movement.

The most serious danger growing out of Communist activities
in the United States is the possibility that the Communists—or
some of them—might serve as a fifth column in case of war between this country and Russia. Espionage, direct physical sabotage, disruption of transportation and communications, and violation of air-raid protection rules might be attempted. Such acts
would, of course, constitute treason in the strict constitutional
sense of the term and could have disastrous consequences. Ordinary prudence suggests that it would be better, if possible, to
prevent them than to punish them.

What Communist treason could accomplish if we were fighting
a full-scale war depends on the circumstances of the war. If this
country were invaded or in imminent danger of invasion or subject to atomic attack, more drastic measures would be necessary
to forestall treason than if the fighting were confined to distant
frontiers. In war, military security is the paramount consideration. But even in war, military security should never be allowed
to serve as a pretext for the needless abandonment of civil processes, institutions, and liberties.

The McCarran Act—adopted by Congress in September 1950
over a courageous and challenging presidential veto—was the
culmination of a number of efforts initiated by the House Committee on Un-American Activities to deal with the Communist
problem through repressive legislation. It embraces three distinct
approaches to the problem: (1) an attempt to deal with the real
and immediate danger of espionage and sabotage by strengthen-
ing the existing statutes which forbid such acts; (2) an attempt to
deal with the contingent but nevertheless serious danger of Communist fifth-column activities in case of war, invasion, or insurrection by providing for the arrest and detention of suspected
spies and saboteurs; and (3) an attempt to deal with the remote

and imaginary danger that Communist propaganda will subvert the devotion of Americans to their own institutions.

The first of these approaches, embodying specific recommendations of the President, involves little, if any, trespass on personal freedom. Vigilant counterespionage and countersabotage measures, together with the most careful protection of classified information and vital installations, can provide an effective check on treasonable activities.

The second approach, authorizing as it does detention on the ground of mere suspicion of an intent to commit espionage or sabotage, involves difficult constitutional questions. It is a drastic measure, repugnant to American traditions. It is contrived, however, to meet an unprecedented situation which, if it should arise, could scarcely be met adequately by any other means. It would probably be necessary, in the event of war with Russia, to arrest summarily the key individuals in the Communist movement in order to render it impotent. Under extreme circumstances, security might require the internment of larger numbers of Communists, especially if they were concentrated in vital defense areas. Attorney General J. Howard McGrath has stated [7] that every Communist in the United States is known to the FBI and other federal law-enforcement agencies. The claim may seem slightly extravagant; but presumably the FBI does know the real leaders of the Communist movement and could round them up swiftly in the event of war, as it rounded up the dangerous Japanese, German, and Italian agents immediately after Pearl Harbor. The job was done so efficiently that, as Mr. Hoover said subsequently, "This nation came through the war with no enemy-directed acts of sabotage." [8] It was, of course, easier to recognize dangerous Bundists than it is to recognize dangerous Communists; and it was easier to deal with them under the law because for the most part they were aliens.

[7] Address to the Fifth National Conference on Citizenship, Washington, May 23, 1950.
[8] *New York Herald Tribune,* November 17, 1947.

Mr. Hoover was reported in the press to have informed a congressional committee early in 1950 that he proposes to arrest some twelve thousand suspected enemy agents immediately following the outbreak of war. The number seems excessive. Such summary action should not, in any case, be left to the discretion of a police chief. If it must be undertaken, it seems preferable that it should be done in conformity with standards formulated by Congress and with provision for prompt hearing and judicial review of each case on an individual basis. Security, not punishment, should be the controlling consideration.

In the present inflamed state of public opinion it is doubtful that reasonable restraint would be possible. Ironically, the FBI has done so much to depict the Communist Party as a terrifying monster that popular anxiety might not be allayed by rational measures, even if they were certified as adequate by J. Edgar Hoover himself. There would be an irrepressible clamor from the Americanist politicians and their journalistic allies to intern not only all the 54,174 Communist Party members on the FBI list but also hundreds of thousands of suspected sympathizers, former sympathizers, and former members who had left the party in disgust. So many innocent and loyal persons would be involved in such a mass incarceration, so many additional persons would become suspect because they had known some of the prisoners or had protested against their arrest, so much fear would be generated, that national unity and security would be disastrously impaired. One defect of concentration camps, apart from considerations of principle, is that they create more trouble than they avert.

It is not to be taken for granted, moreover, that all, or even most, of the persons called Communists by the FBI—let alone those called fellow-travelers—would prove disloyal to the United States in an actual showdown with Russia. Even the most doctrinaire intellectual assumptions may give way in war to the emotional pull of patriotism. The Korean war jolted a number of Americans out of a more or less neurotic somnambulism. Henry Wallace, for instance, after several years of preaching against "Wall Street imperialism," suddenly found that, as he put it, "when my country is at war, and the United Nations sanctions that war, I am on the side of my country and the United Nations."

Dissenting in the cases testing the validity of the non-Communist affidavit provision of the Taft-Hartley Act, Mr. Justice Black pointed out the fallacy of attainting all members of the Communist Party or its "affiliates" on the ground that, as a group, they act in obedience to the commands of a foreign power. "This," he said, "was the precise reason given in sixteenth-century England for attainting all Catholics unless they subscribed to test oaths wholly incompatible with their religion. Yet in the hour of crisis an overwhelming majority of the English Catholics thus persecuted rallied loyally to defend their homeland against Spain and its Catholic troops." [9]

The third approach of the McCarran Act has no relation to internal security at all. It is concerned not with dangerous Communist acts but with Communist ideas. It seeks to shield the American people from these ideas by imposing a variety of disabilities on all members of any group that may be designated a Communist political organization or a "Communist front"—including a requirement that their propaganda be labeled as emanating from a Communist source. Espionage and sabotage are real dangers; subversion is a bugbear. Subversion can be achieved only by inducing a majority, or at least a very large minority, of the American people to renounce their established values and institutions, supplanting them with an alien system naturally abhorrent to them. Communist propaganda, as we have seen, had small success in accomplishing this even in the 1930s when it could represent the Soviet experiment as a hopeful and idealistic one patterned on the principles of American democracy. Now

[9] *CIO* v. *Douds.* He also added an interesting footnote: "35 Eliz. c. 2, for example, was aimed at 'sundry wicked and seditious Persons, who terming themselves Catholicks, and being indeed Spies and Intelligencers, . . . and hiding their most detestable and devilish Purposes under a false Pretext of Religion and Conscience, do secretly wander and shift from Place to Place within this Realm, to corrupt and seduce her Majesty's Subjects, and to stir them to Sedition and Rebellion.' "

that it has revealed itself as an aggressive despotism hostile to the United States, one wonders why there should be any apprehension at all of its widespread acceptance here. The internal security of this country is in no danger from Communist propaganda.

Whether or not Congress may constitutionally restrain the advocacy of Communist ideas, the attempt to do so through legislation such as the McCarran Act is at once foolish and dangerous. It is foolish because it presumes that such advocacy will meet a sympathetic response among an appreciable number of Americans. It is dangerous because it breaches a basic principle on account of an imagined peril. It bears an unmistakable taint of the totalitarianism at which it is aimed. It embraces the very evil it pretends to repel. It represents, in point of fact, the only way in which the Communist program can ever prevail.

Repression of advocacy—even if it is advocacy of violence—is likely to be much more dangerous than the advocacy itself. Pent up, ideas may generate explosive force. Released, they must compete for acceptance with opposing views. The whole foundation of a free society is reliance on the loyalty and good sense of a majority of its members. This at least has been the theory on which political stability has been maintained in the United States for more than a century and a half.

Restraints on Communists as a group ought to be considered, if at all, only in the event of war and a direct military threat to national security. The Korean conflict, although patently the product of Russian-inspired aggression, did not directly threaten the internal safety of the United States. No matter how bitter the antagonism between the United States and the USSR may be—the figure of speech "cold war" should not be permitted to lead us into semantic confusion—we are not now at war with Russia; and to behave as though we were is to end all hope of finding a peaceful solution.

In peacetime the Communist Party can be regarded as a nuisance to be endured for the sake of the great principles that would be flouted if it were suppressed. It can be dealt with by requiring its members to keep their actions within the law and by opposing their evil counsels with good ones. As Mr. Justice Brandeis said in the great opinion from which the motto placed at the head of this chapter is quoted, "If there be time to expose through discussion the falsehood and fallacies, to avert the evil by the processes of education, the remedy to be applied is more speech, not enforced silence. Only an emergency can justify repression." Self-preservation is, of course, the first law of a society as of an individual. Therefore whatever must be done to ward off a threat to its existence will be done. But wanton disregard of its own values can destroy a society no less than the attack of an enemy.

In a dissenting opinion in the Gitlow case, which arose out of the fear of communism after World War I, Mr. Justice Holmes, joined by Mr. Justice Brandeis, argued forcefully against the imposition of needless restraints on advocacy. Benjamin Gitlow was a Left-wing Socialist who later joined the Communist Party and became its candidate for vice-president in 1924 and 1928; still later he left the party, and he is now one of its bitter enemies. In 1919 he had been convicted of violating New York State's Criminal Anarchy Act, under circumstances similar to those under which eleven Communist Party officials were convicted in 1949 of conspiracy to advocate the overthrow of the United States government by force and violence. A frenzied fear of radicalism prevailed in 1919, as it would prevail thirty years later. Gitlow had issued a "Manifesto" pedantically written in Marxian jargon, asserting that "the Communist Internationale calls the proletariat of the world to the final struggle!" It had as much chance of rousing the masses as the unheard trumpetings of the Communist Party in 1950.[10]

The climate of opinion being what it was, Gitlow was sentenced to five years in Sing Sing. He served there, with interludes

[10] Professor Chafee said of Gitlow's pamphlet, "Any agitator who read these thirty-four pages to a mob would not stir them to violence, except possibly against himself. This Manifesto would disperse them faster than the Riot Act." *Free Speech in the United States*, p. 319.

of freedom while his case was being appealed, until he was pardoned by Governor Alfred E. Smith in 1925. The Supreme Court upheld his conviction, Mr. Justice Sanford asserting that the words of the "Manifesto" were "the language of direct incitement." To this Mr. Justice Holmes replied, "Every idea is an incitement. It offers itself for belief, and if believed it is acted on unless some other belief outweighs it or some failure of energy stifles the movement at its birth. The only difference between the expression of an opinion and an incitement in the narrower sense is the speaker's enthusiasm for the result. Eloquence may set fire to reason. But whatever may be thought of the redundant discourse before us, it had no chance of starting a present conflagration." [11]

Who can doubt today that the Republic would have survived if Gitlow's ranting had been left undisturbed thirty years ago? Who, save the frightened Americanists, can doubt that thirty years from now the Republic will have withstood successfully all that the Communist Party can teach or advocate about the duty and necessity of overthrowing the government? The most potent defense against the beliefs of the Communists is an outweighing, affirmative belief in the superiority—and the superior appeal—of American institutions.

In any case, there is no effective bulwark against the ideology of communism that can be erected by law or authority. If the people of the United States want to change their economic system or their form of government, they have an inalienable right and an irrepressible power to do so. "If in the long run the beliefs expressed in proletarian dictatorship are destined to be accepted by the dominant forces of the community," Mr. Justice Holmes went on to say, "the only meaning of free speech is that they should be given their chance and have their way." Loyalty to the United States consists most vitally, perhaps, in a faith that, given their chance in accordance with the pattern of American democracy, they will never have their way.

[11] *Gitlow* v. *New York*, 268 U.S. 652 (1925).

CHAPTER III

PUNISHMENT BY PUBLICITY

If there is any fixed star in our constitutional constellation, it is that no official, high or petty, can prescribe what shall be orthodox in politics, nationalism, religion, or other matters of opinion, or force citizens to confess by word or act their faith therein.[1]

D URING the decade 1939–49 the cult of loyalty found its most characteristic expression in the House of Representatives Committee on Un-American Activities. The members of this body, like the men who conducted the medieval Inquisition, were chosen as judges to determine the existence of heresy and to extirpate it. They identified loyalty with orthodoxy and perfected techniques for the extra-legal punishment of all who questioned their dogma.

No committee in the history of the United States Congress has ever been accorded so vague an assignment and so elastic a definition of its domain. Nothing is foreign to it, nothing is deemed beyond its competence.

When a previously unheard-of individual named G. Racey Jordan confided to a radio commentator late in 1949 that Harry Hopkins had stolen atomic secrets and transmitted them to the Russians in 1943, the Committee on Un-American Activities intervened at once. It might have seemed to an innocent observer

---

[1] Robert H. Jackson, Supreme Court opinion in *West Virginia State Board of Education* v. *Barnette,* 319 U.S. 624 (1943).

that the jurisdiction of the Joint Congressional Committee on Atomic Energy in a matter involving the disclosure of atomic secrets was authoritative, exclusive, and indisputable. It was not.

The Un-American Activities Committee had long since acquired the habit of claiming jurisdiction over any development that promised headlines. Let a charge be made that there were Communists on the federal payroll, and the House Committee on Un-American Activities, not the House Committee on the Civil Service, took charge at once. If someone asserted that public-school textbooks were subversive or that teachers were entertaining dangerous thoughts, the Un-American Activities Committee, not the Committee on Education and Labor, leaped to the rescue. Were the immigration laws inadequate? Congress has two Committees on Immigration and Naturalization. For the past decade, however, the Committee on Un-American Activities has beaten all these rivals to the front page. Like some irritable and incorrigible watch dog, it barks at every passer-by and makes everything its business.

In the dozen years of its existence, the Committee on Un-American Activities has managed to explore almost every phase of American life and to expend close to one and one-half million dollars of public funds in the process. It has established itself as an arbiter of political acceptability. It has published sixty-odd reports about what it dislikes, based on more than twenty-five thousand printed pages of public-hearing transcripts. Writing about the inception of the committee, its former chief investigator, Robert E. Stripling, declared:

In the decade that followed we were to expand to many rooms, to agencies in leading U.S. cities, a staff of 75, and 600 filing cases containing more than 1,000,000 names, records, dossiers, and data pertaining to subversion—including the "pumpkin papers" of Whittaker Chambers. About 20,000 accredited agents of the FBI, Treasury, Army, Navy, Civil Service, Atomic Energy Commission, and other Federal officers have used our growing files and, unless they are destroyed, will continue to do so.[2]

2 Robert E. Stripling, *The Red Plot against America* (Bell Publishing Co., 1949), p. 23.

A file of more than a million names is a fairly formidable black-list; and it is, of course, as a blacklist that the file is used by government officers—and by numerous private employers as well. But this blacklist amounted, in fact, to nothing more than an indiscriminate compilation of the names found on letterheads which the committee's staff patiently collected. Sometimes—as in the case of Secretary of the Interior Oscar Chapman—the names merely appeared in the mailing lists of organizations which the committee considered subversive. A favorable mention of an entertainer or writer in the columns of the *Daily Worker* was enough to get his name included. Anyone who expressed any criticism of the committee was likely to have his name recorded in its voluminous files.

The Committee on Un-American Activities came into being in May 1938, when the House of Representatives adopted by a vote of 191 to 41 a resolution which had been introduced the year before by the Honorable Martin Dies of Texas:

Resolved, that the Speaker of the House of Representatives be, and he is hereby, authorized to appoint a special committee to be composed of seven members for the purpose of conducting an investigation of (1) the extent, character, and objects of un-American propaganda activities in the United States, (2) the diffusion within the United States of subversive and un-American propaganda that is instigated from foreign countries or of a domestic origin and attacks the principle of the form of government as guaranteed by our Constitution, and (3) all other questions in relation thereto that would aid Congress in any necessary remedial legislation.

The adjective "un-American," which is employed twice in this resolution, is its range-finder. The House left the term altogether unfocused. It might have used any of a dozen other terms—"unpatriotic," "unpopular," "unconventional," "undesirable," "unapproved," to suggest but a few. Any of these is as definite and meaningful as "un-American." Addition of the adjective "subversive" in the second clause of the resolution affords no clarification; as used here it appears to be merely redundant. Anything that is "subversive" or that "attacks the principle of the form of government as guaranteed by our Constitution" may be presumed to be "un-American."

What is the form of government guaranteed by our Constitution? In certain circles it has become fashionable to contend that because the authors of the Constitution designated the country a republic they did not intend it to be a democracy.[3] Perhaps, actually, they intended the Constitution to protect what was then generally regarded as an inalienable right of the people to alter the form of their government at will and "to institute new Government laying its foundation on such principles and organizing its Powers in such Form as to them shall seem most likely to effect their Safety and Happiness."[4] No principle lies closer to the heart of the Constitution than that the advocacy of ideas (even when disparaged as "propaganda") should be unabridged by any act of Congress.

The form of government devised by the Constitution is not a parliamentary form. Yet, however un-American the adoption of a parliamentary system might seem, advocacy of it is certainly as American as was, say, advocacy of the abolition of slavery or advocacy of the popular election of senators, or advocacy of suffrage for women, or advocacy of a national prohibition of spirituous liquors, or advocacy of the repeal of such a prohibition. It was because changes in "the form of Government as guaranteed by our Constitution" were foreseen as vital and necessary to its perpetuation that the Constitution not only provided a mechanism for change but also categorically forbade Congress to inhibit the advocacy of change.

It is evident that the Committee on Un-American Activities was authorized to inquire into a great many activities that were un-American only in its own special use of the term. And, lest its

---

[3] Ernie Adamson, a former chief counsel to the Committee on Un-American Activities, once wrote to an organization, Veterans against Discrimination: "I note that you refer to democracy several times. I wonder if you are sufficiently familiar with the history of the United States to be aware that this country was not organized as a democracy. . . ." A similar letter was sent to Drew Pearson because he was in the habit of ending his Sunday evening broadcasts with the exhortation, "Make democracy live."

[4] Declaration of Independence.

grant of authority be construed as restrictive in any way, the final clause of the resolution extends its jurisdiction to "all other questions in relation thereto that would aid Congress in any necessary remedial legislation." The House might just as well have established a "Committee on Activities."

A great deal has been said and written about the manner in which the Committee on Un-American Activities conducts its business. Numerous attempts have been made to correct its commonly acknowledged excesses by reforming its procedure. But the real defect lies deeper than this. It is an incurable defect. It is rooted in the purpose for which the committee was created and in the concept that Congress may properly punish, by publicity, activities which it cannot constitutionally declare criminal.

The effect of this committee, from its inception, has been to censor and to penalize political and economic ideas of which its members disapproved. And this effect has been achieved equally under Republican and Democratic auspices. The change in leadership of the committee occasioned by the Republican victory in the congressional elections of 1946 was no more than nominal. J. Parnell Thomas, who had been the ranking minority member under Dies' leadership, entertained an identical view of its function and an equal disregard for the proprieties and the decencies in regard to procedure. The continuing economic and political philosophy of the committee was pretty accurately formulated by its founder:

If democratic government assumes the responsibility for abolishing all poverty and unemployment, it is simply preparing the way for dictatorship. Such a theory of government is a powerful ally of the Trojan Horses. . . . Government can, of course, abolish unemployment if it is willing to pursue dictatorial methods. Nothing is easier than to put everyone in this country to work if we are willing to pay the price of slavery. . . .

The Fifth Column and the Trojan Horse organizations can never be properly dealt with so long as we retain in the Government service—even in its key positions—hundreds of Left-wingers and radicals who do not believe in our system of private enterprise. . . .

These Left-wingers are scattered throughout the government service and occupy key positions which enable them to oppose any efforts to combat the Fifth Column. They themselves are too deeply compromised to permit any vigorous action against the Trojan Horse organizations with which they have been affiliated. They do not understand that liberty and the Bill of Rights cannot survive the destruction of the American economic system.[5]

Mr. Dies was not referring in this discussion to violent overthrow of the government or to subversion by any unlawful means. He was referring to the advocacy of "a theory of government." Indeed, he was referring to a theory already put into practice in some measure by a duly elected administration—an administration which received repeated popular endorsement of what it had done in successive congressional and presidential elections. However subject to challenge the economic theories denounced by Mr. Dies may have been, they were not incompatible with the arrangements for change provided by the Constitution. Reasonable and patriotic men could espouse them.

Some of the terms used by Mr. Dies, such as "Left-wingers" and "radicals," are, to say the least, imprecise. The Congressman merely found them convenient labels for the designation of persons with whose views he disagreed. But American history has recorded, and not altogether without acclaim, a great many Left-wingers and radicals—the Jeffersonians, the Jacksonians, the Abolitionists, the Populists, the advocates of a graduated income tax, the Trust-Busters, the labor agitators, to name but a few. The notion that the government of the United States ought to guarantee full employment may be visionary. This does not, however, make it un-American; and those who advocate it are at any rate not necessarily "fifth columnists." Their aim could be achieved without so much as a constitutional amendment and, in point of fact, has already been partly achieved by act of Congress.

Mr. Dies was not merely crying, "Turn the rascals out," as any congressman is entitled to do; he was using the committee of

[5] Martin Dies, *The Trojan Horse in America* (New York: Dodd, Mead & Company, 1940), pp. 355, 361, 362.

which he was chairman to stigmatize those with whom he disagreed as disloyal to their country. He made the committee at once a prosecutor, a grand jury, a petit jury, and a judge—inflicting punishment for acts or opinions or even for mere associations that violated no law.

The intent of the committee to punish by publicity has been candidly expressed many times. In one of its earliest reports, it declared: "While Congress does not have the power to deny to citizens the right to believe in, teach, or advocate communism, fascism, and nazism, it does have the right to focus the spotlight of publicity upon their activities." [6] And in a later report, it said: "The purpose of this committee is the task of protecting our constitutional democracy by . . . pitiless publicity." [7] Perhaps the most pungent comment on this concept of the committee's function came from Federal Judge Henry W. Edgerton of the Court of Appeals for the District of Columbia Circuit: "What Congress may not restrain, Congress may not restrain by exposure and publicity. . . . The First Amendment forbids Congress purposely to burden forms of expression that it may not punish." [8]

The only piece of legislation recommended by the Committee on Un-American Activities ever enacted by Congress, prior to inclusion of the Communist-registration provision in the McCarran Act of 1950, was a rider attached to the urgent Deficiency Appropriations Act of 1943, forbidding the payment of salaries to three named individuals, Robert Morss Lovett, Goodwin Watson, and William E. Dodd, Jr. This single legislative fruit of the committee's long study of subversive and un-American activities was found by the Supreme Court of the United States in 1946 to be a violation of the Constitution because it amounted to a bill of attainder.

The rider barring the employment of Messrs. Lovett, Watson, and Dodd emerged from a long speech on the floor of the House by Mr. Dies, attacking thirty-nine named government employees as "irresponsible, unrepresentative, crackpot radical bureaucrats"

[6] H. Rept. No. 2, 76th Cong., 1st Sess., 13 (1939).
[7] H. Rept. No. 1476, 76th Cong., 3rd Sess., 24 (1940).
[8] Dissenting opinion in *Barsky* v. *United States,* U.S. Court of Appeals, District of Columbia, No. 9602.

and affiliates of "Communist-front organizations." Mr. Dies wanted Congress to forbid the payment of salaries to all the thirty-nine, and an amendment to this effect was actually offered to the Treasury-Post Office appropriation bill. The Dies charges were referred to as "indictments." After a good deal of heated debate, it was decided that an Appropriations subcommittee should study these indictments and give each accused employee "his day in court." This special subcommittee held hearings in secret executive session, taking testimony from those charged with subversive beliefs and associations but denying them the aid of counsel. It formulated its own definition of "subversive activity," acknowledging that the offense had not previously been defined by Congress or by the courts. "Subversive activity in this country," the subcommittee declared, "derives from conduct destructive of or inimical to the government of the United States— that which seeks to undermine its institutions, or to distort its functions, or to impede its projects, or to lessen its efforts, the ultimate end being to overturn it all. Such activity may be open and direct, as by effort to overthrow, or subtle and indirect, as by sabotage." The subcommittee found Messrs. Lovett, Watson, and Dodd guilty within its terms.

Attachment of the rider proscribing these men to an urgent deficiency appropriations measure created a difficult problem. The Senate objected to the rider, rejecting the Appropriations Act by a vote of 69 to 0, but was at last compelled to acquiesce in a slightly modified form of it because the funds appropriated were needed to pay salaries, already overdue, of District of Columbia employees. The President felt obliged to sign the measure for the same reason, although he and the Attorney General denounced it as unconstitutional. All three of the proscribed men were considered trustworthy by the federal agencies in which they were employed. Their employment was continued beyond the deadline set by Congress, although they could not be paid. They brought suit in the Court of Claims for the sums due them during this period. The Court of Claims entered judgments in their favor which were upheld by a unanimous Supreme Court.

The language employed by the Supreme Court in an opinion written by Mr. Justice Black is immensely illuminating in respect not only of this particular act of Congress but also of all attempts by a congressional committee to expel federal employees by stigmatization:

We hold that Section 304 [the rider to the Appropriations Act] falls precisely within the category of congressional acts which the Constitution barred by providing that "No Bill of Attainder or *ex post facto* law shall be passed." . . . Section 304 was designed to apply to particular individuals. . . . This permanent proscription from any opportunity to serve the government is punishment, and of a most severe type. It is a type of punishment which Congress has only invoked for special types of odious and dangerous crimes, such as treason; acceptance of bribes by members of Congress; or by other government officials; and interference with elections by Army and Navy officers. Section 304, thus, clearly accomplishes the punishment of named individuals without a judicial trial. . . . When our Constitution and Bill of Rights were written, our ancestors had ample reason to know that legislative trials and punishments were too dangerous to liberty to exist in the nation of free men they envisaged.[9]

The Committee on Un-American Activities did not again attempt, after this judicial rebuke, to embody its punishment of individuals it disliked in any formal legislative act of the kind struck down by the Court. There was no need for it to do so. It could punish quite as effectively by simpler means. It sufficed, in most cases, to denounce a man on the floor of the House or to let his name be blackened by anyone who chose to call him a Communist in a committee hearing under the protection of congressional immunity. Mere inclusion of a name in the committee files, where personnel officials of the Executive agencies could see it, was likely to cripple its owner. Government administrators, obliged annually to come before Congress for appropriations, were not generally so brash as to employ individuals of whom a congressional committee disapproved. Thus, by avoiding the judicial test to which legislation would have been subject, the

[9] *United States* v. *Lovett*, 328 U.S. 303 (1946).

Committee on Un-American Activities systematically continued
to inflict on government employees the very "proscription from
any opportunity to serve the government" which the Supreme
Court had condemned as "punishment, and of a most severe
type."

Between the Americanists of the Un-American Activities Committee and the young men of the New Deal there was a natural
and irreconcilable enmity. Mr. Dies called the New Dealers "Left-
wingers and radicals who do not believe in our system of private
enterprise." The character of the New Dealers in the 1930s deserves some examination in the light of this accusation.

When the history of the New Deal is written by detached his-
torians, they may well set it down as one of Mr. Roosevelt's major
accomplishments that he made the federal government, for a time
at least, a respectable—indeed, a prized—place of employment. It
had not been so for a long while prior to his inauguration. His
administration attracted men who would not previously have
thought of the government as a career. These were the brightest
and most untamed graduates and teachers of the country's colleges and professional schools—young men who, in normal times,
would have been snapped up by the leading law firms, industrial
organizations, and banking houses that had been wont to go
prospecting around college campuses each spring in search of
promising material. In the 1930s the federal government rivaled
and surpassed private enterprise in enlisting this kind of talent.
So far from being scorned, a government job became the aspira-
tion of the ablest young men.

A variety of reasons accounted for this change. One big factor,
certainly, was that at the depth of the depression, the big banking, legal, and industrial firms were contracting rather than expanding, and government salaries began to look exceedingly attractive. But a less materialistic motive played a large part too.
A great many of these young men wanted a kind of compensation that private business could not provide. The New Deal
offered them a chance to participate in a great social undertaking

—the reconstruction and revitalization of the United States along lines that evoked their idealism. It was an administration interested in ideas, hospitable to innovation. Youthfulness was not so much a handicap as an advantage; boldness and imagination were at a premium. Young men could do big things.

As a result, the men who served under President Roosevelt were, whatever their shortcomings, immensely enthusiastic about the jobs they were doing. They worked with prodigious zeal. Not all, but many of them, were dedicated men. Their interest in their work was not confined to conventional working hours. It consumed them. They felt that what they were doing was important—a feeling not common in that period among the privately employed. They talked shop incessantly, discussing the merits of this program and that, arguing, conniving, jockeying for preferment, planning new reforms. They were engaged in nothing less than the regeneration of America.

It could not fairly be said of them in general, however, that they did "not believe in our system of private enterprise." They simply did not believe in Mr. Dies' system. They were imbued with a crusading sense that that system had to be modified in order to make it more responsive to popular needs. In the depth of the depression it seemed relatively easy to isolate the evils and define the issues and identify the enemies. Not capitalism itself but some of the big capitalists appeared to be responsible for unemployment and breadlines and Hoovervilles. And the big capitalists were doing everything in their power, it seemed, to fasten the responsibility on themselves. They used thugs to break strikes; they opposed all the palliatives and innovations advanced by the New Deal; the courts gave the impression of being in bondage to them. And they insisted upon calling every attempt at reform communistic. Small wonder that young men refused to be bothered with distinctions that their elders obstinately obscured.

In the early days of the New Deal the Communists denounced the Roosevelt administration as fascist. They shifted, however, to a "united-front" strategy in the mid-thirties, clamoring for public housing, for utility and stock-market regulation, for public power projects, for a public works program to provide employment, for a wide range of progressive social and economic measures. They vociferously championed the right of labor to organize and bargain collectively. They demonstrated noisily in favor of racial equality. The young liberals of the New Deal were for these measures too—quite independently of the Communists. Franklin D. Roosevelt mobilized the liberals, channeled and directed their enthusiasm, and translated their hopes into concrete projects. The Communists were in the position of being what one might call, without coining a phrase, fellow-travelers.

The New Deal liberals tolerated the company of the Communists, not following them but being followed, just as long as their paths and their immediate destinations coincided. The appearance of companionship could have been avoided only by a departure on the part of liberals from the direction in which conviction impelled them. And it is hard to escape the conclusion today that the powerful social pressures which make even the appearance of keeping Communist company dangerous are operating to make many liberals false to their own beliefs.

Some liberals, it must be admitted, were slow to recognize the true character of the Communists. They obstinately closed their eyes to the realities about life in the Soviet Union, about the aims of Soviet foreign policy, and about the disguised purposes of the Communist Party, USA. Some clung to fictions about communism long after facts had refuted them. But in extenuation, it ought to be recalled that this was at a time when the facts were peculiarly difficult to discern. So many extravagances were published about the Soviet Union that valid indictments were discounted. So many indisputably independent and innocent American groups were called communistic that the epithet lost all validity. When every consumers' cooperative and labor union and organization for civil rights or civil liberties was said to be under Communist domination, it was scarcely surprising that liberals defended them somewhat indiscriminately.

In the years between 1935 and 1939 and between 1941 and

1945, Russian policy was such that the American Communists could support liberal principles. When Russian policy changed, the Communists changed with it. The liberals adhered to the principles they had always professed. This distinction did nothing, however, to deflect the enmity of the Un-American Activities Committee. The committee aimed not so much at Communist ideas as at all ideas; not so much at Communist attempts to change "our system of private enterprise" as at all attempts to change it. From the beginning, liberals were the committee's real targets—because liberals were responsible for the New Deal. This was their besetting sin in the eyes of the Un-American Activities Committee, which regarded conformity as the test of patriotism and "normalcy" as the criterion of the good life.

But the animus of the Committee on Un-American Activities was by no means confined to government employees. It ranged far and wide, affecting individuals in their personal relations and their private employment. Voluntary associations were among its chief victims. In striking at these, the committee struck at the motive force of the democratic process. The diverse and divergent interests of the American people find their most characteristic and effective expression in such organizations—pressure groups designed to make coherent the will of like-minded citizens joined transiently for the achievement of limited common aims. These voluntary associations are much more the levers of public opinion than the major political parties, which deal in generalities and strive to be all things to all men. It is to these groups that the political parties are responsive. It is their pulling and hauling that, in the end, shapes national policy. The powers of government can be derived from the consent of the governed in a continental democracy of a hundred and fifty million people only through a free and fair competition among such associations.

But there can no free and fair competition among them if some are handicapped by an official finding that they are of subversive intent or subject to Communist control. It is a mistake to suppose that any body of men can measure the good faith of a group committed to political purposes in the way that the Federal Trade Commission, for example, measures the honesty of advertising or the Food and Drug Administration measures the purity of a patent medicine. There are no objective standards for the measurement of motive. Purity of political purpose can be tested only in the competition of the market. But the Committee on Un-American Activities has never been willing to leave these matters to the arbitrament of public opinion. By denouncing organizations of which it disapproved, the committee succeeded in reducing their membership and impairing their effectiveness.

The committee utilized its familiar technique of guilt by association in two directions in the case of organizations. A group was contaminated by any "subversive" individual who entered it. And, conversely, every member of the group became "subversive" by the mere fact of membership. Something approaching the pinnacle in this process was reached by the Committee in its report on the Southern Conference for Human Welfare. "Entertainer at the Washington meeting," the report disclosed, "was Susan Reed, employed by Café Society, a night club owned by Barney Josephson, brother of Leon Josephson, leading Communist, Soviet Secret Service operative, charged with passport frauds." [10]

Perhaps the most ambitious and audacious effort of the Un-American Activities Committee to enforce its own ideas of Americanism came in the fall of 1947 when it undertook exposure of subversive propaganda in the motion-picture industry. For here it was attacking not merely individuals and voluntary associations, but the freedom of a powerful medium of communication—an element of the American press guaranteed immunity from governmental control by the First Amendment.

In a room filled with klieg lights, cameras, microphones, re-

[10] H. Rept. No. 592 at 10, quoted by Professor Walter Gellhorn of the Columbia Law School in "Report on a Report of the House Committee on Un-American Activities," *Harvard Law Review*, October 1947—a brilliantly illuminating study of the committee's methods.

porters, and an overflow crowd of the curious, the committee permitted a parade of Hollywood stars and statesmen identified as "friendly witnesses" to give voice, with dramatic gestures, to their personal animosities, resentments, and jealousies. Politically naive actors and actresses were encouraged to recite, without a shred of supporting evidence, their suspicions regarding the political sympathies of their professional colleagues and competitors.

The aim of the hearings was to show that Communists, especially among the screen writers and directors, had injected or would have liked to inject pro-Soviet and anti-capitalist propaganda into the motion pictures they made. No motion picture was shown to the committee, although it was said by some of the witnesses that certain films had displayed some sympathy for the Soviet Union during the wartime alliance with that country against Germany, and that in a few other pictures bankers had been represented in an unfavorable light. This was as far as the committee ever went toward establishing its premise. It had no hesitation, however, in jumping to the conclusion that Hollywood was in the grip of a Red terror.

It had no hesitation, either, in suggesting to the movie-makers quite baldly that their pictures should be slanted differently in the future. The relatively few films made in Hollywood which dealt in any way with contemporary social issues—*Crossfire, Gentlemen's Agreement, The Best Years of Our Lives,* for example— were called communistic in tone because they were critical of some aspects of American life; and the producers were told by the committee to go forth and sin no more.

There was no one to speak for the motion-picture producers as Wendell Willkie had spoken on a comparable occasion a few years earlier, to protest against these proceedings as precisely the kind of abridgment of speech forbidden by the First Amendment and to point out that if the content of films could be made the subject of official condemnation, radio and the press might not long remain immune. Even the newspapers in large part seemed lethargic, unconscious of the implications of this interference for their own freedom. Some of them, notably the Hearst chain, went so far as to demand outright censorship of the movies.

There were some protests, however. Representative Eberharter of Pennsylvania said on the floor of the House, for example:

I cannot escape the conclusion that there is some justification for the charge shared by millions of Americans that the purpose of the Committee was not to destroy an existent subversive threat in Hollywood, but to intimidate and control the movie industry; to secure the production of movies whose Americanism content would be certified by the members of the Committee on Un-American Activities.

A group of Hollywood actors, writers, and directors, assembled hurriedly under the leadership of John Huston and styling themselves "The Committee for the First Amendment," sent a large and glamorous delegation to Washington and expressed their protest against the inquisition with a great deal of eloquence on a radio broadcast. They were certainly more representative of the motion-picture industry than either the "friendly witnesses" or the ten "unfriendly witnesses," whose public pillorying was apparently the object and supplied the grand finale of the whole extravaganza.

Having been denounced from the witness stand by their bosses, the unfriendly ten, writers and directors, were summoned by subpoena, denied any opportunity to make the kind of discursive statement which had been given to the committee by their accusers, and were asked two questions: "Are you a member of the Screen Writers Guild?" and "Are you a member of the Communist Party?" The unfriendly ten refused to answer these questions, arguing that affiliations of this kind are entitled to the same secrecy as the ballot box, and that the questions amounted to an invasion of their constitutional right of privacy. They were promptly cited for contempt of Congress and were subsequently convicted and sentenced to terms in prison.

Ring Lardner, Jr., in response to a series of questions put to him by the *New York Herald Tribune* some time after the Un-American Activities Committee hearings, explained his own reasons for declining to give "Yes" or "No" answers to the questions put to him by the committee:

As the question stands now, if I am a member of the Communist Party I would be exposing myself to the bigotry and inspired hysteria which is forcing not only Communists but all Left-of-Center political groups into a semi-secret status. More specifically, in view of the Motion Picture Association's blacklist statement, I would be banishing myself permanently from the profession in which I have earned my living since I was twenty-one.

If I am not a member, I would be exposing other men to the same bigotry and blacklist by contributing to the precedent that all non-Communists must so declare themselves in order to isolate the actual offenders. Further, it would be clear to everyone, including me, that I had purged myself in order to please my past and prospective employers.

Official inquiry into political belief and affiliation impairs freedom by making belief and affiliation punishable. One need only translate the committee's queries about political belief and affiliation into questions about religious belief and affiliation to see how mischievous and offensive they are. Perhaps men ought to be courageous enough to proclaim their religious faith (or their lack of it). But they do not always have this kind of courage when what they believe is unpopular. And their right to privacy and silence on this score is of the essence of liberty.

One might suppose that private enterprisers of the motion-picture industry, vehemently committed by their own testimony to the system of free private enterprise, would have rebelled, if not against congressional interference with their choice of cinema subject matter, at least against congressional coercion in the choice of their employees. There was, however, no rebellion left in the producers. They surrendered without the semblance of a struggle. The moguls of the industry held a meeting in the Waldorf Astoria Hotel in New York and came out of it with a condemnation of the "unfriendly ten." "We will," they declared, "forthwith discharge or suspend without compensation those in our employ, and we will not re-employ any of the ten until such time as he is acquitted, or has purged himself of contempt, and declared under oath that he is not a Communist. . . . In pursuing this policy, we are not going to be swayed by any hysteria or intimidation from any source."

Mr. Eric Johnston, president of the Motion Picture Association, and one of those who participated in the industry meeting that blacklisted the unfriendly ten, added an interesting postscript to the record of the industry's surrender. In an address [11] on October 27, 1949, he said:

We in the communications industries know what it is to face a threat to freedom of expression. In the motion-picture industry we know it particularly well. I want to give you only one small example tonight.

One of our pictures—a simple little story with a cast of child actors—was banned in Memphis, Tennessee, because it showed white and Negro children in school and at play together. We are fighting that case out in the courts.

The American motion-picture industry isn't taking threats to its freedom lightly. We are not going to be pushovers for outside regulation. We are going to fight back at the threat of official censorship wherever it exists, wherever it is indicated, wherever it is symptomatic. We have more than ourselves to consider, and we are thinking of the danger in those terms.

The issue is broader than the interest of the American motion-picture industry. It is vastly broader. It is the issue of the whole American system—our system of free schools, the free press, free communication, free speech. Here is a case when giving an inch means losing a principle.

It is rather a pity that Mr. Johnston and his colleagues in the motion-picture industry did not act upon this dauntless platform a year before, when giving an inch to the Committee on Un-American Activities meant losing the whole principle of freedom from governmental interference. It was a little late to assert that

[11] Prepared for delivery to the Annual Educational Conference, sponsored by the Educational Records Bureau, the Carnegie Foundation for the Advancement of Teaching, and the American Council on Education, at a dinner meeting honoring the Tenth Anniversary of Teaching Film Custodians, at the Roosevelt Hotel, New York, N. Y. Because Mr. Johnston was unexpectedly delayed in returning from Europe, his address was read by Francis S. Harmon, vice-president of the Motion Picture Association of America.

motion-picture producers will not be "pushovers for outside regulation" after they had been pushed over.

Writing in *The Nation* of November 19, 1949, Carey McWilliams made the following report on conditions in the cinema citadel:

It has always been difficult to take Hollywood seriously, and an observer of the scene today can scarcely believe that the familiar surface gaiety conceals currents of real fear. Fear of the black list is strong, but a more widespread and probably better-founded fear is that of the gray list. . . .

Every relationship in the industry is affected by people's awareness of the gray list. No one is sure where he stands or whom he can trust. Fear determines the proper warmth with which to greet an old friend, the proper line to take on a story, with whom it is wise to be seen having lunch. A social boycott reinforces the graylisting of workers. . . .

There is also, of course, a gray list for themes. One of the finest directors in the industry, an Academy Award winner, told me the other day that the studios have rejected almost every idea he has suggested in the last two years with the remark, "Can't you find a good love story?"

The hearings had painful consequences, of course, for a good many individuals as well as for the industry. The names of actors and actresses, peculiarly subject to injury by adverse publicity, were blackened by allegations made under the committee's protection from suits for slander. So far as the "unfriendly ten" were concerned, they suffered not only the loss of lucrative jobs but fines and jail sentences, because they refused to answer questions put to them by the committee respecting their private political beliefs. They were convicted, as E. B. White pointed out in *The New Yorker*, "not of wrong-doing but of wrong-thinking; that is news in this country and if I have not misread my history, it is bad news."

Another illustration of the committee's punishment of persons for wrong-thinking needs to be presented here because of its apparent wantonness. In the spring of 1949 the committee, then under the chairmanship of Representative Wood of Georgia, turned its attention to subversive activities in the District of Columbia. It was not concerned with propaganda efforts to alter the American way. It was concerned solely with membership in, or affiliation with, the Communist Party on the part of private citizens who happened to be residents of the national capital. And its single purpose, apparently, was to expose individual members.

One of the persons summoned before the committee was Mrs. Rose Edelman Anderson, the owner of a prosperous drugstore known as the Investment Pharmacy. She was asked whether she was or ever had been a member of the Communist Party. On advice of her lawyer, Mrs. Anderson refused to answer the question on the ground that an answer would tend to incriminate her. The avoidance of legal self-incrimination under the protection of the Fifth Amendment resulted, of course, in complete self-incrimination so far as public opinion was concerned. And this, it appeared, was all the committee desired to accomplish.

The "exposure" of Mrs. Anderson was followed immediately by a boycott of her drugstore. One month after her appearance before the Committee on Un-American Activities, Mrs. Anderson, who had built the business up over a period of twenty-two years, sold it at a price far below what it would normally have commanded and left the District of Columbia.

Thus Mrs. Anderson was punished for a presumptive political association the legality of which was never brought into question. She was punished on the supposition that she had done something that Congress, under the Constitution, would, in any case, be powerless to prohibit. And the punishment, at least in this case, seemed to have been inflicted for the sheer sake of punishing. No public purpose was served by it.

One more case deserves to be cited in this connection. In the summer of 1948 Elizabeth Bentley, a confessed former Soviet espionage agent, appeared before a subcommittee of the Senate Committee on Expenditures in the Executive Departments and charged that a Commerce Department employee, William W. Remington, had been a member of the Communist Party and had met her frequently in a clandestine manner in 1942 and

1943 to give her classified data of the War Production Board, where he was employed at the time. As a result of her testimony Mr. Remington was suspended from his Commerce Department job, and the Fourth Regional Loyalty Board decided that, on all the evidence, reasonable grounds existed for belief that he was disloyal to the United States.

When his case was heard on appeal by the Loyalty Review Board of the Civil Service Commission, Miss Bentley was invited by the board to appear as a witness. She accepted but failed to appear on the date of the hearing. She was invited again—the board has no power to subpoena witnesses—accepted again, and again failed to appear. A third invitation was extended to her; this she ignored entirely. Mr. Remington, after presenting such proofs as it is possible to present of one's own *bona fides,* was exonerated by the Loyalty Review Board and returned to the Commerce Department payroll.[12]

In the meantime, Miss Bentley had made a tactical mistake. Dared by a newspaper reporter in the course of an interview on a television program to repeat her charges concerning Remington without benefit of congressional immunity, she rashly did so. Remington gave her a chance to retract and then brought suit for defamation against her, against the sponsor of the program, and against the broadcasting company. The defendants did not choose to go to trial. The case was settled out of court with the payment of substantial damages to Remington.

Long before the Senate subcommittee heard her, Miss Bentley had made the same charges about Remington to a grand jury in New York. The grand jury called Remington before it but declined to indict him. He may fairly be said, therefore, to have won three distinct forms of vindication. One might have supposed that his ordeal in the name of national security was at an end. It was not. Two years later, in the spring of 1950, the House Committee on Un-American Activities discovered two individuals who testified before it in secret session that they had known

[12] For a detailed and sensitive account of Remington's experience, see *The New Yorker,* May 21, 1949, "A Reporter at Large," by Daniel Lang.

Remington in 1936 when he was an eighteen-year-old messenger boy working for the Tennessee Valley Authority in Knoxville— and that he had belonged to the Communist Party at that time. They knew for the usual reason, of course: they had been Communists then themselves.

Remington was at once hailed before the committee and confronted with the accusation. He denied it. Whereupon he was summoned once more by a grand jury in New York, was once more asked if he had ever been a Communist, and, upon answering the question negatively, was indicted for perjury.

Observe the immunity of the informers in this procedure: they were not accused of bearing false witness or put to the expense and ignominy of standing trial. Observe, too, that the substantive act in question—that is, joining the Communist Party—was not criminal; if it had been a crime in 1936, it would certainly have been protected from prosecution in 1950 by any rational statute of limitations. For it is not always possible to procure records or documents or witnesses bearing on events so far in the past; and recollection may be extremely uncertain after fourteen years. Observe, finally, the peculiar difficulty of proving that one was not a member of a political organization at some remote period in the past. A man falsely accused of robbing a bank on the night of June 16, 1936, may be able to find someone who can swear that he was at a different place on that particular date. But no one except himself can swear that he was not secretly a Communist at some indefinite time years ago. In such circumstances a jury can do no more than weigh the credibility of an accuser, who has no apparent motive for lying, against the credibility of an accused, who obviously has everything to gain by denial of the accusation.

In other times, and in different circumstances, a man's reputation in his community, a record of decent, law-abiding conduct, might have carried some weight in his favor against the testimony of admitted ex-Communists. But it is well known that Communists use good works as a disguise. Since denial of party affiliation is the usual tactic of Communists, no one who makes such a denial is now believed. As Louis Francis Budenz, the most prolific and successful of the ex-Communist informers, has pointed out, party members are instructed to deny all affiliation with the party and to denounce their accusers—even, if possible, to sue them for slander. Thus, to resist stigmatization is simply to draw the noose tighter about one's throat. To the now familiar technique of establishing guilt by association, the Committee on Un-American Activities has added—as others have pointed out—the novel doctrine of guilt by dissociation. By its logic, a denial of guilt is tantamount to a confession. Only those who have admitted at least past membership and have turned informer are granted any credence. This is the era of the apostate. The Committee on Un-American Activities has elevated him to the status of a national hero and transformed his role into a profession.[13]

A review of the cases outlined here suggests that the Committee on Un-American Activities has contrived a complicated kind of Procrustes' bed for those who incur its wrath. Accused of being Communists, its victims can choose among four courses of action:

1. They can, like Ring Lardner, refuse on grounds of principle to deny or acknowledge the charge. The price of this course is conviction for contempt of Congress and a term in prison.

2. They can, like Rose Anderson, plead immunity from self-incrimination under the Fifth Amendment. The price of this is disgrace and probable loss of livelihood. And it is no longer clear that even this plea will avoid a contempt citation.

3. They can, like Louis Budenz, admit past or present mem-

---

[13] ". . . the Inquisition was not bound by the ordinary rules of procedure in its inquiries; the accused was surprised by a sudden summons, and as a rule imprisoned on suspicion. All the accused were presumed to be guilty, the judge being at the same time the accuser. . . . No witness might refuse to give evidence, under pain of being considered guilty of heresy. . . . The accused swore that he would tell the whole truth, and was bound to denounce all those who were partners of his heresy, or whom he knew or suspected to be heretics. If he confessed, and denounced his accomplices, relatives or friends, he was 'reconciled' with the Church, and had to suffer only the humiliating penalties prescribed by the canon law . . . 'there was never any case of an acquittal pure and simple' (H. C. Lea)." From the *Encyclopædia Britannica*, XIth edition, article entitled "Inquisition," Vol. XIV, pp. 589-90.

bership in the party; but the consequence of this is that they must then themselves become informers and betray all others of their acquaintance who were once party members, or suffer the penalties of contempt proceedings. There hangs over their heads also the threat of prosecution under the Smith Act for participation in a conspiracy to advocate overthrow of the government by force or violence.

4. They can, like William Remington, deny the charge and undertake the long, painful, expensive, and hazardous effort to refute an indictment for perjury. The price of this decision may be pretty high for them. In times of public excitement their innocence is hard to establish in court; and conviction for perjury carries a five-year term in jail.

What contribution has the Committee on Un-American Activities made, through the use of these methods, to the security of the country? It must be credited with having promoted awareness of the evil purposes of the Communist Party and with having put the public on its guard against a number of organizations carrying on the party's work under false labels. It must also be credited with having exposed, in 1948, certain prewar espionage activities within the government—an accomplishment that will be discussed in the succeeding chapter.

But in its treatment of the Communist Party it so grossly distorted and exaggerated the danger as to inspire panic rather than realism. By denouncing liberal individuals and progressive measures as "communistic," it spread confusion rather than caution. By punishing unorthodox opinion, it put a halter on expression, making Americans wary of what they say, wary of their associations, in ways that are incongruous to a free people. Such results, quite apart from their injury to innocent individuals, impair rather than promote national security.

Like the judges commissioned to extirpate witchcraft in seventeenth-century Massachusetts, the members of the Un-American Activities Committee invited all manner of persons to come into

court and "cry out" against their fellow-citizens. How much subversion of American values they effected can be measured in their
apotheosis of the informer. Not since the days when women in
Salem were investigated—and hanged—on suspicion of unearthly
activities have Americans endured so grave a corruption of their
best traditions.

CHAPTER IV

"COLD-WAR TREASON"

It is also true that in many instances the crimes of treason and espionage are so difficult to punish by conviction because of technical devices and the necessity of so tightly defining these crimes, that if near treason and "virtual espionage" and "cold-war treason or espionage" are to be guarded against, it is imperative that not only must the power of public opinion be marshaled against these disloyal and self-serving practices but legislation must be enacted which will provide appropriate punishment for these specific derelictions.[1]

THE COMMITTEE on Un-American Activities scored its greatest triumph in 1948. In the summer of that year it turned its attention to espionage within the government. Its spy hearings were the most sensational in its career—and also the most significant. They culminated in production of the notorious "pumpkin papers." Thus they revealed to the American people for the first time that Soviet agents, using American sympathizers within the government, had succeeded in obtaining classified information from the Department of State—at least in the year 1938.

The situation revealed by the committee was already well known to government officials and had already been corrected but not publicized. All but two of the individuals accused before

[1] *Interim Report of the House Committee on Un-American Activities on Hearings Regarding Communist Espionage in the United States Government,* August 28, 1948, p. 3.

the committee of Communist connections had resigned or had been removed from the government before the hearings. And the stringent measures of the Federal Employee-Loyalty Program had been put into effect by the President more than a year before. The Federal Bureau of Investigation had long been aware of the facts that the committee made public. Indeed, it had presented its information to a federal grand jury in New York, which had summoned, and taken testimony from, nearly all the witnesses who appeared before the committee. To a great extent, therefore, the committee may fairly be said to have usurped, or at any rate duplicated, the role of the FBI and of the grand jury. It is a reasonable question whether its publication of charges that would otherwise have been kept secret should on the whole be considered a public service in this situation. The committee itself drew an interesting distinction between its function and the functions of the FBI and the grand jury:

... The FBI is a fact-finding and investigating agency and not an exposure agency. ... It is not a vehicle for reporting to the public on the extent of nefarious activities. ... Grand Jury proceedings are conducted in the greatest of secrecy. ... At best, the Grand Jury is not a vehicle for reporting to the public on the extent of Un-American Activities in a free republic. As contrasted with the FBI and the Grand Jury, the House Committee on Un-American Activities has a separate and very special responsibility. It functions to permit the greatest court in the world—the court of American public opinion—to have an undirected, uncensored, and unprejudiced opportunity to render a continuing verdict on all of its public officials and to evaluate the merit of many in private life who either openly associate and assist disloyal groups or covertly operate as members or fellow-travellers of such organizations. It is as necessary to the success of this committee that it reveal its findings to the public as it is to the success of the FBI that it conceal its operations from the public view.[2]

This distinction deserves some examination. A grand jury, like a congressional committee, is an instrument of inquiry. Being concerned with violations of the law rather than with the fram-

[2] Ibid., pp. 1-2.

ing of legislation, it functions *in camera* for two reasons: first, because witnesses are more likely to tell what they know if their testimony is protected by secrecy; second, because of the presumption of innocence attending an accused person under American law. Operating in secret, it may explore all aspects of a situation without doing wanton injury to innocent persons. It accuses no one until it becomes convinced that a sufficient body of evidence exists to justify an indictment. The grand jury in New York had been in session for about a year before the hearings of the House Committee on Un-American Activities began. The FBI presented to it all the facts it had been able to gather concerning violations of law. Apparently the grand jury did not believe that these facts warranted any indictments. What the House committee did, then, was to make public what the grand jury had kept secret, and to punish by publicity those the grand jury had concluded were not subject to punishment under the law.

The committee's hearings revolved around two accusatory witnesses—Elizabeth T. Bentley and Whittaker Chambers—both, by their own account, former Communist couriers and undercover agents of the Soviet Union. Some of the individuals accused by them had had distinguished careers in the government and enjoyed reputations not alone for integrity but for devoted service to their country; some were obscure; some had long been the objects of gossip and suspicion.

In her appearance before the committee Miss Bentley described the manner in which she came to Washington, met agents of two spy rings for which she said she served as courier, and took back to New York the material they gave her. In positive terms she identified thirty individuals who were or had been government employees; twenty-seven of them, she said, were members of the Communist Party; all of them, she said, had consciously and purposefully transmitted information of a classified character in violation of the express terms of the Espionage Act.

It must be remembered that no statute of limitations protected the targets of Miss Bentley's charges. Their case was radically different from that of the persons named as Communists at about the same time by Whittaker Chambers. Mr. Chambers told about a period in the mid-thirties when the United States was at peace. The three-year statute of limitations applicable to peacetime violation of the Espionage Act made the persons named by him in 1948 immune from prosecution under that Act. But Miss Bentley talked about a period in the early 1940s when the United States was at war. Wartime violation of the Espionage Act entails a death penalty and thus is not protected by any statute of limitations. The grand jury could have indicted any or all of the persons Miss Bentley named. Yet it did not consider her testimony substantial enough to warrant indictment in a single instance.

The persons accused by Miss Bentley may fairly be divided into three categories on the basis of their behavior toward the Committee on Un-American Activities. Seventeen of them, either because they were never subpoenaed or because they never requested a chance to be heard, did not appear before the Committee to make any formal responses to the charges. Six of the thirty were subpoenaed but declined to answer most questions put to them by the committee on grounds of the protection against self-incrimination afforded by the Fifth Amendment. They were stubborn, uncooperative, uncommunicative witnesses, with attitudes ranging from abject terror to outright defiance of the committee. They refused to acknowledge acquaintance even with one another —in some cases when close association through employment in the same agency was a matter of public record. The third category among those charged by Miss Bentley embraced seven persons who answered all the committee's questions and categorically denied Communist Party membership or any divulgence of classified information. Five of the seven asserted that they had never previously met or heard of Miss Bentley; the other two admitted acquaintance with her and agreed in the impression that she was a neurotic, unhappy woman who pressed her friendship upon them until it became an embarrassment from which they endeavored to free themselves. They denied any knowledge that she was a Communist or a Soviet agent.

The most prominent of the accused witnesses were Lauchlin

Currie, who had been an administrative assistant to President Roosevelt, and Harry Dexter White, who had been an assistant secretary of the Treasury during the Roosevelt administration. Miss Bentley did not claim personal acquaintance with either of them. Of Mr. Currie she said: "The man was not a Communist but he did give information. . . . He furnished inside information on this government's attitude toward China, toward other governments. He once relayed to us the information that the American government was on the verge of breaking the Soviet code." [3]

Mr. Currie at once requested, and was granted, an opportunity to be heard by the committee. He acknowledged that he had, of course, talked with a great many people about China, since he had twice gone there on official missions. But he denied emphatically that he had ever discussed confidential matters "with anyone other than officials of the government officially charged with responsibility in connection with China." [4] Obviously anything that he said about China, any personal opinion he expressed about its military or economic situation, might have been repeated to Miss Bentley and regarded by her as "inside information." She did not disclose the nature of the information she said she garnered. As for the breaking of the Soviet code, Mr. Currie testified: "I did not know during the war, nor do I know now, that any branch of the government or of its military forces attempted to or was about to break the Russian code. I knew nothing and I know nothing about whatever work was done in connection with our own or foreign codes." [5]

At the conclusion of his testimony Mr. Currie was asked if he thought he had been treated with due consideration by the committee and given a full and fair chance to answer the charges that had been made against him. This was a pattern commonly adopted toward accused persons who came before the committee at their own request. It was much as though an innocent pedes-

---

[3] Ibid., p. 519.
[4] Ibid., p. 855.
[5] Ibid., p. 853.

trian spattered with mud by a passing vehicle were expected to thank the driver for permitting him to wipe the mud off his face and clothes. If the committee, before publicizing sensational hearsay by a confessed Soviet agent, to whom Mr. Currie was admittedly a total stranger, had accorded this respected public official a chance to refute the allegations in private, some expression of appreciation might have been in order. But the committee heard him only after his name had been irremediably besmirched —and then with scant courtesy. Nevertheless, Mr. Currie gave thanks. In the circumstances they seemed a testimonial only to the committee's boundless power to injure anyone failing to win its favor.

Harry Dexter White proved a less complaisant witness. He behaved, indeed, like a man indifferent to the opinion of the committee and unafraid of its power. There was no cringing in his manner; no taint of equivocation, no accommodation to the committee's prejudices. He seemed prepared to rest on his record and his conscience.

Harry White was called a Communist by Whittaker Chambers as well as by Elizabeth Bentley, although neither asserted that he was an actual member of the Communist Party. Miss Bentley said: "He gave information to Mr. Silvermaster which was relayed on to me." [6] Mr. Chambers, in direct contradiction of Miss Bentley, said that Mr. White had belonged to an elite group separated from the Communist "apparatus" to which most of the other accused persons were supposed to have been attached. "I should perhaps make the point," Mr. Chambers added, "that these people were specifically not wanted to act as sources of information. These people were an elite group, an outstanding group, which it was believed would rise to positions—as, indeed, some of them did—notably Mr. White and Mr. Hiss—in the government, and their position in the government would be of much more service to the Communist Party." [7]

[6] Ibid., p. 511.
[7] Ibid., p. 577. In the course of the perjury trial of Alger Hiss, Chambers changed his mind about this and testified that he had received documents from Harry White. Four memos, said to be in White's handwriting, were

Mr. White denied any affiliation with the Communist movement and any acquaintance with either Miss Bentley or Mr. Chambers. But he was not a man who would turn his back on friends because they happened at the time to be in trouble. Personal loyalty is an American trait no less than loyalty to the State. Perhaps a few excerpts will convey something of the flavor of Mr. White's testimony:

Mr. Stripling: Mr. White, the names that I read to you a few moments ago, were the people Elizabeth T. Bentley testified comprise the so-called Silvermaster group. A number of these people worked for you. I believe you admitted knowing all but one.

Mr. White: Not admitted; affirmed, if you do not mind, Mr. Stripling.[8]

. . .

Mr. Stripling: Now Mr. Perlo and Mr. Ullmann, as well as your friend Mr. Silvermaster—

Mr. White: Yes.

Mr. Stripling: Have all been accused.

Mr. White: Mr. Ullmann is also my friend.

Mr. Stripling: Make him your friend, too.

Mr. White: Yes.

Mr. Stripling: What about Mr. Perlo?

Mr. White: Not that I would not wish him to be a friend. I just do not happen to know him very well.

Mr. Stripling: Regardless of friendship involved, they have all been before this committee and have all refused to state under oath whether or not they were members of the Communist Party. Do you have any attitude on their refusal to answer that very pertinent question since two of them were former employees in your department and the other a very close friend of yours whom you interceded to keep in the government?

Mr. White: No; I do not think I would know what the situation is. Apparently they have had the advice of counsel. I suppose it depends

---

offered in evidence by the prosecution but were not admitted. Subsequently, Representative Nixon read the contents of these memos into the *Congressional Record* of January 31, 1950.

[8] Ibid., pp. 882-83.

on what counsel you have. I do not happen to have any counsel that I would seek advice of that kind from. I do my own thinking.[9]

.   .   .

The Chairman: How do you feel about Mr. Silvermaster today in view of the testimony that has been given before the FBI and Federal grand jury and before this committee, and what you have read in the newspapers? Do you think Mr. Silvermaster was ever a member of the Communist Party?

Mr. White: You cannot erase 7 or 8 years of friendship with a man that way, unless I see evidence, unless the court declares he is; and until they prove he is guilty, I believe he is innocent. I am sorry, Mr. Chairman, this applause is not my fault.[10]

When Harry White first took the witness chair he passed a scribbled note to the chairman, Representative J. Parnell Thomas. Then, in the course of his testimony, he had occasion to mention that he had played baseball and ping-pong. Mr. Thomas interrupted him suddenly and spoke with heavy sarcasm.

The Chairman: Just a minute, right there. Let me see that note. One thing I cannot reconcile, Mr. White, you send me a note and you say that: "I am recovering from a severe heart attack. I would appreciate it if the chairman would give me 5 or 10 minutes rest after each hour."

For a person who had a severe heart condition, you certainly can play a lot of sports.

Mr. White: I did not intend that this note should be read aloud. I do not know any reason why it should be public that I am ill, but I think probably one of the reasons why I suffered a heart attack was because I played so many sports, and so well. The heart attack which I suffered was last year. I am speaking of playing ping-pong, and I was a fair tennis player, and a pretty good ball player, many years prior to that. I hope that clears that up, Mr. Chairman.

The Chairman: Yes, sir. (Applause) [11]

Three days later Harry White died of a heart attack. He was regarded by his colleagues in the Treasury as a brilliant econo-

[9] Ibid., p. 883.
[10] Ibid., p. 898.
[11] Ibid., p. 881.

mist who had built the Division of Monetary Research into an efficient and effective unit of government. As an assistant secretary of the Treasury, he had served his country devotedly during the war years. He was the principal author of the American proposals presented—and in large part adopted—at the International Monetary Conference at Bretton Woods, New Hampshire, in 1944; and he carried the main burden of representing American interests in the conference as a technical expert, the opposite number of Britain's Sir John Maynard Keynes. His great contribution to the conference brought him appointment as an executive director of the International Monetary Fund, representing the United States. But perhaps no public service in his distinguished career was so significant as that rendered at the close of his life when he gave the House Committee on Un-American Activities a lesson in essential Americanism.

The members of the Un-American Activities Committee confused themselves not only with a grand jury but with a petit jury as well. They repeatedly referred to themselves as constituting a court—not a court which could afford accused persons any of the protections which would have been theirs by right in a court of law, but nevertheless a court which would pass judgment upon them, determining their guilt or innocence. The witnesses, committee members said repeatedly, were before the great court of public opinion. For example, Representative Hebert told one of the witnesses:

. . . Dr. Silverman, you are now before the greatest open court in this country, I believe, beyond the confines of any limited courtroom in this country. You are now in the presence of probably 1,000 or more people in this committee room. You are in the presence of an invisible audience of millions of American people who listen to the radio. You are in the presence of millions of American people who see moving pictures. You are in the presence of competent and able representatives of the American press, which is free.

I now tell you, Dr. Silverman, you are facing Miss Elizabeth T. Bentley, who may be known to you under the name of Elizabeth T.

Bentley, or perhaps under the name of Mary or under the name of Helen. I tell you, Dr. Silverman, that this lady standing here, whom I have described by name, accuses you in open court before the American people of being an espionage agent, or rather of having given her secret documents, confidential documents, which you, Dr. Silverman, obtained through your connections with the Army Air Forces. She accuses you of disloyalty to your government, and she tells you that you were untrue to your trust.

You face your accuser, Dr. Silverman. What is your answer? Is she telling the truth or isn't she telling the truth, and do you recognize her?

Mr. Silverman: In my opinion, she is telling a huge web of lies.

Mr. Hebert: You tell Miss Bentley here—that is contradictory now to the fact that you refused to answer because it might incriminate you. Are you waiving that now?

Mr. Silverman: With respect to the charge of espionage and any other criminal conduct, I waive.

Mr. Hebert: You waive any charges right now—

(Mr. Silverman confers with Mr. Jaffee.)

Mr. Hebert: Wait a minute. You can answer by yourself. You are a doctor of philosophy and had access to all this. You didn't ask advice of counsel when you handed these documents to Miss Bentley, did you?

Miss Bentley has made these charges and you are familiar with them. Now, you have your opportunity in open court to tell this lady that you have never seen her before, that you have never received anything from her, that you never knew her as Helen, Mary, or Elizabeth Bentley, and tell her that she never gave you any documents that were confidential or in violation—rather, that she—you have got me confused—(laughter)—that you, Dr. Silverman, never handed to her any documents, and you further tell her that you never gave documents to any unauthorized person with the intent and purpose of transporting them to other unauthorized persons.

Now, you have got your chance.

Mr. Silverman: That is too complex. I do not consider this to be a court.

Mr. Hebert: You are hedging. You asked for an open court. I am giving it to you.

The Chairman: Let him go ahead.

Mr. Silverman: I didn't ask for an open court. I asked for a court.[12]

12 Ibid., pp. 846-47.

Perhaps it is not altogether beyond understanding in the light of this colloquy that Mr. Jaffee, who was Mr. Silverman's lawyer, advised him against giving any testimony in such a court. "On advice of counsel," Mr. Silverman said, "I refuse to answer that question in the exercise of my constitutional privilege against self-incrimination under the Fifth Amendment."

During Mr. White's appearance Representative Karl Mundt asserted that the witnesses there were appearing "in the best court of this country, which is the court of public opinion." Mr. White responded promptly, "If it is properly presented, Congressman Mundt. If the whole story is presented, I agree with you. And the public could read something beside the headlines, Congressman Mundt, you know that, as well as I." [13]

Frank Coe, after a categorical denial that he had ever known Miss Bentley, made the following observation:

One of the members of this committee has been reported as saying that these hearings would leave the decision to public opinion. If public opinion is to decide, surely the committee ought to hear witnesses on behalf of the accused. Such witnesses should be heard and cross-examined. The public would not find such testimony as exciting as the original accusation, but at least all the facts would be available. . . . Before this committee there are accusers and accused, just as in a court. The accused are punished. The grave and sensational charges which are made here are given wide publicity, and that is a cruel punishment. It hurts the accused, his family, and his friends and associates. The peculiarity of this court is that all who are accused before it are punished—the innocent and the guilty alike. Under present methods of the committee, that result is inevitable.[14]

Later in the course of the hearing Mr. Coe said to Representative Mundt, who was at that time acting as chairman, "If Miss Bentley is here, I would like to ask her some questions." To this Mr. Mundt replied without any apparent loss of composure:

The position of this committee has been—and you explained it very clearly in your statement—that we are not functioning as a court, don't

13 Ibid., p. 892.
14 Ibid., p. 916.

have the power, unfortunately, that a court does have, and so we have not made it a policy to cross-examine witnesses or to permit counsel to do so.

Had we the full authority of a court, certainly it would be easier to get down into the disputed evidence in this particular case. Since we do not have, we cannot adapt ourselves to part of the rules of the court without having the authority that goes with being a court. Unfortunately, we cannot accept your request.[15]

The committee's conception of itself as a court became even more pronounced when, after a considerable amount of pyrotechnical display in hearing other accused persons, the espionage investigation narrowed down to a duel between Whittaker Chambers and Alger Hiss.

The early testimony of Whittaker Chambers differed materially from that given by Miss Bentley in content and quality. He accused the men identified by him only of being members of what he termed a "Communist apparatus designed to influence government policy." He did not represent himself as a spy or charge the members of the "apparatus" with espionage. And it is especially noteworthy that he neglected entirely to name Henry Julian Wadleigh, who subsequently confessed that he had actually given him confidential documents. Indeed, in all its exhaustive interrogation of Mr. Chambers, the Un-American Activities Committee, although its hearings purported to be on the subject of "Communist Espionage in the United States Government," did not discover that he had been engaged in espionage until he dramatically produced some stolen official papers in the course of a pretrial hearing of Alger Hiss's libel suit against him.

Whittaker Chambers' story as it gradually unfolded was more detailed, more circumstantial, and therefore more impressive, than Miss Bentley's. There was a conspiratorial air about him that made it relatively easy to believe he had actually been, as he asserted, a disciplined agent of the Communist underground. Moreover, there was an articulate repentance about what he said that gave his words something of the weight of a Judgment Day

[15] Ibid., p. 926.

confession. "It is ten years since I broke away from the Communist Party," he told the Committee.

During that decade I have sought to live an industrious and God-fearing life. At the same time I have fought communism constantly by act and written word. I am proud to appear before this committee. The publicity inseparable from such testimony has darkened, and will no doubt continue to darken, my effort to integrate myself in the community of free men. But that is a small price to pay if my testimony helps to make Americans recognize at last that they are at grips with a secret, sinister, and enormously powerful force whose tireless purpose is their enslavement.[16]

The most impressive aspect of Chambers' testimony, of course, is that eventually it was bolstered by documentary evidence. He produced the "pumpkin papers." And his possession of those papers demonstrated conclusively that the Espionage Act had been violated by someone in 1938.

Initially, however, Chambers appeared to be just another in the long, long list of professional ex-Communists dredged up by the committee to make reckless charges about the Roosevelt administration. His recital had a painfully familiar sound. It seemed an echo of the voice of Martin Dies crying out against the "Trojan Horses" in the New Deal. It was natural that men who had been sympathetic to the New Deal and who had come to regard the Committee on Un-American Activities as an evil influence should have reacted to Whittaker Chambers with anger and incredulity.

Alger Hiss was the first of the persons accused by Chambers to request a hearing before the committee; his vigorous denial of any affiliation with the Communist movement and of any acquaintance with his accuser made him seem, in a sense, a representative of the New Deal challenging the committee in the name of all his former colleagues. Thus, from the beginning, there was intense partisanship over the Hiss-Chambers duel. On either side, far greater meaning was attached to the outcome than the real status of either protagonist warranted. Nothing could actually

16 Ibid., p. 565.

be proved by this spurious test beyond the guilt or innocence of the two individuals involved.

With the dramatic production of the "pumpkin papers," Chambers' story took on a new significance and a greatly augmented credibility. Hiss was indicted for perjury by the New York grand jury as its final official act. But by that time most liberals had experienced so strong a sense of identification with him that they could not escape the feeling that they themselves—or at least what they believed in—were in some measure on trial with him. They insisted that he must be innocent because they desperately wanted him to be innocent. If they could prove that Whittaker Chambers was lying, they would be able finally to discredit the Committee on Un-American Activities and win a triumphant vindication of the New Deal. So they believed what they wished to believe and let the trial assume an importance out of all relation to its real significance.

Those hostile to the New Deal were even more disposed to regard the perjury trial as a decisive test, not alone of Alger Hiss as an individual, but of the loyalty of all those who had been associated with him and had professed faith in him. They wished ardently that Alger Hiss would be proved guilty of espionage through a conviction of perjury, because it seemed to them that this would prove the Roosevelt administration as a whole guilty, as they believed it to be, of betraying the United States to Russia. If they could prove that Alger Hiss gave classified material to a Soviet agent, they would have succeeded, the more extreme among them felt, in proving by implication that the National Labor Relations Act, the Social Security Act, and all the other social welfare legislation of the 1930s constituted a betrayal of the United States to Communist ideology.

In this embittered conflict there was no room for doubt as to the sympathies of the Un-American Activities Committee. In one of the most revealing interchanges of the long proceedings, the chairman, J. Parnell Thomas, said to John Rankin, "You know, Mr. Rankin, well down deep in your heart that this Committee is not going to whitewash anybody or anything, and you also know that this Committee has done a very big job—a very big job—and especially a big job in the last two years. We have been unearthing your New Dealers for two years, and for eight years before that."

To this gambit Mr. Rankin responded, "I know the Senate is busy now nagging the white people of the South, and all of the FEPC, and all this communistic bunk." [17]

As the duel between Hiss and Chambers developed, members of the committee tended more and more to refer to the latter as "our witness," and to speak of the accumulation of evidence against Hiss as "our case." In *The Red Plot against America*, Robert Stripling tells of a despondent moment when he was mistakenly informed that the "pumpkin" microfilms were made on celluloid manufactured in 1946. "Our case lay in ruins around our feet," he said. "It had rested wholly on our charge that these documents had been stolen from the State Department in the 1930s, and photographed at that time for transmission to Russia. I felt like taking a dry dive out the nearest window." [18]

Mr. Stripling's disappointment at receiving information which seemed to support the word of a trusted and respected former State Department official against the accusation of a confessed Soviet spy was relieved by subsequent news that the microfilm was actually made in 1937. His jubilation, naturally, was immense. [19] The committee, after all, had a tremendous investment in Whittaker Chambers. Its own reputation was on trial quite as much as Alger Hiss. Its whole function of "unearthing" New Dealers was being put to the test.

No doubt Alger Hiss received a fair trial—as fair a trial as any could be in an atmosphere impregnated with suspicion and bitter political conflict. He was found guilty by a conscientious jury sitting under the authority of a just judge. No better means of determining guilt has yet been devised. The evidence against him was comprehensive and compelling. But the fact remains that he

[17] Ibid., p. 548.
[18] Stripling, op. cit., p. 149
[19] Ibid., p. 150.

was tried first by a committee of Congress and second by the newspapers before he ever came to trial in a court of law. When he came into court he was tried for espionage on a charge of perjury, and this charge was contrived to circumvent the statute of limitations, which would otherwise have afforded him immunity from prosecution for a crime that was so far in the past as to make the recollection of events difficult and uncertain.

No one reading the record of this trial can think that it uncovered the whole story beneath the surface circumstances disclosed to the jury—in the sense of fitting these circumstances into a rational and understandable pattern. Accepting the verdict of the jury as valid in terms of the evidence available to it, we are left with all the larger and more significant questions raised by the case still unanswered. What impelled Whittaker Chambers, more than a decade after the conspiracy had ceased and when Hiss no longer had any connection with the government, to destroy a person he described as his closest friend in the party and as "a man of great simplicity and a great gentleness and sweetness of character"? [20] What could have impelled Hiss to enter into a conspiracy so apparently inconsistent with all the rest of his career?

In the latter part of the 1930s there was a bitter struggle within the Roosevelt administration over the direction of foreign policy. To many of the New Dealers, the Department of State, dominated then by career foreign service officers, seemed exasperatingly insensitive to the rise of fascism—particularly in connection with the Spanish war. They sought in various ways to prod the Department into more militant action against Germany, Italy, and Japan. One of the standard techniques in the internal feuds of that period was the calculated leak to newspapers—designed to arouse public opinion for or against a given policy. When one faction in the administration wanted to spike a project contemplated by another faction, the simplest method was to tell some eager reporter or columnist all about it—in strict confidence, of course; sometimes it was expedient to show the newspaperman a

[20] Hearings, p. 666.

confidential memorandum or the preliminary draft of a proposed
set of regulations or the contents of a report meant for official
eyes alone. Security rules were very lax at that time, or at any
rate very laxly enforced; indeed the term had not yet come into
vogue. Violation of the rules was rationalized by those who indulged in it as a kind of in-fighting required in the public interest as they saw it. The only sin was getting caught.

The best that can be said of the practice is that it was generally
harmless—and, in a sense, innocent, or at least free from sinister
motivation.[21] The trial of Alger Hiss revealed, however, that
some persons went beyond this—went so far, indeed, as to divulge
classified information to foreign agents. The rationalization that
could lead an American citizen to such folly and disloyalty is
hard to understand. One interpretation of it is to be found in
the words of Henry Julian Wadleigh, a State Department employee who was confessedly guilty of the crime. He put it this
way in the first of a series of newspaper articles describing his
double life in the State Department:

Something drastic had to be done [about the rise of fascism and
nazism], and I felt there was a need for me to help. But what should
I do? I had no idea. I was as diffident in making practical decisions as
I was confident in handling theories. But of one thing I was convinced.

Civilization was menaced by a highly organized and disciplined
enemy. The defense must be disciplined and well coordinated. As far as
I could see, the only disciplined group of people in the world offering
any vigorous resistance to the growth of fascism was the Communist
movement.

[21] A more recent comparable instance of this attitude is the case of Captain
John G. Crommelin, Jr., the Navy's most outspoken critic of a unified defense
organization. He acknowledged in a public statement, October 5, 1949, that
he had given newspapermen copies of classified letters from high naval com-
manders to Secretary of the Navy Francis P. Matthews. "I consider," he said,
"my release of the letter of Vice Admiral Bogan with the endorsements of
Admirals Radford and Denfeld necessary to the interest of national security.
. . . My action in this vital matter may have been a technical violation of a
regulation, but it had to be done." (Quotation from *The New York Times,*
October 6, 1949.) Captain Crommelin was reprimanded but not court-
martialed for this breach of security, and in certain quarters he was warmly
applauded.

After much hesitation, I suddenly decided to offer my services to the Communists, and to do faithfully whatever task they might assign to me.

This decision was a practical one, not based on theoretical convictions. To be sure, I thought, I can pick all kinds of holes in their theories and dogmas, but that isn't the point. This is a world emergency. Narrow-minded dogmatism is a common weakness of people who passionately consecrate their lives to a cause, just as an incapacity for disciplined action is a common weakness of independent thinkers like myself. . . .

They wanted facts about foreign countries collected by the United States and perhaps not available or so readily available elsewhere. They wanted to use this government as a window for spying on other countries. . . .

Technically, I was giving out some of the secrets of my own government to agents of a foreign country. However, I did not regard my action as contrary to the interests of the United States, but definitely the opposite. Anything that would help the Russians, or anyone else, to resist German or Japanese aggression would not only foster United States interests, but benefit the whole of mankind on the purely nationalistic level. The expansion of the aggressor powers was proceeding unchecked, and might soon become a direct military menace to this country.[22]

How largely this apologia reflects real recollection of past motives and how largely it is contrived in the convenient light of subsequent developments can only be conjectured. It affords, in any case, a beautiful subject for the psychoanalysts. Neurotic insecurity and the yearning for flight from independence into discipline and submergence are writ large in it. But so, too, is a kind of idealism, however mistaken and misplaced. The sense that because "something drastic had to be done," he, personally, had to do it, is a sense out of which saints as well as sinners, great patriots as well as base traitors, are made.

Perhaps, like Wadleigh, Alger Hiss was infected in that decade of uprooted faith, the 1930s, with the tragic delusion that the

[22] Published in the *Washington Post,* July 24, 1949; copyright, 1949, New York Post Corp.

struggle against fascism could best be advanced by service to the Soviet Union and that such service would promote the real interests, as distinguished from the official policy, of the United States. If so, he deserves punishment, of course, for the crime into which that delusion led him.

But the crime itself, if this be accepted as its motivation, deserves to be judged in the context in which it was committed. The United States Attorney who prosecuted Alger Hiss likened him to Benedict Arnold and to Judas Iscariot. What Arnold committed was treason in the strict constitutional sense of the term: a general in the American Revolutionary Army, he was led by pique and personal bitterness to make regular reports to the British in 1779 and attempted a year later while the war was still in progress to deliver West Point to the enemy for a promised reward of twenty thousand pounds. Judas, a disciple, betrayed Jesus to Caiaphas and the chief priests for thirty pieces of silver. Whatever Alger Hiss did, he did not do it for money, and he did not do it in aid of an enemy with which his country was at war. All this does not mitigate the offense or make it less of a threat to the country's safety; but, if mischievous inferences are to be avoided, the facts have to be remembered when we evaluate the meaning of his act.

"Obviously the decisive fact about Chambers," Arthur Koestler wrote in an article deploring the hostility of American liberals to this Communist renegade, "is that he has performed a service of great social utility." [23] In the light of subsequent events, this is by no means so obvious. There is always social utility, to be sure, in disclosure of the truth. Insofar as Chambers may be credited with having told the truth—he made many assertions that remain unverified—and insofar as his disclosures illuminated the extent and the deviousness of the Communist conspiracy, he may be said to have rendered a service to his readopted country. But some of the results have been far from socially useful.

The members of the Un-American Activities Committee and other Americanists interpreted the verdict in the Hiss trial as a

[23] *New York Times Magazine,* February 19, 1950.

condemnation of all the best that Alger Hiss had come to represent as well as all the worst. He had been one of the dedicated young men of the New Deal; therefore the whole social program of which he had been a part was tainted. He had risen to attend the conference at Yalta with President Roosevelt; therefore Yalta must have been a betrayal of the United States. He had played a minor part in the evolution of American policy in the Far East; therefore the whole of that policy and everyone else who had a share in it must be suspect. Secretary of State Dean Acheson and Supreme Court Justice Felix Frankfurter had been his friends; therefore they deserved to be hounded out of office. The irrationality of this reaction is explicable only in terms of the blind rancor that motivated it.

In nothing was the hatred of the Americanists so nakedly revealed as in the attack upon Dean Acheson because he refused to "turn his back" upon a friend in distress and disgrace. What can loyalty have come to mean in the United States if it forbids friendship and even Christian charity? The fair-weather friend has not hitherto been a hero in America. Jury verdicts are not so infallible that free men may not disagree with them—which the Secretary of State was careful not to do—or believe that evidence not yet uncovered might lead to a different decision.

The wave of embittered suspicion and extravagant name-calling that grew out of the Hiss case had no social utility whatever. It suggested nothing so much as a national nervous breakdown. The Americanists and the professional ex-Communists joined in a sadistic-masochistic orgy of denunciation, "crying out" against their fellow-Americans. The ex-Communists, conscious of their betrayal of American values, wanted the comfort of company; they had to show that many others, even many who were highly respected, had been as recreant as they. And they had to prove that they were more American than the Americanists by plunging us into more and more extravagant loyalty purges. The Americanists—or at least a portion of them—had been no less guilty of disloyalty in a different form. When faith in democratic and libertarian principles was at its ebb in the 1930s, their search for an escape from freedom had taken some of them far in the direction of fascism. Among them were carriers of infections—the doctrine of racial supremacy, the poison of anti-Semitism, the notion that the people could not be trusted and needed disciplined submission to an elite authority in which they themselves, of course, would be leaders. They cheered Franco in Spain, they reminded us that Germany and Italy had, after all, been regenerated, and they preached the doctrine of isolationism. If fascism had had an international organization comparable to that of the Communist parties, some of these men might well have been its agents here as they were, indeed, its fellow-travelers. The cynicism and despair of the 1930s found expression in more than one form of totalitarianism.

The men who fought the Revolutionary War were not so benighted as to consider George Washington a traitor because he had befriended and sponsored Benedict Arnold in the Continental Congress. They knew what the Committee on Un-American Activities has never understood, that guilt is personal, that it cannot be transferred by mere association. If they had allowed suspicion to disunite them and to paralyze all policy, they would never have achieved independence.

Whatever the guilt of Alger Hiss and whatever the utility of exposing and punishing it a decade later, national security is not likely to be achieved by vilifying all who worked with and trusted him. It is not likely to be achieved by regarding the State Department as a haunted house from which evil spirits must be exorcised by the ritual of incessant purges. It is not likely to be achieved by inventing crimes called "virtual espionage" and "cold-war treason" and punishing them outside the law. Nothing that the agents of communism have done or can do in this country is so dangerous to the United States as what they have induced us, through the Americanists, to do to ourselves.

CHAPTER V

THE GOVERNMENT'S LOYALTY PROGRAM

... we must consider the two objects of desire, both of which we cannot have, and make up our minds which to choose. It is desirable that criminals should be detected, and to that end that all available evidence should be used. It also is desirable that the government should not itself foster and pay for other crimes, when they are the means by which the evidence is to be obtained. . . . We have to choose, and for my part I think it a less evil that some criminals should escape than that the government should play an ignoble part.[1]

SECURITY is never an absolute. It is attained in its optimum state not when all risk has been excluded, but when risk has been brought into rational balance with the ends which security is supposed to serve. The government of a free people must take certain chances for the sake of maintaining freedom which the government of a police state avoids because it holds freedom to be of no value.

Any parent knows that he exposes a child to some degree of danger by granting him the freedom indispensable to growth. There are risks in going off to school, in playing with friends, in the whole process of development to maturity and independence. These risks can be reduced by wise guardianship; but they cannot

[1] Oliver Wendell Holmes, Jr., dissenting opinion *Olmstead* v. *U.S.*, 277 U.S. 438 (1928).

be wholly avoided except at the cost of inhibiting and frustrating growth altogether. Excessive protection can destroy its own object.

Every government must take measures, of course, to protect itself from untrustworthy individuals, particularly in the ranks of its own employees. The totalitarian governments aim at total security. This is sought in Russia, for example, by placing the government itself within the Kremlin, a walled city that is inaccessible to the Russian people; by recruiting government functionaries exclusively from a single disciplined party and on the basis of an undeviating adherence to orthodoxy; by cutting them off from contact with foreigners and the ideas of the outside world. Such divorcement of the government from the governed is an identifying characteristic of the police state. But judging from the frequency of Russian purges and treason trials, these precautions cannot be considered an infallible technique of assuring loyalty or achieving security.

A democratic government cannot, in any case, take such precautions without ceasing to be democratic. It is undoubtedly desirable, to paraphrase Mr. Justice Holmes somewhat loosely, that disloyal persons should be kept out of government employment and to that end that all available means should be used. It is also desirable that the government should not itself resort to means destructive of the ends for which governments are established among free men. We have to choose, and perhaps it is a lesser evil that some risks should be run than "that the government should play an ignoble part."

The risks involved in the employment of disloyal persons are obvious enough. A disloyal employee might disclose important confidential information to an agent of a foreign government; he might, in certain circumstances, give false information to the United States government; and he might, conceivably, influence American policy to the advantage of another country. Similarly, employees who are indiscreet or emotionally unstable or of bad character might be persuaded or coerced into serving foreign interests. Great care in the selection of government employees is manifestly a vital element of national security.

Since 1947 the United States government has certainly exercised great care, through the Federal Employee-Loyalty Program, in selecting its personnel. But this program involves certain risks of its own which ought to be examined conscientiously and weighed in the balance. A consideration of these risks—and of whether the program leads the government to "play an ignoble part"—will be the business of this chapter. The chapter which follows will consider the effectiveness of the loyalty program in terms of its stated objectives; the value of other proposals for protecting the government from undesirable employees; and a personnel policy which seems to the writer better adapted to this end.

Before 1939 the American people took it for granted that the fellow-Americans they employed as government servants were loyal to the United States. They set certain standards for appointment to the classified Civil Service designed to exclude the criminal and the incompetent. They endeavored to have government jobs awarded on a merit basis rather than through political patronage. They established a number of checks and regulations, sometimes referred to as red tape, to prevent abuses and irregularities and to assure a reasonable amount of industry on the part of employees. But so far as loyalty was concerned, they asked only that federal workers take an oath on assuming office to support and defend the Constitution of the United States against all enemies, to bear true faith and allegiance to the same, and to discharge their duties well and faithfully.

Tests of political orthodoxy are repugnant to the American tradition. So far as government employees are concerned, indeed, they were expressly banned by a Civil Service rule promulgated in 1884. This rule stated:

No question in any form or application or in any examination shall be so framed as to elicit information concerning the political or religious opinions or affiliations of any applicant, nor shall any inquiry be made concerning such opinions, or affiliations, and all disclosures thereof shall be discountenanced.

A number of factors combined by the end of the 1930s to make stricter standards seem desirable. The Un-American Activities Committee was telling the public that the government was filled with Trojan horses. The Communist Party stood revealed as a microphone for Soviet propaganda. The German-American Bund was patently an agency of the Third Reich, and war seemed imminent. Accordingly, in 1939, Congress adopted as a provision of the Hatch Act a clause forbidding any person employed in any agency of the federal government to hold membership in any political party or organization advocating the overthrow of our constitutional form of government. This was interpreted as applicable specifically to the Communist Party and the German-American Bund. It was justified on the ground that a Civil Service procedure designed to prevent political discrimination among loyal Americans should not be allowed to protect those who gave their allegiance to a foreign power.

The origin of the prohibition against advocating overthrow of the government is an interesting one. It grew out of fears that antedated the Russian Revolution—fears of anarchism. The first statutory use of the phrase was in the Immigration Act of 1918 when it was applied to that most impotent of all minorities, aliens seeking admittance to the United States. No one who advocated overthrow could come in—as though the American form of government would topple at the first suggestion of a foreign agitator. In 1920 the barrier was broadened to include the first legislative recognition of the doctrine of guilt by association. Congress in that year provided a legal basis for Attorney General A. Mitchell Palmer's xenophobia by making it a deportable offense for any alien to have *membership in or affiliation with* any organization "advocating or teaching opposition to all organized government, or the overthrow by force or violence of the government of the United States or of all forms of law. . . ."

Because aliens were and are without any status, there was no protest against this restraint on advocacy or against adoption of the idea that guilt could be established through mere imputation of belief. And once imbedded in the statute books, these lega-

listic catch phrases were available for more extensive and mischievous employment. In 1939, through the Hatch Act, they were
applied to citizens who worked for the government. In 1940 the
Alien Registration Act forbade all Americans to teach or advocate
the duty or necessity of overthrowing by force or violence a government created by just such advocacy. Thus the United States
returned for the first time since the abandonment of the Alien
and Sedition Acts of 1798 to a peacetime sedition statute. It is
no accident that this repression was achieved through an amendment to a statute nominally aimed only at aliens. The extension
of this restraint on advocacy from the few to the many is an
object lesson in the danger of countenancing any encroachment
on liberty. Those who imprison the helpless are likely in the end
to find themselves inside the walls they have erected.

This is by no mean a unique illustration of the point. Aliens
are often merely the initial victims of restraints subsequently applied to citizens. To cite another instance, the Attorney General
has absolute discretion under the Immigration Act to exclude
any alien from the United States without giving him a hearing
or even a statement of charges. Thus, in 1949, Ellen Knauff, the
wife of an American civilian employee of the occupation establishment in Germany, was detained at Ellis Island and denied
admission to the United States on the basis of "confidential information." Neither the nature nor the source of the charge was
made known to her—a denial of due process which, whatever the
merits of the particular case, leaves a good deal of room for prejudice or error. A divided Supreme Court upheld the authority
of the Attorney General to act in so arbitrary a manner—although
the language of its opinion could scarcely have been comforting
to him. The procedure in this case—or lack of procedure—is not
markedly different, however, from the now prevalent practice of
excluding American citizens from government service as "security
risks," without a hearing and without charges, on the basis of
anonymous accusations.

The Hatch Act of 1939 was supplemented in 1941 by a rider
tacked to all appropriation measures stipulating that no part of

the funds provided should be used to pay the salaries or wages of any person "who advocates or who is a member of an organization that advocates the overthrow of the government of the United States by force or violence." Additional legislation intended to protect the government from disloyal employees had already been adopted in 1940 in the form of an authorization to the Secretary of War and the Secretary of the Navy to remove summarily, without regard to any other provisions of law governing the removal of employees, anyone who in his opinion constituted a risk to the security of the country. Subsequently the Secretary of State and the Atomic Energy Commission were given the same power. In 1942 President Roosevelt issued war service regulations specifying that one of the grounds on which an applicant could be barred from the Civil Service was the existence of a reasonable doubt as to his loyalty.

A general though somewhat haphazard loyalty program was begun in all the federal agencies with the issuance of the 1942 war service regulations. But the Civil Service Commission lacked funds and personnel to investigate more than a fraction of the great mass of employees brought into the government during the war and in the years immediately preceding it. Moreover, the standards of disqualification were vague and uncertain. Some undesirable individuals were employed. Employees were sometimes dismissed on tenuous charges of disloyalty without any chance to defend themselves. To supplement the work of the Civil Service Commission, the Attorney General in 1941 had directed the FBI to investigate complaints made against federal employees alleged to be disloyal. The FBI reported its findings to the various employing agencies, leaving disciplinary action entirely within their discretion. To correct the defects of this system, or lack of system, the Attorney General created in 1942 a special Interdepartmental Committee on Investigations. This committee endeavored to achieve some standardization among the federal agencies and offered its services to review the records in individual cases and to render advisory opinions.

A year later the Attorney General's committee was replaced by a new interdepartmental committee on employee investigations, established by the President. This group, too, functioned only on an advisory basis. The Supreme Court has held that authority to remove or retain an employee rests exclusively with the employing agency. The Interdepartmental Committee confined itself, moreover, to incumbents, and regarded an employee as removable on loyalty grounds only if it was established that he personally advocated overthrow of the government by force or violence, or belonged to an organization advocating such a program. The Civil Service Committee of the House of Representatives turned its attention to the problem in 1945, establishing a special subcommittee to study and report on employee loyalty and employment policies in the government. This subcommittee's report declared that "there are many conditions called to the committee's attention that cannot be remedied by mere changes in techniques or issuance of directives. Adequate protective measures must be adopted to see that persons of questioned loyalty are not permitted to enter into the federal service. These protective measures should of course be absolutely fair and impartial, but doubts must, in the nature of things, be resolved in favor of the Government."

In response to this report, President Truman in 1946 created the President's Temporary Commission on Employee Loyalty, which made an extended study of the situation and submitted a set of recommendations which led to the promulgation on March 21, 1947, of an executive order establishing a full-scale loyalty program for the Executive branch of the federal government.

The executive order had a double aim: (1) that "maximum protection must be afforded the United States against infiltration of disloyal persons into the ranks of its employees," and (2) that "equal protection from unfounded accusations of disloyalty must be afforded the loyal employees of the government." There was certainly a most pressing need for the second of these aims. Extravagant accusations of widespread disloyalty in the Executive branch of the government were again coming from the House

Committee on Un-American Activities. In 1947 the Republican Party had control of Congress, while a Democratic president remained in the White House. And it can scarcely be doubted that, in part at least, attacks on the administration were politically motivated. Conversely it seems equally clear that there were political motives for establishing the loyalty program as a means of disarming criticism and forestalling the adoption of repressive legislation by Congress.

The President's order provided for "a loyalty investigation of every person entering the civilian employment of any department or agency of the Executive branch of the federal government." The investigation was to take the form in the first instance of a name check against the files of the FBI, the Civil Service Commission, and the military and naval intelligence services. It involved reference also to "the files of any other appropriate government investigative or intelligence agency and to the files of the House Committee on Un-American Activities; and reference, in addition, to local law-enforcement files at the place of residence and employment of the applicant, including municipal, county, and state law-enforcement files, to schools and colleges attended by the applicant, to former employers, to references given by an applicant, and to any other appropriate source."

Under the terms of the loyalty program "a full field investigation" must be conducted with respect to the loyalty of any applicant or employee concerning whom "derogatory information" is uncovered through reference to these sources. What this means is a probe of his past by agents of the Federal Bureau of Investigation, aimed at discovering his sympathies, his attitudes, his motives, and his intentions. The FBI interviews his associates. It seeks opinions respecting his loyalty from neighbors, from former employers and from former employees, including sometimes janitors and housemaids. It inquires into the organizations he has joined, the sentiments he has expressed about public issues. The fruits of this harvest are then delivered to a loyalty board which has the task of evaluating them and determining whether "on all the evidence, reasonable grounds exist for belief that the person involved is disloyal to the government of the United States."

The executive order takes cognizance of the danger that men may be mistakenly or maliciously accused of disloyalty. To offset this danger, it provides an elaborate procedure of review. If a loyalty board considers charges warranted on the basis of the FBI report, it affords the individual an opportunity to appear before it, with counsel or a representative of his own choice. It allows him also to present witnesses and affidavits in his own behalf; it supplies him, if he is an incumbent, with a specification of the charges, and, if he is an applicant, with an interrogatory designed to acquaint him with the character of the suspicion under which he has fallen. The order provides that an employee shall be informed "of the nature of the charges against him in sufficient detail, so that he will be enabled to prepare his defense. The charges shall be stated as specifically and completely as, in the discretion of the employing department or agency, security considerations permit. . . ."

If an agency or regional board makes a recommendation of ineligibility, the accused individual has a right of appeal to the head of the agency. And if, as is generally the case, the board is sustained by the agency head, the individual may then appeal for a review of the record to the Loyalty Review Board established in the Civil Service Commission under the terms of the President's order. Again, before this board he may appear personally with counsel and may present witnesses and affidavits. The President's order also provides that:

. . . the investigative agency may refuse to disclose the names of confidential informants, provided it furnishes sufficient information about such informants on the basis of which the requesting department or agency can make an adequate evaluation of the information furnished by them, and provided it advises the requesting department or agency in writing that it is essential to the protection of the informants or to the investigation of other cases that the identity of the informants not be revealed.

The executive order also itemizes a number of activities and associations which loyalty boards may consider in the determination of disloyalty. Most of these are rather obvious. Sabotage; espionage; treason; sedition; intentional unauthorized disclosure of confidential documents—these not only indicate disloyalty; they are criminal and therefore subject to prosecution in a court of law. Acting "so as to serve the interest of another government in preference to the interest of the United States"; "advocacy of revolution or force or violence to alter the constitutional form of government of the United States"—these are not so much standards as a redundant expression of the very issue to be determined. The executive order goes on then to add still another ground which loyalty boards may consider:

Membership in, affiliation with, or sympathetic association with, any foreign or domestic organization, association, movement, group or combination of persons, designated by the Attorney General as totalitarian, fascist, communist, or subversive, or as having adopted a policy of advocating or approving the commission of acts of force or violence to deny other persons their rights under the Constitution of the United States, or as seeking to alter the form of government of the United States by unconstitutional means.

The President made it clear in a statement about the loyalty program on November 14, 1947, that "membership in an organization is simply one piece of evidence which may or may not be helpful in arriving at a conclusion as to the action which should be taken in a particular case." Thus membership in a disloyal organization is not necessarily a proof of individual disloyalty. What is plain, however, from the inclusion of this standard among the criteria used in determining loyalty is that the executive order aims at exclusion from the government service not alone of the disloyal but also of the potentially disloyal. There is a distinction here too vital to be glossed over. It is one thing to disqualify for government service a person who has committed espionage against the United States or who advocates the overthrow of the government by force. But it is something different in both magnitude and kind to disqualify from government service a person who might be guilty of such an act or of such advocacy in the future.

Loyalty tests were necessarily very different in character from the tests which had previously been applied to applicants for federal jobs. It is possible to set up fairly objective standards to determine competence. Civil Service examinations are no doubt an imperfect measurement of ability. They serve well enough, however, at least to promote a survival of the fitter. A conviction of crime is a matter of fact readily established. Scrutiny of an employee's record, of his recommendations, of his performance in past employment, may not always disclose his full potentialities or his weaknesses, but it affords a reasonable basis for judgment respecting his character and his suitability for a particular job.

A determination of loyalty necessarily goes far beyond this. It involves inquiry into past associations, into opinion, into relations which Americans have been wont to consider private. It demands the most subtle evaluation of motive and intent and sincerity. And of course a disqualification on grounds of disloyalty has an effect upon the individual concerned vastly different from a disqualification on any other grounds. It constitutes, as the Supreme Court said in the Lovett case, "punishment, and of a most severe type."

Once the government of the United States assumed that it could set standards to determine the loyalty of its employees, the development of the whole complex machinery of investigation and trial now known as the loyalty program became inevitable. If "subversives" were to be kept out of the government, inquiry into political belief and affiliation was necessary. If persons who responded to such inquiry falsely were to be detected, investigation of the most searching character had to be undertaken. If investigation was to be genuinely effective, it had to resort to the use of informers. If the continued effectiveness of informers was to be assured, their identity had to be concealed and their information had to be kept confidential. If individuals were to be safeguarded from the errors incident to investigation conducted in such a manner, an elaborate system of hearings and reviews and appeals had to be contrived.

The procedures of the loyalty program obviously fall far short of what has been established in this country as due process of law. The standards it employs for the measurement of guilt are wholly lacking in the definiteness usually required for official condemnation of American citizens. There are risks in these defects: (1) the risk of injustice to innocent individuals; (2) the risk of injury to the morale and efficiency of the Civil Service—an important factor in national security; (3) the risk of injury to the nation through corruption of its fundamental values.

Let us look critically, first, at the procedural defects of the loyalty program as they affect individuals.

The mandate which the executive order gives the Attorney General to designate voluntary associations as subversive is perhaps the most arbitrary and far-reaching power ever exercised by a single public official in the history of the United States. By virtue of it, the Attorney General may stigmatize and, in effect, proscribe any organization of which he disapproves. The executive order imposes no check upon his exercise of this power. It does not require him to hold hearings in arriving at his decisions, nor does it provide for any judicial review of them. The two Attorneys General who have wielded this power to date have done so with considerable restraint; that is, they have acted in accord with widespread popular feelings. They have judged the American Youth Congress, for example, to be a subversive organization and have placed it on their index; but apparently they have had no fault to find with the Young Men's Christian Association or the Federal Council of Churches. Yet who knows what an A. Mitchell Palmer might do with this authority?

The consequences of this grant of power go far beyond the loyalty program and far beyond the confines of the government itself. Blacklisting of this kind was not originated by the executive order. Earlier, Attorney General Francis Biddle had compiled a list of subversive organizations for the guidance of federal administrators in determining the loyalty of employees; and indeed a list of this sort is virtually indispensable if associations are to be taken as an indication of disloyalty and if the various government agencies are to observe uniform loyalty standards. Mr. Biddle's list was intended to be strictly confidential. It remained so, however, only until Representative Martin Dies obtained a copy and inserted it into the *Congressional Record*. Whether it is preferable to have such a blacklist kept secret or made public presents a nice question. Secrecy means complete irresponsibility, but publication has resulted in an extremely widespread use of the list for unintended purposes. The executive order authorizes no more than a consideration of membership in the listed groups as one factor to be taken into account in evaluating eligibility for government employment. However, membership in a listed organization has been made a justification for the dismissal of teachers from schools and universities, of clergymen from their pulpits, of ordinary citizens from ordinary private jobs. Thus it has become inevitably a kind of official blacklist.

Membership in a listed organization, while still permissible, involves, in these circumstances, a very costly defiance of authority—so costly that few save the already outcast can afford it. The listed organizations are injured even more grievously than through stigmatization by the Committee on Un-American Activities. This power to destroy voluntary associations may be an aid to security; but it is scarcely less at variance with American traditions than a power on the part of any official to imprison an individual in the name of security without any process of law. It is difficult to see in this anything less than a direct negation of what has always been a principal source of pride to Americans—that they live under a government not of men but of laws.

One of the organizations placed on the list by Tom Clark when he was Attorney General is the Socialist Workers Party. This is a bitterly anti-Stalin splinter group reflecting the Trotskyist deviation from what is now orthodox communism. It is a legal political party which polled about thirteen thousand votes in the 1948 national election. It advocates production for use, socialization of all industry, and creation of a workers' and farmers' government. It resolutely denies that it seeks to achieve these ends by violence or any other unconstitutional means.

But, somewhat ironically, the Attorney General classified the Socialist Workers Party not only as "subversive" but also as "Communist" and as an organization which seeks "to alter the form of government in the United States by unconstitutional means." Thus membership in it entails mandatory dismissal from the government service under the terms of Section 9-A of the Hatch Act. One result of this ruling was that James Kutcher, a clerk in the Newark branch office of the Veterans' Administration, lost his job in 1948 and was officially declared disloyal to the United States.

In 1943 James Kutcher, as a private first class in the Army of the United States, lost both his legs in the Battle of San Pietro in Italy. He has never made any attempt to conceal his membership in the Socialist Workers Party; he merely denies that he personally, or the party to which he belongs, advocates the violent overthrow of the government. The Attorney General's ruling makes him, therefore, the victim of a dual arbitrariness. The organization to which he belongs has been arbitrarily held to advocate what it denies advocating. And this advocacy was imputed to Mr. Kutcher through the mere fact of his membership—an assumption of guilt by association which the Supreme Court in the Schneiderman case denounced as invalid and repugnant to American law. This arbitrariness, moreover, has cost Kutcher much more than his job; it has cost him a reputation for loyalty to his country earned at considerable sacrifice in its military service.

As this is written, a civil suit is before the federal courts challenging in Kutcher's name the constitutionality of the loyalty program and the constitutionality of Section 9-A of the Hatch Act. The one, he charges, imposes punishment without due process of law; the other limits freedom of speech in contravention of the First Amendment so far as government employees are concerned.

In passing judgment on individuals concerning whom "derogatory information" has been discovered in one or another of the various reference files, the loyalty boards are dependent almost entirely on the investigative reports furnished them by the FBI. These reports contain statements of fact and opinion culled by the investigator from a variety of sources. As previously noted, the President's order says that "the investigative agency may refuse to disclose the names of confidential informants"—thus depriving the accused employee of the benefits he might gain through confrontation and cross-examination of his accusers, and depriving the boards of an invaluable means of weighing the credibility of the accusation.

No investigative agency discloses any more than it is required to disclose. The FBI is understandably reticent about its sources of information. Given discretion to withhold the identity of its informants, it naturally tends to do so whenever that seems expedient. It solicits information from all sorts of persons on a confidential basis; and when it designates its source by some cryptic symbol such as T-13, the loyalty board reading its report has no independent means of knowing whether this source is a paragon of veracity, a knave, or the village idiot. Some of its information comes of course from undercover operatives or, to use a more common police term, stool pigeons, who may or may not be above embroidering the facts here and there for the sake of seeming to be worth their keep. In practice, there is a close liaison between the Loyalty Review Board and the FBI. The board often asks the FBI to appraise the reliability of its confidential informants. In doing so, however, it manifestly gives to that police agency judicial powers which ought to be exercised, if at all, by itself—and ought certainly never be entrusted to the police in a free society.

At the inception of the loyalty program, the Loyalty Review Board faced the difficult task of determining to what extent it would make use of information from informants who could not be subjected to cross-examination by the accused employee, and whose identity could not be made known even to the board itself.

It is a mistake to blame J. Edgar Hoover for the board's decision
to rely on unidentified informants. Had it elected to do so, the
board could have instructed him to furnish information only
from persons who could be called upon to testify under oath
and submit to cross-examination. The board did not choose this
course for reasons which its chairman, Seth Richardson, set forth
candidly soon after he took office:

. . . it will be observed that the FBI report occupies an exceedingly
important position in the establishment of the facts upon which an
ultimate determination as to loyalty will be made. It should be clearly
understood that the FBI reports are not binding on the Board. Indeed
the fact of non-confrontation of witnesses, since it operates to the dis-
advantage of the employee, is a fact to be considered in the adjudication, and such fact will be weighed with other facts in determining
whether or not an individual is disloyal. It is important, therefore, to
observe that for reasons noted hereafter the employee will not be permitted to examine or inspect this report of the Bureau, at any time,
and such deprivation gives rise to one of the very controversial points
involved in the operation of the entire loyalty program.

The point has been vigorously presented to us as follows: "Every employee accused of disloyalty should be given the right to confront his
accusers, and subject them to cross-examination." This contention has
obvious force, and presents grave considerations to us. Why have we
been unable to accept it?

In nearly all cases the Bureau secures the facts for inclusion in its
reports from confidential sources, many of them closely connected with
considerations sounding in national security. We are advised by the
Bureau, that, in its experienced opinion, practically none of the evidential sources available will continue to be available to the Bureau if
proper secrecy and confidence cannot at all times be maintained with
respect to the original source of information, and that if the source of
such information is to be disclosed—save in the exceptional case—the
Bureau can be of much less service to the Board in making the essential
basic investigation.

In cases where sources of evidence are not confidential, and disclosure
of sources, possibly with pertinent oral testimony, will not tend to
hinder or impede the investigative work of the Bureau, we will make
every reasonable effort to extend the scope of the evidential source dis-

closure, to the affected employee, at the hearing. But it must be appreciated that in the great majority of the cases, we apprehend that disclosure of evidential sources to the employee, and the resulting opportunity of cross-examination of such sources by him, will probably not be practicable.   .

The importance of confrontation in determining the validity of evidence is illustrated by the record in the Dorothy Bailey case —a case which the accused employee herself made public after accounts of it had leaked to newspapers and had been widely published. Miss Bailey, a graduate of the University of Minnesota and a graduate student in the field of labor relations and employment management at Bryn Mawr College, went to work in 1933 as a junior clerk-typist in the United States Employment Service of the District of Columbia at a salary of $1440 a year. The following year she was transferred to the national office. She served in this agency continuously for fourteen years, rising to the position of supervisor of the Training Section at a salary of $7911. In June 1947 she was separated as a result of reduction in force and was re-employed in March 1948. Thus her status was technically that of an applicant, and her hearing on loyalty charges came before a regional loyalty board.

The interrogative sent to Miss Bailey informed her that "the Commission [Civil Service Commission] has received information to the effect that you are or have been a member of the Communist Party or the Communist Political Association; that you have attended meetings of the Communist Party, and have associated on numerous occasions with known Communist Party members." It said also that the Commission had information to the effect that she was or had been a member of the American League for Peace and Democracy and of the Washington Committee for Democratic Action, both of them organizations on the Attorney General's list. She denied membership at any time in the Communist Party or Communist Political Association and said she had never attended a meeting of either save once as part of a graduate seminar in Social Economy at Bryn Mawr in 1932. She also denied membership in the Washington Committee for Democratic Action but admitted that she had belonged to the American League for Peace and Democracy and had attended two of its meetings in 1938 or 1939.

In the course of the Regional Board hearing, however, Miss Bailey was questioned about organizations not referred to in the interrogative and not on the Attorney General's list—the Southern Conference for Human Welfare and the League of Women Shoppers among them. She was even asked by one of the board members: "Did you ever write a letter to the Red Cross about the segregation of blood?" [2] And the bulk of the hearing was taken up with a discussion of her activities as president of Local 10, United Public Workers of America, a CIO union widely referred to as Communist-dominated but not on the Attorney General's list.

Miss Bailey had been extremely active in the union. Indeed, she had been involved in a bitter intra-union fight and expressed a suspicion that the information alleging that she had had Communist associations came from members of a minority faction which had unsuccessfully opposed her re-election. In her own defense, she presented evidence of positions taken by her that ran directly counter to the Communist Party line; and a number of reputable persons who knew her well professionally and socially testified or filed affidavits in her behalf. In due course, however, the Regional Board found her ineligible for government employment because of doubts respecting her loyalty.

When Miss Bailey's appeal was heard by the Loyalty Review Board, her counsel charged that the allegations against her were "a result of malicious, irresponsible, reckless gossip which has no foundation whatsoever in fact and stems from an internecine union controversy that we shall develop." Then came the following exchange between Seth Richardson, chairman of the Loyalty Review Board, and Paul Porter, counsel for Miss Bailey:

[2] Harry W. Blair, the Regional Board member who asked this question, was subsequently elevated to the Loyalty Review Board by presidential appointment.

Chairman Richardson: I can only say to you that five or six of the reports come from informants certified to us by the Federal Bureau of Investigation as experienced and entirely reliable.

Mr. Porter: We would like to have their names, and I would challenge any one of them to state it publicly in a non-privileged form.

.   .   .

Mr. Porter: Mr. Chairman, would we be privileged to obtain at least this much information? Those informants which are judged reliable by the Federal Bureau of Investigation, have they been active in the Federal Workers Union activity?

Chairman Richardson: I haven't the slightest knowledge as to who they were or how active they have been in anything.

Mr. Porter: I think that is very relevant.

It was more than relevant; it was indispensable to any fair evaluation of the charges. The difficulty of combating anonymous allegations was later made even plainer through a series of questions asked by Mr. Seasongood, a member of the board:

Mr. Seasongood: Let me ask you now. Here is a statement that it was ascertained you were a member of the Communist Party in the District of Columbia as early as 1935, and that in the early days of her Party membership she attended Communist Party meetings. What do you say to that?

Miss Bailey: I have never been a member of the Communist Party. I have never attended a Communist Party meeting except the one I mentioned in the interrogative when I was in college. I cannot understand how this allegation could be made. It seems to be completely unsupported. At the hearing we asked for examples of what Communist meetings I was supposed to have attended. Is there any evidence given by the person who made the charge that I was a member of the Communist Party? We weren't able to obtain any evidence or any examples or instances and I find it extremely hard to defend myself in a case like this.

Mr. Seasongood: You can say it is not true.

Miss Bailey: Other than to say under oath that it is not true, that I have never been a sympathizer, and anyone who knows me could not help but corroborate this statement.

Mr. Seasongood: Then another one says that it first came to the informant's attention about 1936, at which time she was a known member of the so-called "closed group" of the Communist Party operating in the District of Columbia.

Miss Bailey: First of all, I didn't know, or don't know, that there is a "closed group." This terminology is unfamiliar to me. I can say under oath and with the strongest conviction that I was not then and have never been a member of the Communist Party.

Mr. Seasongood: Here is another that says you were a member of the Communist Party, and he bases his statement on his knowledge of your association with known Communists for the past seven or eight years. That is part of the evidence that was submitted to us.

Mr. Porter: It is part of the allegations. I don't think that can be considered evidence.

Chairman Richardson: It is evidence.

Mr. Porter: We renew our request, even though we recognize the futility of it, that some identification of this malicious gossip be given this respondent or her counsel.

Chairman Richardson: Of course, that doesn't help us a bit. If this testimony is true, it is neither gossip nor malicious. We are under the difficulty of not being able to disclose this.

Mr. Porter: Is it under oath?

Chairman Richardson: I don't think so.

Mr. Seasongood: It is a person of known responsibility who has proferred information concerning Communist activity in the District of Columbia.

Miss Bailey: You see that point in it worries me, because if I am convicted here that will make the person who has made these charges considered a reliable witness; and they are not, because the charges are not true, and whatever is said here should not add to their reliability.

There is literally no way for a defendant to refute such charges. The need to protect anonymous informants makes the charges devoid of all specificity. Had there been information as to the specific dates and places of the meetings she was alleged to have attended, or as to the names of other alleged attendants, perhaps she could have produced witnesses of her own to prove that she had been elsewhere or to prove that the meetings were not in fact

Communist meetings. Had she known the identity of her accusers, perhaps she could have shown them to be prejudiced or irresponsible. But in the circumstances she was able to offer nothing save the good opinion of her friends and office associates (who testified under oath), her record as an employee, and her own word.

The Loyalty Review Board made an adverse finding. It is indisputable from the record that this finding was based entirely on the assertions of five unidentified, unsworn informants characterized as "reliable" by the FBI. Not only was Miss Bailey denied any opportunity to confront and cross-examine these accusers; but the board itself was denied any independent means of checking their reliability. It did not even know if they were disinterested. In point of fact, it did not even know if they were real and living persons.

To brand Miss Bailey disloyal to her country on such evidence alone—and despite an abundance of sworn testimony as to her trustworthiness by known, reputable witnesses, supported by a record of fourteen years of service in the government—was to fly in the face of the President's order that eligibility should be determined "on all the evidence." More, it was to fly in the face of every standard of fairness that has gone to make up the American concept of due process. It is immaterial whether Miss Bailey was actually a Communist or not. A lynching is a lynching no matter whether its victim is innocent or guilty.

Another instance of loyalty board procedure may help to clarify the difficulties under which it places an accused person. Here is a colloquy that took place before a regional loyalty board weighing the eligibility of a scientist who had worked for six years on the atomic-energy project, had a "Q" clearance from the AEC, and continued to serve it as a consultant, but desired a transfer to another agency of the government. The hearing occurred in 1949 and was concerned largely with associations and attitudes during the years 1934–38 when the witness was a graduate student working for a doctoral degree.

Question: [By the examiner.] The Commission's information is also to the effect that you have admitted to a close associate that you were attending Communist meetings at the time. [That is, in the period 1934–38.] Do you have any explanation for that?

Answer: No, none. This just can't be true. May I ask, can it be found out who this person is?

Question: I do not know at this time.

Answer: Because this is just impossible. Whoever it was must have confused some other attendance at some open public meeting with this, but it just can't be true. I would like to know who this person is and confront this person.

Question: You understand that under this program we cannot always do that. We can only give you this information at this time, giving you every opportunity to explain it and bring out any matters that may explain it.

Counsel for the Witness: I would like to ask what knowledge you have as to the individuals involved who reported. I realize the importance of keeping the names confidential, but I was wondering if there had been any check on the individual who gave this information to ascertain the character of the person who gave it.

Examiner: There has been considerable check.

Counsel: Has that been checked by this board or is that only the—

Examiner: You understand that all our investigative work is done by the FBI.

Counsel: I have understood that the FBI would when questions were raised about confidential informants, that the FBI would give information they had to the Loyalty Board involved, telling them about the reliability of the person and giving them some background information, so that they might better appraise the informant even if the name of the informant remained anonymous.

Examiner: I do that when I can.

The most cursory cross-examination would have served to disclose to the board whether this informant was, in fact, "a close associate" of the witness or not; whether there was any mistake in identity; whether the informant could cite specific occasions on which the witness had attended "Communist" meetings; whether these meetings were, in fact, "Communist," or "Communist" only in the mind of the informant; whether the informant was motivated by some ancient grudge or prejudice. In the absence of any cross-examination, the board could proceed only by a species of divination. In this case it divined that the witness was not disloyal.

The plain fact is that the loyalty order's redundant system of appeals designed to protect unjustly accused individuals affords very limited protection. It amounts, indeed, to little more than a ritual of review. If the appeals permitted under the program were doubled or trebled—or even multiplied by ten—they would be no more effectual. They make possible so far as the employee is concerned nothing more than a reiteration of denial. They afford no public record by which the validity of a decision may be appraised. From the founding of this Republic—indeed from its earliest days as a colonial dependency—men accused of such petty crimes as pocket-picking have been granted the right to confront their accusers in open court and to require these accusers to testify under oath and to submit to cross-examination. The practice is rooted not in theory but in Anglo-Saxon experience running back to Magna Charta. It grew out of the knowledge that accusations are sometimes made falsely—perhaps out of malice, perhaps out of prejudice, perhaps out of innocent error. And confrontation affords the best means, is indeed an indispensable means, of uncovering this falsity.

A hearing before a loyalty board is not an agreeable experience for an innocent man. It involves, in the first place, an accusation of a sort that injures in a most intimate way anyone who has a love of country and a sense of having served it faithfully. It involves, in the second place, the humiliation of having to appeal for testimonials to friends, to former employers, to acquaintances prominent in public life, whose willingness to offer an endorsement may make the difference between survival and ruin; and this appeal for help means naturally the painful admission that the supplicant is under suspicion of disloyalty by his own government. It involves, in the third place, a long and sometimes costly process in which it is desirable to retain legal counsel. It cannot be an easy matter for a man who considers himself a loyal American to appear before a group of strangers and attempt to justify opinions or conduct, admittedly lawful, which may run counter to the prejudices of his judges. It must be even more painful when the appellant is obliged to grope blindly in a desperate attempt to discover what part of his past has brought him under suspicion. This is an ordeal much easier for the sycophant than for the person of independent outlook. There is required in these proceedings a humility and a groveling protestation of innocence not too difficult perhaps for a Uriah Heep, but galling and degrading to self-respecting human beings.

It is the rule rather than the exception for loyalty boards to range far outside the frame of reference laid down by the executive order. The very difficulty of resolving questions raised by anonymous informants leads board members to probe a witness's private convictions and political philosophy. In the case of the scientist just cited, the board was led, as in almost all such inquiries, into an attempt to elicit professions of patriotism and denunciations of communism that ran against the grain of the witness's scientific training. It is scarcely surprising that a natural independence of spirit coupled with a resentment at being subjected to this sort of inquisition should have produced a stubborn resistance to giving the easy, expected, orthodox answers.

A Member of the Board: I'd like to ask one more question, if I may. Frankly, I have gained the impression from your answers to questions asked that you did not categorically deny that you have any communistic sympathies.

The Witness: I do not know what you mean by communistic sympathies.

Board Member: I know, I agree with you.

The Witness: You say what you mean and I will answer. Please say it.

Board Member: Are you favorable to any of the Communist philosophies of government?

The Witness: Please enumerate these.

Board Member: Don't you know anything about communistic theories of government?

The Witness: I know something, but please enumerate them and I will answer your question. Please do. I'm anxious to get this straight.

Board Member: I asked you whether there were any of them that you favor.

The Witness: I asked you to please enumerate what they are because I don't know in detail.

Board Member: Do you categorically say that you have no sympathies with communism?

The Witness: I asked you to answer my question.

Board Member: I'm not going to ask any further questions. I just wanted to—

Counsel: Let me ask you a question. Have you ever voted for a candidate for a political office?

The Witness: Yes.

Counsel: Communist candidate?

The Witness: Oh, no. I've voted for lots of candidates.

Counsel: Would your inclination be to vote for a candidate for political office who is a Communist?

The Witness: No. I think that you don't understand the natural reluctance of somebody trained scientifically to deny things categorically. If you will state specific things and ask me whether I believe them, I will tell you. If you make a broad, vague, general thing and say do I believe this—something connected with this, I just find that temperamentally it is impossible to make a categorical denial.

This kind of recalcitrance could prove very costly. In the end, it is upon general impressions that a loyalty board rests its decisions. A case in point is that of another scientist—in the field of medicine—whose services were sought for a research project by an agency having no conceivable relation to military security. In the course of his hearing before a panel of the Loyalty Review Board, it was made clear that none of the panel members was concerned with the trivial charges set forth in the interrogatory which had been given to him. Their concern was with his general outlook. The hearing resembled nothing so much as a college classroom discussion in political science.

Chairman of the Panel: What do you mean now by saying that you believe in the right of any individual to advocate the overthrow of our government by force?

The Witness: I believe that an individual must have the right to express any opinions, whether they're cockeyed or reasonable, whether they're agreed to by his fellows or not. . . . I think I would honestly have to stick by the statement that people have a right to advocate; but they have no right to plan or plot, or to organize action. Thinking is one thing, speaking is one thing; action is quite a different thing. . . . I believe that the values in democracy and the values in the country that we've built here have come out of the conflict and the mixture of all sorts of opinions, and all sorts of advocacy of points of view; and I believe that even this opinion—advocacy of the opinion of the right to overthrow—itself builds up contrary opinions, itself forces us to show the ridiculousness and the unreasonableness, or the lack of value to a system, in advocating that sort of a thing. I think that anything that forces us to stereotype our thinking or forces us to try to follow a particular channel of thinking is stultifying and deadening.

The chairman complimented the witness, observing that "we appreciate your frankness; you have been a commendably frank witness"—and then returned to the interesting debate.

Chairman: Doesn't it come down to this very fine distinction—I'm afraid it's a dangerously fine distinction—they have a right to get together and advocate anything, and therefore they have a right to get together and advocate a political doctrine which includes the overthrow of the government of the United States, but they don't dare to get together, or have any right to get together, for the purpose of engaging in any conspiracy that would overthrow the government of the United States, or to engage in any overt act along that line? Is that right?

The Witness: I think that states it pretty fairly.

Panel Member: But how can you do both? If you belong to a group that has as part of its creed and policy the overthrow of the government by force, as the Communist Party clearly does, and you say, "I'm in favor of that, but let's not do it," why what's the use in saying it?

The Witness: I'm not in favor of advocating it or of doing it.

Chairman: But you would protect the right of anyone else to advocate it if they so wished?

The Witness: Yes, sir.

A little later in the hearing the following exchange occurred:

Chairman: Well, now, let me ask you about that. You certainly have given us the impression that you believe in the right of a political party to advocate—your emphasis has been on advocacy. You still be-lieve, do you not, unless I grievously misunderstood you, in the right of a group of people to get together to advocate a political theory even if such advocacy includes the overthrow of the United States govern-ment by force?

The Witness: But I also said, previously, that if such advocacy has the possibility of inciting violence or disorder, at that time it is not—it should not be legally possible to do it, just as you can yell "Fire!" out in a field and that's all right, but yelling "Fire!" in a crowded theater is not right.

Chairman: Well, taking the situation of today, 1950, do you think that a Communist Party group has the right to get together and form a political party which advocates communism, even if that includes the violent overthrow of the government?

The Witness: I think I would say that they do not have the right if they preach that when there is an apparent danger of that preach-ing causing disturbance and violence.

Chairman: Well, does that danger exist today?

The Witness: Well, I don't know.

Chairman: So that you're not—

The Witness: It does more today than it did ten years ago.

Chairman: But you're not sure that as of today the calling together of a group for the advocacy of such principles would necessarily be unlawful or wrong?

The Witness: You say it would not necessarily be unlawful or wrong for them to do that today? Not necessarily, yes. I wouldn't be the one to judge whether there was that danger.

Chairman: And it would become wrong only when there was a pretty clear danger of some kind of an upheaval resulting from it?

The Witness: Yes.

Chairman: I have again stated your position pretty fairly, have I?

The Witness: Yes, sir, I think so.

At this point counsel for the witness attempted to bring the discussion back to the charges contained in the interrogatory. The chairman responded:

Chairman: You're dealing with a phase of the case that doesn't con-cern me at all. . . . It's not those peripheral things that cause us con-cern. What causes us concern is your basic philosophy, which seems to go so far as to defend the right of advocacy even to overthrow the government of the United States, unless the conditions at the time are such that that would probably incite a dangerous upheaval. It is not all of these marginal things that concern me; it's your basic philosophy that concerns me.

As the hearing drew to a close the issue was restated and sharpened in these words:

The Witness: I do feel that I've had as adequate a hearing as it's possible to have. I do not feel that I have explained to you adequately my position. I have the feeling that you have very strong doubts as to whether at some time I would irrationally espouse some cause—

Chairman: No. Now, let me explain. I'm not concerned about that. I don't believe that you would advocate communism personally. I'm not at all sure that you believe in communism.

The Witness: Well, I don't believe in communism.

Chairman: That's not the point. Let's get this clear. The point that I'm disturbed about is that while you would neither advocate communism nor do anything consciously to implement it, nevertheless you would go the limit in defending the right of other people, or groups of people, to advocate communism, through political parties or otherwise, even though that includes the overthrow of our government by violence, and the only limitation that you placed on that right, as I understood you, was that you would limit it, or forbid it, if the conditions at the time happened to be such that a political upheaval of some kind might result.

In due course, the panel concluded that the witness was ineligible on grounds of disloyalty for employment by the United States; and the full Loyalty Review Board sustained the finding. Yet there were no objective criteria at all in this case; there was merely a determination by the panel that the witness entertained dangerous thoughts. It is perhaps beside the point that the same thoughts have been expressed over and over again by the Supreme Court of the United States and reflect the most authoritative interpretation of the scope of the First Amendment. The panel would be required by its own logic to find almost every present member of the Court disloyal. What the witness did in this hearing was to attempt a restatement, somewhat awkwardly, of the "clear and present danger" doctrine enunciated by Mr. Justice Holmes for a unanimous court in 1919.[3]

The kind of questioning developed in these two cases grows almost inescapably out of the nature of a loyalty board's function. How else is loyalty to be established except in terms of orthodoxy? In the final analysis, loyalty boards are forced to adopt the standards of the House Committee on Un-American Activities. An unorthodox view of the Communist Party or of the character of American-Soviet relations or even of the capitalist system is liable to be looked upon as disloyal. At least it raises a doubt. And if the members of the board consider the doubt to be a reasonable one, it is their obligation to resolve it in what is supposed to be the interest of the government—which is to say, against the interest of the individual. Charged as they are with assuring the safety of the United States, they dare not take what they consider chances. Moreover, they are subject to an incessant and formidable pressure from critics in Congress to produce more and more victims. They must keep the tumbrels filled—or be charged themselves with a disloyal want of vigilance.

The task imposed on the loyalty boards is an altogether impossible one. It is the task of judging inscrutable motives on the basis of imponderable evidence. These boards are expected to search out the hidden defects of character which may, under certain circumstances, lead a man to behave disloyally. But of course every man has hidden defects of character. The combination of psychoanalysis and clairvoyance required to foretell how they may reveal themselves in a given individual under unforeseeable future conditions is beyond the competence of any board, how-

[3] What Holmes said was: ". . . the character of every act depends on the circumstances in which it is done. The most stringent protection of free speech would not protect a man in falsely shouting fire in a theater and causing a panic. . . . The question in every case is whether the words used are used in such circumstances and are of such a nature as to create a clear and present danger that they will bring about the substantive evils that Congress has a right to prevent. It is a question of proximity and degree." *Schenck* v. *U.S.*, 249 U.S. 47 (1919).

ever just. How to weigh an anonymous allegation, how to weigh evidence that a man has expressed radical opinions or that he has Leftist tastes in literature or that he has associated with persons whose own loyalty has been made suspect by just such tests —these are matters too subtle and delicate for any tribunal. And when they entail a judgment that may destroy a man's reputation and career, they ought not to be attempted under a government of laws.

Those who defend the loyalty program are fond of repeating that nobody has a right to a government job. But every American has a right to equality of opportunity to work for the government; and he has a right not to be punished arbitrarily or capriciously. The Supreme Court ruled in the Lovett case that a proscription foreclosing opportunity to federal employment amounted to a punishment. How much more, then, is it a punishment when the proscription is coupled with an official, formal finding of disloyalty which operates to foreclose not only government employment but private employment as well. "Men might as well be imprisoned," John Stuart Mill observed, "as excluded from the means of earning their bread." Disloyalty, to be sure, is not a crime, and a finding of disloyalty by an administrative tribunal is not the same as a conviction by a court of law.[4] But it is a cruel and bitter punishment nonetheless, the more cruel, the more bitter, and the more violative of basic American rights because it is inflicted without the essential elements of due process of law.

The loyalty program entails, then, the risk of injustice to individuals. It can be argued that this risk must be run for the sake

[4] "Some may urge that a determination that the accused was in sympathetic association with a group designated by the Attorney General as subversive is not a finding of guilt against the accused, and that in any event no one has a vested right to public employment. But in practical effect the result of a finding of such association is analogous to that of a criminal conviction—loss of occupation, lasting disgrace to the individual, and a continued impairment of his ability to earn a livelihood. In fact, there is something peculiarly sinister and insidious in even a charge of disloyalty. Such a charge all too frequently places a stain on the reputation of an individual which is indelible and lasting, regardless of his complete innocence later proved." John Lord O'Brian, "Loyalty Tests and Guilt by Association," *Harvard Law Review*, April 1948.

of national security. But the program entails also a risk to the caliber of the Civil Service—a risk that has a direct bearing on national security.

In point of fact, the government is injured by the loyalty program in real and substantial ways. The program puts a premium on conformity. It almost automatically certifies any individual who has habitually associated with the "right" people, thought the "right" thoughts, belonged to the "right" organizations, and who, in short, has unquestioningly accepted things as they are. As a rule, only the unorthodox come before loyalty boards. They come before loyalty boards because someone has charged them with expressing the "wrong" opinions, associating with the "wrong" people, belonging to the "wrong" organizations, and in general criticizing or seeking to change the existing patterns of American life.

It is easy to see danger in unorthodoxy; at least it is hard to be certain whether the motive behind a challenge of accepted ideas is loyal or disloyal. The consequence of this uncertainty is that the loyalty program, even if it serves to weed out those who are unfit because they are unpatriotic, operates at the same time to weed out those who are most fit by reason of intelligence, initiative, and independence. In short, the loyalty program applies a kind of intellectual means test under which only the indigent in ideas can qualify.

Defenders of the loyalty program assert that it has not amounted to a "witch hunt" because it has found disloyalty in only a tiny percentage of incumbents and applicants for government jobs. At the end of May 1950, when the program had been in operation for three years, only two hundred and twenty-five individuals had been dismissed as a result of ineligible determinations by loyalty boards. Of these, a hundred and twenty-six were incumbents and ninety-nine were persons who had been conditionally appointed in the competitive service on or after October 1, 1947, or were applicants for government jobs. This is a testimonial to the conscientious restraint with which the Loyalty Review Board has discharged its difficult task. If the burden of the program fell only on this handful of individuals, it could perhaps be considered an expedient propitiation of the congressional lust for human sacrifices. But this is a calculation that leaves entirely out of account the impact of the program on the rest of the Civil Service. The loyalty investigation leaves its mark on those who survive it as well as on those who do not. It leaves its mark, indeed, on the whole character of the government.

In the three-year period to May 31, 1950, 12,272 individual cases were received by agency and regional loyalty boards. Of this total, 1464 employees left the government service while investigation of their loyalty was in progress, and an additional 1068 left the government after the investigation but prior to an adjudication of their cases. It can scarcely be assumed that all these employees were disloyal to their country. A number of them, no one can guess how many, quit the government because they had at one time belonged to an organization or expressed opinions which they feared might lead a loyalty board to judge them disloyal. By evading the danger of such a judgment they spared themselves, at least in part, a stigmatization that would have made private employment very difficult to obtain. There is no way to estimate how many good men were lost to the federal service through this pressure. A number of resignations occurred also, of course, on account of health, age, curtailment of particular government activities, or the opening up of desired employment opportunities in private industry.

Of the 8026 cases adjudicated by regional and agency loyalty boards, 7558, or 94 per cent, resulted in clearance of the individuals involved. Of the approximately 6 per cent that went on appeal to the Loyalty Review Board, about half were reversed. So it may be said that an enormous amount of waste motion was involved in the program. This was the consequence of regarding as suspect every person concerning whom any derogatory information—which is to say, any bit of idle or malicious gossip—was discovered in the catch-all files to which reference was required. And one may reasonably wonder whether the results were worth the time and effort of a vast number of FBI agents who might otherwise have been investigating violations of federal law or devoting themselves to real counterespionage.

The impact of the loyalty program is by no means confined, however, to the twelve thousand or so subjected to intensive FBI investigation because of "derogatory information." None of the two million individuals who work for the United States today can consider himself safe from an ordeal of this kind.[5] He needs to be guarded in his utterances, for any criticism of official policy may be mistaken as an indication of disloyalty. He needs to be ruthless in his associations, for a friendship with anyone who may become enmeshed in a loyalty investigation could result in his own undoing. Conventionality and conformity are his safest guides. But these are not necessarily guides to good service as a government employee.[6] The government of the United States is entitled to expect of the men who work for it not only trustworthiness but also precisely the kind of initiative and criticism which the loyalty program makes perilous. Dissent and diversity are the sinews from which a free government draws strength.

The loyalty program operates equally to deter men of ability from entering the service of the government. Consider, for example, the case of a university professor with special skills which lead a government administrator to seek him for a particular job. If he agrees to tackle the job, he must go to the president of his university and ask for a leave of absence; he must rent his house and make arrangements to move his family and live in Washington. And when he has done all this, he may very well find his

---

[5] "No one familiar with the administration of a government department . . . can doubt that the mere existence of any law or order authorizing secret investigations will encourage suspicion, distrust, gossip, malevolent tale-bearing, character assassination, and a general undermining of morale." O'Brian, ibid.

[6] "A state of things in which a large portion of the most active and inquiring intellects find it advisable to keep the general principles and grounds of their convictions within their own breasts, and attempt, in what they address to the public, to fit as much as they can of their own conclusions to premises which they have internally renounced, cannot send forth the open, fearless characters, and logical, consistent intellects who once adorned the thinking world. The sort of men who can be looked for under it, are either mere conformers to common-place, or time-servers for truth, whose arguments on all great subjects are meant for their hearers, and are not those which have convinced themselves." John Stuart Mill, On Liberty.

loyalty called into question because in the course of his lectures he denounced the Committee on Un-American Activities, or expressed doubts about the infallibility of J. Edgar Hoover, or asserted that the Truman Doctrine was not the best possible foreign policy for the United States. He runs the risk of being obliged to go back to his college president and to say that he no longer wants the year's leave of absence because his government has found him ineligible for employment on grounds of disloyalty.

Men of ability who have been heterodox in the expression of opinion, or who have joined organizations somewhat incautiously, or who have had colleagues and friends whose names have fallen into the files of the Un-American Activities Committee or the FBI may understandably be reluctant to run such a risk when called upon to accept government jobs for which their training and experience make them peculiarly qualified. Government service may be, as it is so often called, a privilege not a right; but it is a privilege liable to be so costly under contemporary conditions that patriotic men may understandably decline it.

The risk inherent in the loyalty program so far as the caliber of the government service is concerned is that it will force on that service a dead level of mediocrity and complacency. It is a program that tends to eliminate or silence individuality. It tends, too, to undermine the morale of federal workers by making their tenure uncertain, by making them distrustful of their colleagues, and by making them subject to constant anxiety. At a time when the government imperatively needs the best talent procurable, this is a serious risk to national security. There are better ways of checking the qualifications of government employees, as the next chapter will try to show.

Now let us consider the effect of the loyalty program on the fundamental values which the government of the United States was instituted to secure. Does this program lead the government, in Mr. Justice Holmes' phrase, to "play an ignoble part"?

It is no overstatement to say that the loyalty program fundamentally alters the traditional American relationship of the individual to the State—a relationship that is the key characteristic of a free society. "Because of the great variety of investigations in different fields," John Lord O'Brian observed, "there exist today vast numbers of governmental secret dossiers filled with information as to the private lives and activities of public employees. . . . What must be the inevitable effect of this kind of institutional practice, with its secret investigations and vast numbers of secret dossiers, upon the freedom of the individual?" [7]

The inevitable effect is a corruption of the traditional American right of privacy and the development of a dangerous police power. When investigators undertake compilation of a record upon which the loyalty of an individual is to be determined, they necessarily include in it a great deal of information, some of it authentic, some of it unreliable hearsay, concerning his moral conduct, his personal relationships, and other matters that used to be considered part of his private life. Much incidental information is likely to be recorded, too, concerning associates who are not themselves direct subjects of investigation. The maintenance of such dossiers about citizens who have never been charged with any violation of law and who have no means of refuting misinformation that may have been collected concerning them is an invitation to abuses of the gravest sort. Secret dossiers are paraphernalia of a police state. They are not proper instruments of a democratic government.

To enumerate the features of the loyalty program is to suggest the description of an authoritarian society. Any American hearing of a foreign country in which the police were authorized to search out the private lives of law-abiding citizens, in which a government official was authorized to proscribe lawful associations, in which administrative tribunals were authorized to condemn individuals by star-chamber proceedings on the basis of anonymous testimony, for beliefs and associations entailing no criminal conduct, would conclude without hesitation that the country was one in which tyranny prevailed. And the most shock-

[7] O'Brian, op. cit.

ing aspect of the whole business is that we have accepted these curtailments of essential liberty for ourselves with no outcry, with no apparent sense of their implications.

It does not matter that these invasions of what were once deemed inalienable rights have been adopted for the sake of national security. It does not matter that the Attorney General exercises his power with restraint and that the FBI happens to be directed by a man free from sinister intentions. It does not matter that the loyalty boards are made up of high-minded and conscientious men. Dictatorship always has its origin in the assumption that men supposed to be benevolent may be entrusted with arbitrary authority. The American Republic was born in rebellion against such authority; it was nurtured on the doctrine that governmental power must be jealously circumscribed and kept, in particular, from interference with individual freedom of expression and association. The risks inherent in a disregard of this doctrine are graver by far—and more menacing to the real sources of American security—than the risks that would be run if the whole spurious system of evaluating loyalty were abandoned.

CHAPTER VI

"SECURITY RISKS"

It is of the essence of the institutions of liberty that it be recognized that guilt is personal and cannot be attributed to the holding of opinion or to mere intent in the absence of overt acts. . . .[1]

CONSIDERED in terms of its stated objectives and its results, the loyalty program suffered a serious breakdown in the spring of 1950. Its first objective was to afford the United States "maximum protection . . . against infiltration of disloyal persons into the ranks of its employees." There is no evidence that it failed to provide this protection; that is, no proof has been presented that a single "disloyal" employee passed through its rigorous screening procedure. But it was certainly a corollary purpose of the program to give the American people confidence in the trustworthiness of their federal employees. And in this the program cannot be said to have been more than partly successful.

Through no fault of the loyalty boards but as a result of persistent congressional attacks, notably by Senator McCarthy, a great deal of public anxiety developed over the effectiveness of the program. Although the McCarthy charges were probably not widely believed in detail, a good many people tended to apply the adage that where there was so much smoke there must be some fire. Their anxiety manifested itself in demands for more

[1] Charles Evans Hughes, quoted by O'Brian, op. cit.

stringent clearance procedures and for replacement of the loyalty program by a security-risk program throughout the government.

The second stated objective of the loyalty program was to give loyal employees of the government "protection from unfounded accusations of disloyalty." In this, the program—again through no fault of the loyalty boards—must also be said to have failed, at least in part. Clearance by loyalty boards did not shield John Service or Haldore Hanson or Esther Brunauer of the State Department from being called Communists and Soviet agents by Senator McCarthy or from being subjected to another "trial" by a Senate subcommittee. Clearance by loyalty boards did not save Michael Lee from a public attack by Senator Malone, or William Remington from reinvestigation by the Un-American Activities Committee; it did not even save either of them from being summarily ousted from their jobs by the Secretary of Commerce.

Although the Americanists are responsible for the breakdown of the loyalty program, the Truman administration shares responsibility for creating a climate of opinion in which the Americanist extravagances could flourish. The administration resorted, in dealing with the Communist problem, to techniques that did violence to settled standards of fairness. Thus it undercut the moral basis of its resistance to McCarthyism. It was a little thick to hear administration spokesmen denounce Senator McCarthy for imputing guilt by association when the loyalty boards, operating under a presidential order, had for two and a half years been condemning men on grounds of "sympathetic association" with organizations arbitrarily called "subversive" by the Attorney General. No doubt Senator McCarthy deserved to be excoriated for calling as witnesses against reputable men discredited ex-Communists and professional informers; but the loyalty boards from the beginning used anonymous, unsworn testimony from just such sources.

All that McCarthy did was to carry to its cynical extreme the debasement of American values begun by the administration for lofty purposes. McCarthyism is an illustration of the force of the argument *ad horrendum*. The river is liable to flow quite beyond control once the dam has been breached.

From its beginning the loyalty program has been under attack from two directions: critics on the one side have complained that in its emphasis on protection of the government it rode roughshod over individual rights; critics on the other side considered it insufficiently tough in excluding from the government anyone upon whom the slightest shadow of a doubt had been cast.

The most common demand of the more liberal critics is that confrontation and cross-examination of accusers be assured in loyalty board hearings. This would, it is true, eliminate one of the most obnoxious features of the present procedure. It would be vastly preferable to condemnation on the basis of unsworn testimony by unidentified informants. But it would also, it must be admitted, leave the boards with comparatively little material for their purposes. Persons who are willing to make whispered allegations that their acquaintances or neighbors harbor dangerous thoughts or keep unhallowed company are not disposed to come forward and face the rigors of cross-examination. And the FBI is certainly not going to endanger its undercover operatives by disclosing their identity for the mere purpose of keeping an individual of doubtful loyalty out of a clerical job in the Agriculture Department's Bureau of Entomology and Plant Quarantine. That game, from the FBI's point of view, is plainly not worth the candle.

Moreover, affording accused persons the right of confrontation would not resolve the deeper dilemma of the loyalty boards—the dilemma inherent in their inability to define even the symptoms of the disease they are supposed to isolate. How are they to judge disloyalty when they do not know whether it manifests itself in an opposition to segregated blood banks or in adherence to the "clear and present danger" doctrine or in pacifism or in personal loyalty to outcast individuals? Even if all the safeguards of judicial procedure were observed in loyalty hearings, the task of the loyalty boards would be an impossible and an improper one. Free men may not be judged, and punished, for conduct which violates no law.

Another common suggestion from the liberal side is that the loyalty program ought to be confined to those positions in the government which, in fact, affect the national security. Certainly this is at least the beginning of common sense about the matter. It is a sheer waste of time and effort to investigate the loyalty of employees in the Interior Department's Fish and Wildlife Service or in the Labor Department's Bureau of Veterans' Re-Employment Rights or in any of a hundred other specialized agencies of the government. The inference is inescapable that the inclusion of such employees in the loyalty program was undertaken not to safeguard the government but to punish Communist sympathizers who might have secured such jobs. So far as security is concerned, it would be hard to think of any safer place to sequester them.

Indeed, only a minor fraction of the jobs in government have any significant relation to security. It would not be easy to catalogue these jobs; admittedly, it could not be done by a careless or blanket classification in terms either of job status or of agency function. It ought to be done, however, if only for the sake of determining the true dimensions of the security problem.

Critics on the other side contend that the loyalty program as now constituted does not protect the government from dangers that are at once more prevalent and more serious than disloyalty. There is indubitable force to this contention. As the program has conclusively demonstrated, disloyalty is extremely rare; with all their tendency to impute disloyalty on the basis of heterodoxy, the loyalty boards have made ineligibility findings in only a tiny percentage of the three million cases they have screened.

The loyalty program is not calculated to catch deliberate foreign agents. Throughout its course, as Seth Richardson told the Tydings subcommittee investigating Senator McCarthy's charges, "no case has been reported involving espionage, and the great majority of cases relate to the connection of the employee with organizations which have been certified by the Attorney General as subversive." Professional spies do not join such organizations. Even amateurs who intend to commit disloyal acts keep clear of them. Henry Julian Wadleigh, for instance, never joined the Communist Party. And for the sake of protective coloration he also kept out of "Communist fronts." According to his published "confession," he was not even a convinced Marxist, and he disguised such Leftist views as he may have held by talking like a conservative. He was not in the least interested in overthrowing the government by force, violence, or any other means. It is doubtful whether any study of this young man's past, save perhaps by a psychiatrist, could have afforded a warning of his unreliability.

Similarly, Judith Coplon's background gave no indication that she would be found guilty of removing, for motives which remain inscrutable, classified material from Justice Department files and attempting to give it to a Soviet agent. Her disloyalty became apparent only after it had found expression in an overt act. It is, of course, no reflection at all on the competency of the loyalty boards that they do not uncover spies; that is not their function.

Neither is it their function to deal with those who might become dupes of spies—the weaklings or drunkards or mercenaries or fools. These are the persons properly called "security risks" as distinguished from "disloyalty cases." They are much more dangerous, if only because they are much more common, than the deliberately disloyal. Professional spies, operating in obscurity outside the government and the scrutiny of loyalty boards, can use such persons to glean isolated, seemingly trivial bits of information which, pieced together, provide the real substance of foreign intelligence activities. Great care needs to be exercised to keep such persons out of the federal service. A security-risk program supplementing the loyalty program has been in force since 1940 in the Armed Services and since 1947 in the State Department, Atomic Energy Commission, and Central Intelligence Agency. Representative Richard Nixon suggested a general extension of the security-risk system as a substitute for the loyalty program in a speech to the House on January 30, 1950:

It is necessary that we completely overhaul our system of checking the loyalty of federal employees. Mr. Hiss would have passed the present loyalty tests with flying colors. The loyalty checks are based primarily on open affiliations with Communist-front organizations. Underground Communists and espionage agents have no open affiliations and it is therefore almost impossible to apprehend them through a routine loyalty investigation under the President's order. Serious consideration should be given to changing the entire approach under the loyalty order and placing the program on a security risk basis. In this way, where there is any doubt about an individual who has access to confidential information, that doubt can be resolved in favor of the government without the necessity of proving disloyalty and thereby reflecting on the character of a possibly loyal but indiscreet government employee.[2]

The security-risk system, as it has been put into practice in the so-called "sensitive" agencies, differs from the loyalty program in two principal particulars: (1) it is designed to eliminate unintentionally as well as intentionally dangerous employees—the indiscreet as well as the disloyal; (2) it empowers the head of an agency to reject applicants and dismiss employees summarily without the procedural protections of the loyalty program. It is meant to have the virtue, on the one hand, of avoiding an official designation of an applicant or employee as disloyal, and, on the other hand, of enabling doubt, as Representative Nixon put it, to "be resolved in favor of the government without the necessity of proving disloyalty."

But the appealing simplicity of this arrangement is illusory. When it was first used in the State Department in 1947 it was applied in an extremely arbitrary manner to ten employees; the Department simply told them they were dismissed as security risks without giving them any indication of the charges against them or any chance to refute those charges. The shocking nature of such a procedure was made obvious when the *New York Herald Tribune* published the transcript of a hearing granted one of

[2] *Congressional Record*, Appendix, A657, January 30, 1950.

the employees, identified only as Mr. Blank, after his dismissal. The Department's security officer opened the hearing with this candid statement:

Mr. Robinson: . . . The proceedings which were taken are final so far as the Department is concerned and, under those circumstances and under its terms of reference, the Committee is not going to ask you any questions, except such as we may feel helpful to your presentation for explanatory purposes, nor are we able to answer any questions, and so we are delighted to listen to any statement that you care to make on that basis.[3]

Later on Mr. Robinson offered this help:

Mr. Robinson: I don't think we can suggest to you things that you ought to discuss. I think it's up to you to decide. As I say, we are trying to help by making suggestions to you, in a general way, which may make your record more complete when it all comes together. But so far as saying you ought to talk about this or you ought to talk about that, I don't see how we can do that. This is your opportunity to say anything you want.

Mr. Blank: Gentlemen, it's my "opportunity" to say anything, but really, to be frank—you gentlemen aren't responsible—it's really not an opportunity. I don't know what to talk about. I mean, I am—

Mr. Robinson: All right, I withdraw the statement it was an opportunity, if you prefer.[4]

The distinction between "disloyalty" and a "security risk" was explained by Mr. Robinson with great lucidity.

Mr. Robinson: I think I might just say for the record here one thing which I believe is worth pointing out, and that is that it is fairly clearly indicated in the press release that this action was taken on the ground of a doubt as to security, and what I would like to say for the record is that we carefully bear in mind in all these cases that there is a very definite difference between the word "security" and the word "loyalty." I just want that to be on the record.

Mr. Blank: May I ask what the difference is? It's not clear to me.

[3] Quoted by Bert Andrews, *Washington Witch Hunt* (New York: Random House, 1948), p. 27.
[4] Ibid., pp. 37-38.

Mr. Robinson: There's a vast difference between security and loyalty.

Mr. Blank: I think—may I ask that question?

Mr. Robinson: Yes.

Mr. Blank: To clear up the difference between them, I mean to me, I think one—

Mr. Robinson: Well, I'll point out a difference. I think loyalty must necessarily be a conscious proposition. Security, or lack of it, might be conscious or unconscious. And I think that probably serves the purpose of what I am trying to do, but I am making the statement for the record without any implication as to any conclusion that you should draw from that statement, but you made several statements about that and I just want to make clear that this action was based, as the press release stated, as a matter of security.[5]

"Could I explain this difference between security and loyalty to some kind of college where I am trying to get a teaching job?" Mr. Blank asked pathetically. In the end, as a result of vigorous representations by his legal counsel and protests in the press, Mr. Blank and six others of the unfortunate ten were allowed to resign "without prejudice," instead of being dismissed. But Mr. Blank found door after door slammed in his face when he sought employment in universities and private industry.

Summary dismissals of this sort left the door wide open to grave injustices resulting from erroneous or malicious information in investigators' reports. Accordingly, after Mr. Blank's experience, the State Department, along with the other sensitive agencies, revised its procedure in order to permit specific charges, a formal hearing before a security board, and an appeal to the head of the Department in security risk cases. The procedure became identical with that in loyalty cases, save that no appeal to the Loyalty Review Board of the Civil Service Commission was permitted.

But the security-risk program then became subject to the same defects as the loyalty program: (1) it involved a formal finding by an administrative tribunal which, if adverse, amounted to severe

[5] Ibid., pp. 41-42.

punishment without due process of law—that is, proscription from all opportunity to serve the government and an indelible stigma; (2) reliance on information from unidentified and perhaps prejudiced sources; (3) a lack of clear-cut standards of judgment; and (4) the proliferation of secret investigations and secret dossiers respecting the private lives of law-abiding citizens. Let us look at these defects in brief detail.

First, substitution of security for loyalty as a qualification for government employment does not really remove the stigma of an adverse finding. To be designated a security risk to one's government is not appreciably preferable to being designated disloyal. In most cases, to be sure, as the security-risk program is now put into effect, employees disqualified under it are allowed to resign. But the reasons behind such resignations are always known to colleagues and are certain to be the subject of gossip and speculation. Besides, the disqualified employees know that suspicion will follow them through the rest of their lives. Prospective private employers who inquire about their records in the government would be told, as they are told in disloyalty cases, that they were discharged or resigned under fire.

Second, the special concern of the security-risk program with personal associations and private morals puts even greater emphasis than does the loyalty program on the lowest form of gossip-mongering. It invites allegations of sexual irregularities from the naive, the prurient, and the malicious—allegations which are at once unprovable and irrefutable and which generally have little real relevance to an employee's fitness for government service.

Third, the tests for determining security risks are as indefinite and confused as the tests for determining disloyalty. Indeed, they are in large part the same tests merely applied with greater stringency. Although the former are meant to be aimed more directly at eliminating the instability or indiscretion or impetuosity that might result in some unintentional act of disloyalty, the line between the two is altogether blurred. The State Department's

Regulations and Procedures on the subject say that "an officer or employee constitutes a security risk when he falls into one or more of the following categories":

a. A person who engages in, supports, or advocates treason, subversion, or sedition, or who is a member of, affiliated with, or in sympathetic association with the Communist, Nazi, or Fascist Parties, or of any foreign or domestic party or movement which seeks to alter the form of government of the United States by unconstitutional means or whose policy is to advocate or approve the commission of acts of force or violence to deny other persons their rights under the Constitution of the United States; or a person who consistently believes in or supports the ideologies and policies of such a party or movement.

b. A person who is engaged in espionage or who is acting directly or indirectly under the instructions of any foreign government; or who deliberately performs his duties, or otherwise acts, to serve the interests of another government in preference to the interest of the United States.

c. A person who has knowingly divulged classified information without authority and with the knowledge or belief or with reasonable grounds for the knowledge or belief that it will be transmitted to agencies of a foreign government, or who is so consistently irresponsible in the handling of classified information as to compel the conclusion of extreme lack of care or judgment.

d. A person who has habitual or close association with persons known or believed to be in categories a or b to an extent which would justify the conclusion that he might, through such association, voluntarily or involuntarily divulge classified information without authority.

The security boards, like the loyalty boards (they are the same in most of the sensitive agencies), are made up of earnest, devoted men striving conscientiously to protect the government from dangerous employees and at the same time to deal justly with accused individuals. Their task is an impossible one. The rule under which they operate comes down in the end to saying that anyone shall be deemed a security risk who might "reasonably" be deemed a risk to security. Quite naturally, the most circumspect and conventional employees seem the safest. The security-risk program accentuates the tendency of the loyalty program to eliminate from the government all originality, initiative, and independence.

The fourth and most dangerous defect of the security-risk system is that it extends the compilation of secret dossiers. The FBI makes only loyalty and not security investigations, although its loyalty reports may serve as a basis for security-risk charges; each of the agencies having summary dismissal powers has its own investigators to supplement the work of the FBI. It should be particularly noted in this connection that, unlike the loyalty program, the security-risk system as now constituted provides no procedural protection for job applicants. An applicant may be rejected without a hearing or a chance to defend himself. No reasons are given for the rejection. This means that if the report contains false accusations, they remain unchallenged and uncorrected. And the report, however erroneous it may be, becomes a permanent record available to the personnel officers of other agencies, foreclosing other possibilities of government employment and stamping the applicant as a risk to the security of his country. This arrangement places in the hands of real enemies of the United States an easy means of keeping able, useful men out of public service.

In 1950 the power of summary dismissal on security grounds was given a permanent statutory basis by Congress, and the President was authorized to extend it to any executive agency. If the whole federal establishment is put on a security-risk basis, it will mean virtual abandonment of the 1912 Civil Service Act, which gives government employees such protection of tenure as they now possess. This is all too likely to result in capricious discharges on the pretext of security both for patronage reasons and on account of political pressure by members of Congress. It may bring an end to the merit system in government employment.

Protection of the government from dangerous or undesirable employees need not entail either a disregard of individual rights or a profligate waste of available talents. There are tested methods of personnel selection in common use throughout private industry that will adequately serve the government's needs. These methods are prosaic and old-fashioned and, indeed, obvious. But since they seem so largely to have been forgotten, it may be in order to mention them briefly here.

The government needs trustworthy, intelligent, tough-minded, and devoted workers. Finding them is essentially a recruitment problem. It ought to be approached, therefore, in terms of a search for affirmative, desired qualities rather than in terms of a negative policy of exclusion. For the government, as for any private employer, the best index to an applicant's capabilities is his record of past performance. That record ought to be scrutinized in every case with great care. Previous employers should be consulted. Recommendations should be required from persons of known character, responsibility, and stature in the applicant's home community and from professional or business associates—and those recommendations should be weighed judiciously. Beyond this, it should be ascertained that the applicant has not been convicted of any crime and that he is not financially irresponsible. Most important of all—just as it is most important in the personnel work of any private enterprise—the applicant should be interviewed at first hand both by personnel officers of the agency and by the particular official under whom he is to serve, with a view toward determining his attitudes respecting the policies and functions of the agency. It is important to select persons enthusiastic about the work they are to do. A great deal can be learned about the personality and capabilities of a prospective employee through such simple, aboveboard techniques.

Other appropriate techniques have been developed for the assessment of personality and capacity which can be applied usefully to the screening of government personnel. General William J. Donovan, wartime director of the Office of Strategic Services, has told a little about the experience of the Assessment School of that extremely sensitive agency in selecting overseas personnel in terms of their physical, mental, and emotional aptitude for the tasks to which they would be assigned.[6] The Armed Services have made use of comparable techniques; and they are widely utilized by some private employers. There are, of course, limits to the utility of psychiatric and psychological tests for predicting character, fitness, and integrity under stress; but they are certainly at least as reliable in disclosing instability, disloyalty, and other dangerous personality defects as evaluation by wholly untrained loyalty or security boards on the basis of police interviews with anonymous informants.

The degree of care to be exercised in selecting government employees must depend, of course, on the importance—in security terms—of the jobs they are to fill. Perfect loyalty and absolute incorruptibility would be desirable throughout the Civil Service; but since these are attainable only in heaven, most positions on earth must be filled by ordinary human beings. This is less threatening to national security than might be supposed even by those most distrustful of their fellow-citizens. Most positions, even in the sensitive agencies, afford very little opportunity for weakness or folly or disloyalty to impair national security. It is not necessary to circulate confidential cables to every employee of the Department of State or to grant indiscriminate access to secret codes. Few workers in the Atomic Energy Commission need to know the critical mass of uranium or plutonium; few would understand it even if they were told. The blueprints of the latest jet bomber can be reserved for a handful of senior officers and technicians in the Bureau of Naval Aeronautics. Classified memoranda do not have to be left lying about carelessly on desktops. Espionage is neither so prevalent nor so easy as the romantic and the fearful tend to suppose. It is never as important, even in wartime, as the readers of spy-thrillers are inclined to believe. Nine-tenths of good intelligence work is not the acquiring of secret information but the organization of readily available non-secret

[6] William J. Donovan and Mary Gardiner Jones, "Program for a Democratic Counterattack to Communist Penetration of Government Service," *Yale Law Journal*, July 1949. The authors refer for a more extended treatment of the subject to *Assessment of Men* by a group of scholars, scientists, and professional men under the direction of Dr. Harry Murray, Harvard Medical School.

information. The seemingly trivial bits of inside gossip carelessly and innocently divulged may, it is true, give important aid to spies. But the only cure for carelessness is care.

Government secrets can be effectively protected through strict, yet rational, security regulations. It is indisputable, of course, that particular care needs to be exercised in the selection of persons to fill certain key positions involving the formulation of policy and access to vital classified material. Yet it is precisely in respect of these positions that the routine investigation of FBI agents is least applicable and reliance on unidentified informants is most dangerous. What is needed in filling these positions is not a record of orthodoxy and conformity but a record of initiative, imagination, and individuality. It is not unreasonable to assume that persons who have shown such qualities and won the confidence of their colleagues in previous governmental service, in private business, or in their professions are neither traitors nor fools. It is on this basis that private industry chooses its most trusted and responsible employees. The government, too, has done so throughout most of our history—and with few occasions to regret its faith at least in the loyalty of its citizens.

The best way to find out about an applicant's fitness for a sensitive position is to ask for estimates of him, in confidence, from known, reputable colleagues, past employers, teachers, and business associates or competitors. Such opinions are very different from gossip picked up at random by police investigators. If there are any doubts about a prospective employee's trustworthiness and discretion as a result of such inquiries, he should be rejected, of course; there is no need to label him disloyal or a security risk and therefore no need to put him "on trial." It is important that the decision about him be made before he is appointed and before any publicity that he is under consideration for appointment. This may cause delay in filling vital positions, but it is a delay worth incurring for the sake of caution and fairness.

Once an applicant has been appointed and has served a probationary period, the only rational determinant of his tenure is his performance on the job. If he engages in espionage or sabotage, obviously he should be dismissed—and prosecuted in a court of law. He should be dismissed if he violates security regulations—by loose talk or improper handling of classified material or association with persons whom he has specifically been warned to avoid. He should be dismissed if he drinks excessively or behaves immorally or performs his work carelessly or attempts in any way to thwart the policies of his agency. There is nothing in the Civil Service rules to prevent the prompt discharge of criminal, insubordinate, or incompetent employees. But the test should be conduct. So long as an employee does his work faithfully and well, he is entitled to immunity from anonymous accusations about his past associations and beliefs. Adherence to this standard is dictated as much by expediency as by principle. High morale and a sense of independence among government workers are tremendous assets to national security. They cannot be maintained in an atmosphere of suspicion and anxiety.

A decent and democratic personnel policy of this kind will not eliminate all errors of judgment. But neither will it fling the employment door wide open to spies, saboteurs, perverts, blabbermouths, and deadbeats. There is no need to suppose that administrators will hire the worst among competing applicants for subordinate positions or be heedless of security considerations. They want able and trustworthy subordinates and can be counted upon to exercise ordinary prudence in selecting them. It is true that Communists and Communist sympathizers are not always identifiable; in rare cases they may enjoy high repute in thoroughly respectable circles. A few may escape the vigilance of the most conscientious employing officers—just as they now, no doubt, occasionally slip through the elaborate network of the loyalty program. The risk has to be run for the sake of avoiding graver risks inescapably involved in a resort to anonymous informants.

There is no use blinking at the fact that, when the utmost reasonable care has been exercised, dangerous and damaging leaks may still occur. The British experience with Dr. Klaus Fuchs is perhaps the most alarming instance in point. Yet it is hard to say how it could have been avoided without incurring even more damaging consequences. "There has been a great deal of loose talk in the press suggesting inefficiency on the part of the security service," Prime Minister Clement Attlee told the House of Commons in commenting on the Fuchs case.[7] "I entirely deny it. It was said in 1933 when Fuchs came into the country that he was a Communist. But the source of that information was the Gestapo. There was no responsibility for it at all."

It is true that if the British security service had acted on the Gestapo's information, Fuchs would have been prevented from giving classified atomic energy data to the Russians. But he would also have been prevented from making his rather considerable contribution to the Anglo-Canadian-American wartime priority in creation of an atomic bomb. During the war the American atomic-energy project utilized the services—and most profitably— of Dr. Frank Oppenheimer,[8] who admitted that he had once been a Communist Party member; in his case the presumption of loyalty was fully vindicated. Absolute security is likely to result in nothing save absolute sterility.

"I am satisfied," Mr. Attlee went on in his remarks to the House of Commons, "that unless we had here the kind of secret police they have in totalitarian countries, and employed their methods, there was no means by which we could have found out about this man."

Here, then, is the choice. It is a choice between the evil that some risks should be run and the evil that the government should "play an ignoble part." Risk is an inescapable element of freedom.

[7] AP dispatch from London, March 6, 1950, in the Washington *Evening Star*.
[8] Not to be confused with his better-known brother, J. Robert Oppenheimer.

CHAPTER VII

THE GROWTH OF THE FBI

Experience should teach us to be most on our guard to protect liberty when the government's purposes are beneficent. Men born to freedom are naturally alert to repel invasion of their liberty by evil-minded rulers. The greatest dangers to liberty lurk in insidious encroachment by men of zeal, well meaning but without understanding.[1]

THE FEDERAL BUREAU OF INVESTIGATION is undoubtedly the most popular of all federal agencies. No government administrator commands greater confidence and respect among the American people than John Edgar Hoover, who has been director of the FBI for more than a quarter of a century. He and the bureau alike have won an almost legendary status as models of rectitude, efficiency, and nonpartisan devotion to the public service.

There is testimony to the prestige of the FBI in a Gallup Poll published in the *Washington Post* on August 21, 1949. Dr. Gallup asked his sample of the American public, "Will you tell me what the initials 'FBI' stand for?" He reported that a total of 78 per cent gave "accurate or reasonably accurate answers." All who identified the FBI initials correctly were asked, "What is your opinion of the FBI?" Dr. Gallup gave the following tabulation of responses:

[1] Louis D. Brandeis, dissenting opinion, *Olmstead* v. *U.S.* 277 U.S. 438 (1928).

Very high, excellent, it does wonderful job	32%
Good, approve it	41
Mild disapproval	2
Derogatory	1
No opinion	2
	78%

This overwhelming approbation has for many years been mirrored in Congress. Mr. Hoover is perhaps the one bureaucrat whose requests for appropriations are granted almost without question—indeed, with expressions of anxiety lest they be over-modest. He is certainly the only bureaucrat whose appearances before congressional committees are treated with a reverence usually reserved for utterances from the throne.

When he testified before the Committee on Un-American Activities on March 26, 1947, the chairman made this comment at the conclusion of his formal statement: "Mr. Hoover, the chair wishes to express for the committee our deep appreciation for your acceptance of our invitation to come here today. . . . Now, Mr. Hoover, if it meets with your pleasure, the members of the committee would like to ask questions." Congressman Mundt opened the questioning by observing that, "I have read all of your speeches and articles on this subject which you correctly refer to as Red fascism, and I have profited from them all, but I think that today you have made the most masterful and conclusive statement of your career on the subject of this very definite menace."

Congressman McDowell, when his turn came to pose questions, added only, "Mr. Chairman, I merely want to compliment this great American public servant for a very substantial contribution to good government. Thank you, sir."

Congressman Bonner, after asking a few questions, said, "Mr. Hoover, I am very proud of your record. I admire you personally as a man, and I appreciate the great service you have rendered and are rendering this country." After this, the chairman brought the ceremony to a close by remarking, "Mr. Hoover, we deeply appreciate your coming here today, and we certainly hope that it has not interfered with your work."

It is no reflection on Mr. Hoover that he commands such deference from a congressional committee notorious for its incivility to witnesses. But Mr. Hoover is, after all, a cop; and a deferential regard for cops has not, until recently, been an American characteristic. The attitude is a testimonial not alone to his integrity and competence but in part also to his power. It has disquieting as well as desirable implications.

"Cop" has never been a term of endearment in America, and the policeman has not hitherto been a heroic figure here. He is frequently referred to as a flatfoot. In plain clothes, as a detective, he is usually represented on radio, stage, and screen as something of a clown. The more popular murder mysteries do not deify him; after he has fumbled ponderously and missed all the clues, the crime is customarily solved by a lawyer or a newspaper reporter or some other amateur investigator. The FBI is an exception to this general depreciation of the police—a somewhat anomalous exception in a country inaugurated in distrust of national authority.

Disrespect for authority is one of the most deep-rooted of American traditions. It has deplorable aspects, of course. No doubt it accounts, in part at least, for the lawlessness that has always been so prevalent in the United States. But it may also account, in part, for the American resistance to men on horseback; the absence of such disrespect among Germans probably had something to do with their ready submission to a Führer. This impatience with the duly constituted forces of law and order comes naturally to a nation born in rebellion, antipathetic to rulers, and suspicious of all organized government. It is an expression of the individualism nurtured by the frontier, where, as Frederick Jackson Turner observed, "To the pioneer, government was an evil." If it has to some extent impeded law enforcement, it has at the same time been a source of the inventiveness, self-reliance, and readiness to try new methods, which we like to think of as American traits.

More disturbing than the general reverence for the FBI is a widespread feeling, fostered to some extent, it must be said, by Mr. Hoover himself, that any criticism of the bureau is a form of lese majesty or an expression of downright disloyalty to the United States. Despite the overwhelming enthusiasm for the federal police agency among politicians, press, and public, there is now an appreciable number of Americans—and not all of them dupes or minions of Moscow—who view the growth and expanded authority of the FBI with genuine anxiety. But anyone who is bold enough to express such a view runs the risk of having his motives impugned and his patriotism questioned. After it was revealed in the course of the trial of Judith Coplon that the FBI had been tapping private telephones, a number of responsible citizens protested that this wiretapping was in violation of the law. The protests were denounced by the director of the FBI as "motivated for the purpose of confusing the public." [2] In a reply to an article critical of the FBI in the *Yale Law Journal,* Mr. Hoover indulged in the observation that, "I find such opinions most frequently expressed on the pages of the *Daily Worker,* the publication of the Communist Party." [3] It is not healthy in a democracy that any governmental agency—and least of all a police agency—should be considered above criticism. Even captious criticism is preferable to unrelieved adulation.

The present Federal Bureau of Investigation was created by Attorney General Harlan F. Stone (later Chief Justice of the Supreme Court) in 1924, as a result of a reorganization that abolished the Division of Investigation, which had played an ugly part in the arrest and deportation of aliens under the at-

[2] Quoted by Joseph L. Rauh, Jr., chairman, National Executive Committee, Americans for Democratic Action, in a speech before the National Civil Liberties Clearing House, Washington, February 24, 1950. "The obvious implication," Mr. Rauh went on, "is that anybody who criticizes the FBI is a Communist or a fellow-traveler of the Communists. It is true that the Communists and their fellow-travelers do criticize Mr. Hoover. As far as I am concerned, the Communist attacks neither discredit nor exalt him. But honest and sincere criticism is needed and deserves a hearing on merits, not motives."

[3] "Comment" by Mr. Hoover, *Yale Law Journal,* February 1949, p. 410.

torney generalship of A. Mitchell Palmer. It has been charged
that Mr. Hoover had some responsibility, as an assistant to Attorney General Palmer, for the extravagances of that period. But Mr.
Hoover has given an effective answer to this allegation. "The late
Chief Justice of the United States, Harlan Fiske Stone," said Mr.
Hoover, "raised his voice in vigorous protest of the manner in
which the raids were carried out long prior to his appointment as
Attorney General in 1924 to reorganize the Department of Justice. He had investigated the raids in detail, and I am sure he
would never have appointed me director of the bureau in May
of 1924 had I been responsible for the manner in which the raids
were carried out." [4]

Attorney General Stone defined the function of the new bureau
in a manner designed to set at rest criticisms then prevalent that
the federal police had engaged in political activities. The bureau,
he said, would confine itself exclusively to investigating violations
of the laws of the United States. In a statement of May 15, 1924,
he said:

> There is always the possibility that a secret police system may become
> a menace to free government and free institutions. It carries with it the
> possibility of abuses of power which are not always quickly appre-
> hended or understood.
>
> The enormous expansion of federal legislation, both civil and crimi-
> nal, in recent years, however, has made a bureau of investigation a
> necessary instrument of law enforcement. But it is important that its
> activities be strictly limited to the performance of those functions for
> which it was created and that its agents themselves be not above the
> law or beyond its reach.

The FBI remained within this orbit for fifteen years. It won a
reputation as the scourge of kidnapers and bank robbers and automobile thieves and prohibition-era gangsters. Its laboratories and
crime-detection techniques were generally acknowledged to be the
most advanced and comprehensive in the world. It served as a
model for municipal police departments and state bureaus of investigation. Youngsters aspired to join it when they grew up, and

[4] Quoted by Andrews, op cit., p. 102.

the term "G-man" came to be a synonym for fearless, implacable law enforcement. If Mr. Hoover's publicity methods seemed now and then a trifle on the theatrical side, they nevertheless served a useful public purpose by making the federal forces of law and order universally respected.

On September 6, 1939, however, President Roosevelt issued the following statement:

The Attorney General has been requested by me to instruct the Federal Bureau of Investigation of the Department of Justice to take charge of investigative work in matters relating to espionage, sabotage, and violations of the neutrality regulations.

This task must be conducted in a comprehensive and effective manner on a national basis, and all information must be carefully sifted out and correlated in order to avoid confusion and irresponsibility.

To this end I request all police officers, sheriffs, and all other law enforcement officers in the United States promptly to turn over to the nearest representative of the Federal Bureau of Investigation any information obtained by them relating to espionage, counterespionage, sabotage, subversive activities, and violations of the neutrality laws.

This directive not only tremendously expanded the bureau's work, but also radically changed its focus. It brought the FBI into an area quite outside the scope of Attorney General Stone's definition. It brought it, indeed, back into the area from which he had taken it. Counterintelligence is not the normal work of a law-enforcement agency; and subversive activities are essentially political activities which may or may not be criminal. In 1941 the bureau's jurisdiction was further extended when the Attorney General directed it to investigate allegations of disloyalty in connection with federal employees. In 1947 President Truman gave it full responsibility for investigation under the Federal Employee-Loyalty Program. The step from investigation of conventional crime to investigation of espionage, sabotage, subversive activities, and disloyalty was a step that raised the most delicate questions respecting the compatibility of authority and freedom.

One measure of the magnitude of the step can be found in the

FBI's budget and personnel statistics. For the federal fiscal year 1924, it received an appropriation of $2,242,240 and employed 441 special agents. Its appropriation in 1939 amounted to $6,643,778 with 785 designated special agents on the payroll. For the fiscal year 1951, Congress gave the bureau $57,400,000, and the number of special agents had grown to 4602. But these indications of dramatic growth tell only a portion of the story. Like any police agency, the FBI uses, in addition to its known personnel, under-cover agents whose number is not ascertainable and whose relation to the agency is exceedingly obscure. Some of these, perhaps, are mere occasional informants; some may be regular, paid opera-tives. In several instances of late, men who designated themselves former FBI agents testified before the House Committee on Un-American Activities respecting what they called subversive groups into which they said they had infiltrated. One of them, by his own account, played a principal part in organizing the American Slav Congress and in leading it into what he called subversive activities—fulfilling the classic role of the *agent provocateur*. The FBI, however, neither acknowledges nor denies the status these men claim. In the New York trial of eleven Communist Party leaders in 1949, a number of FBI undercover operatives who had joined the party appeared as prosecution witnesses. How widely such agents have been dispersed in labor unions, in lawful voluntary associations, and in political groups is a matter of mere conjecture. But it is certainly a matter of legitimate concern to Americans who care about preservation of the traditional rights of privacy.

The lumping together in a single agency of responsibility for investigation of conventional crime and of espionage, sabotage, subversive activities, and disloyalty has produced some extremely unhappy confusions. The investigation of conventional crime entails the detection and apprehension of persons who have com-mitted overt unlawful acts; it is the normal, proper business of a law-enforcement agency. The fruits of such investigation are turned over to prosecutors who present them to courts; and those proved guilty are punished in accordance with the law. Counterespionage and countersabotage may be preventive as well as punitive; they are concerned with the detection, surveillance, and frustration of spies and saboteurs much more than with their immediate arrest and prosecution. This is more an intelligence operation than a police operation.[5] The investigation of subversive activities and of disloyalty is not a police operation at all—save in those countries where political police are countenanced.

At a time of international tension, particularly at a time when Russian agents are known to be active in this country, a vigilant and skilled counterintelligence corps is an indispensable element of national security. It is a reasonable question, however, whether national security is best protected by entrusting so delicate a function to a police force—even to so expert a police force as the FBI. In England it is entrusted not to Scotland Yard but to a special branch of the military. Counterintelligence calls for knowledge, skills, training, and techniques altogether different from those required for the detection of conventional crime. It calls, to begin with, for almost absolute anonymity on the part of the head of the corps as well as on the part of its agents. It calls for familiarity with a world wholly different from the underworld of crime. It calls for the highest kind of political sophistication—something which even the best of policemen is unlikely to possess.

FBI special agents are recruited in accordance with standards extraordinarily exacting for a police force—standards no doubt admirably adapted to the task of detecting and apprehending criminals. An applicant for one of these jobs must be a graduate either of a resident law school and a member of the bar or of an accounting school and possess a certified public accountant's cer-

---

5 "Counterespionage assignments of the FBI require an objective different from the handling of criminal cases. In a criminal case, the identification and arrest of the wrongdoer are the ultimate objectives. In an espionage case, the identification of a wrongdoer is only the first step. What is more important is to ascertain his contacts, his objectives, his sources of information, and his methods of communication. Arrest and public disclosure are steps to be taken only as a matter of last resort. It is better to know who these people are and what they are doing and to immobilize their efforts, than it is to expose them publicly and then go through the tireless efforts of identifying their successors." Testimony of J. Edgar Hoover before a Senate Appropriations Subcommittee, February 7, 1950, p. 160.

tificate. Before being appointed he is rigorously investigated by
the FBI itself, and before being assigned to field duty he is given
a twelve-week period of special training. It cannot be said, however, that either the salary of a special agent or the type of work
he is required to perform attracts the best graduates of the country's professional schools.

Some FBI alumni—there is a Society of Former Special Agents
of the FBI, Inc.—have risen in public life, in some instances to
prosecutory positions in the Department of Justice, in one or two
cases to membership in the House of Representatives; collectively
they constitute a formidable FBI claque. A greater number have
moved on into remunerative protective jobs in private industry
or have set up shop for themselves as private investigators or have
undertaken to merchandise their recollections.

The beginning of effective counterintelligence today is a realistic appraisal of Soviet resources in the United States, including
the true nature of the Communist Party and its potentialities for
Soviet purposes. Such an appraisal must be quite free from emotional judgments respecting the odiousness of Communist views
on religion or foreign policy or even the free enterprise system. It
cannot be based on unverified conjectures that "for every party
member there are ten others ready, willing, and able to do the
party's work." [6] It cannot indiscriminately identify communism
or "communistic tendencies" with espionage and sabotage. It cannot confuse heterodoxy with disloyalty and disloyalty with espionage and sabotage. Above all, it cannot confuse espionage and
sabotage with subversive propaganda or a disposition to overthrow the government by force or violence. Counterintelligence
must be focused with the precision of a microscope on the particular germs it aims to isolate.

The FBI fixed its eye on espionage and sabotage with admirable precision in the war against the Axis dictatorships. It did not
make the mistake of supposing that everyone who spoke with a
German accent or who was anti-Semitic or who hailed Adolf

[6] See testimony of J. Edgar Hoover before Senate Appropriations Subcommittee quoted in Chapter II, p. 36.

Hitler's "regeneration" of the Fatherland was a potential spy or saboteur. It should be set down as a matter of everlasting credit to the FBI that it had no part in the tragic stupidity which led the Army to drive eighty thousand American citizens from the West Coast of the United States on the sole ground that they were of Japanese ancestry. Promptly after Pearl Harbor the FBI rounded up the small number of actual enemy agents who endangered the security of the United States—and did it so discriminatingly that enemy espionage and sabotage were forestalled without violence to the rights of great numbers of aliens and citizens who might otherwise have fallen under suspicion. The FBI accomplished this because it knew what to look for. It accomplished this because it was governed by its intelligence instead of by its emotions, and because it had not then helped to create—as it has with respect to the Communists today—an atmosphere of panic, foreclosing restraint and rationality.

There are disturbing signs that the FBI does not now know what to look for and that it is looking in erroneous directions. The signs are that it is looking for disloyalty—even among law-abiding citizens who have no connection with the Federal Employee-Loyalty Program—and that this search is leading it down innumerable blind alleys and into areas which are not a proper part of any police agency's business. To see these signs, one does not need to give credence to the myriad stories that FBI agents ask whether subjects under investigation read *The Nation* or the *New Republic* or oppose racial segregation; these anecdotes are probably often exaggerated and are, in any case, unverifiable. The signs are to be seen indisputably enough, however, in the official reports of FBI agents which were made public in the course of the trial of Judith Coplon for espionage in the summer of 1949.

Miss Coplon was charged with having tried to transmit to a Russian agent abstracts culled from certain classified documents vital to the security of the United States—confidential files of the FBI. One of the shocking aspects of her trial was the attempt by the Department of Justice to secure her conviction without disclosing the character of these documents. They were essential evidence, since one of the significant questions to be determined by the jury was whether they were, in fact, vital to the national security. Federal Judge Albert Reeves, who presided at the first trial of Miss Coplon in Washington, ruled, over the vehement protests of Justice Department attorneys, that if the government wished to prosecute Miss Coplon, it would have to produce in court the evidence on which its prosecution was based. "I regretfully have to state," said Judge Reeves, "that a judge is charged with a responsibility—to see that justice is done. If it turns out that the government has come into court exposing itself, then it will have to take the peril. If it embarrasses the government to disclose relevant material, then the government ought not to be here."

In sober truth, it embarrassed the government greatly. It embarrassed the government, in the first place, because publication of the FBI files may have revealed the identity of certain confidential and strategically-placed informants—a high price to pay for the punishment of a young woman who had ceased to be a danger as soon as her espionage activities had been discovered and she had been removed from her job. Publication of the FBI files was embarrassing in another way as well. It disclosed that the FBI had been collecting much "information" of dubious value and that it had been investigating the private lives of citizens who were neither criminals nor threats to the security of the State.

The published files contained, for example, an assertion that one of the assistants to the President of the United States had given some help in obtaining a passport for a trip to Mexico to a friend with whose wife, according to an informant, the presidential aide had once been in love. The files contained a statement by an informant that his next-door neighbors entertained Army and Navy officers up to the rank of colonel "under suspicious circumstances"; that these neighbors "engaged in parties which lasted throughout the night and sometimes into the following morning"; that "approximately once a month an unknown individual in civilian clothes, appearing to be a foreigner, attended the gatherings," and that "when this individual appeared, great secrecy was maintained at the house, and all curtains were drawn"; that, according to the informant, on different occasions the neighbors were observed "moving around the house in a nude state"; that the informant's eleven-year-old boy said he saw one of these interesting neighbors go out on the porch, undressed, to get the newspaper. The identity of the newspaper was not disclosed.

It seems legitimate to ask what an agency of the United States government is doing with gossip of this sort as part of a permanent record. One answer customarily given by law-enforcement officers is that information which may seem valueless today has a possible future utility when considered in the light of additional data which may be uncovered at some later date. Perhaps so. But it also has a possible future danger which it would be folly to ignore. Records are the blood plasma of every modern police system. When they are confined to criminals, they are undoubtedly an effective means of suppressing crime. When, as in the case of the Gestapo and the Italian OSNA and the Russian NKVD and MVD, they involve persons innocent of crime, they may be an effective means of suppressing political dissent or unorthodoxy. They invite misuse. Indeed, the likelihood that they will be misused is far greater than the possibility that they will at some time, as the saying goes, come in handy. It cannot be taken for granted that all future directors of the FBI will have Mr. Hoover's integrity. The possession of great numbers of dossiers on individual citizens could put into the hands of some future police chief a malevolent power.

The FBI makes no pretense that its files contain only tested, reliable material. On the contrary, it has declared candidly on innumerable occasions that they are made up of unchecked and what it calls "unevaluated" information. "The files," Mr. Hoover said in testimony before a Senate Foreign Relations subcommittee, protesting against that body's demand for confidential investigative reports, "do not consist of proved information alone. The files must be viewed as a whole. One report may allege crimes of a most despicable sort, and the truth or falsity of these charges may not emerge until several reports are studied, further investigations made, and the wheat separated from the chaff. Should a given file be disclosed, the issue would be far broader than concerns the subject of the investigation. Names of persons who by force of circumstance entered into the investigation might well be innocent of any wrong. To publicize their names without the explanation of their associations would be a grave injustice." Nor is there anything new about the inclusion of such unchecked data in FBI reports. In 1941 Robert H. Jackson, then Attorney General, offered much the same argument against surrendering any of these reports to another congressional committee. "Disclosure of information contained in the reports," he said, "might also be the grossest kind of injustice to innocent individuals. Investigative reports include leads and suspicions, and sometimes even the statements of malicious or misinformed people."

These reports are supposed, then, to be inviolably secret. If they are kept secret, the argument runs, they cannot do any damage. The first fallacy in this has already been made apparent: they are not necessarily kept secret. Secrecy is an elastic term. The files of the FBI are available to a number of the employees in the Department of Justice. Judith Coplon, for example, evidently had access to them. She conveyed a knowledge of their contents outside the Department. The Department itself, when it undertook the prosecution of Miss Coplon, decided that the confidential character of the FBI files was not so inviolable as to forbid their disclosure for the sake of convicting Miss Coplon. President Truman, after protesting that he would never, never, never make FBI loyalty reports available to the Senate subcommittee investigating Senator McCarthy's charges, nevertheless allowed subcommittee members to inspect them.

The contents of some of the files are leaked occasionally—it would seem almost necessarily with the connivance of someone in the FBI itself—to congressional investigators and to newspaper reporters. A portion of the FBI's loyalty report on Dr. Edward U. Condon, for instance, was made public by Representative J. Parnell Thomas. The FBI, like any other government agency, has its turnover of personnel. There are indications that some former FBI agents have made use for private purposes of their knowledge of the bureau's files. The weekly newsletter called *Counterattack,* published by former agents of the FBI, sometimes exhibits a remarkable knowledge of the private activities and associations of persons it "exposes" as "Reds." And there is the possibility, finally, that some FBI alumni will use their memories of FBI files for blackmail or for political pressure. Buried in rows upon rows of jealously guarded steel filing cabinets, these dossiers rest like little guided missiles, each with its designated target, waiting to be launched toward the destruction of a reputation and a human life.

Even if knowledge of the contents of these files never passed beyond the portals of the Department of Justice, they would have a cancerous influence upon American life. The most serious danger in these compilations of random hearsay on the private lives of private citizens is the anxiety and inhibitions they inspire. One thing is quite clear: the files are kept secret from their subjects. No man knows, therefore, whether the FBI has a dossier on him, culled perhaps from unfriendly sources and full of unevaluated untruths. No man can gauge the hidden mischief that may be wrought by such a dossier. Who can tell what avenues of public employment have been closed to him because an administrator has discovered that there is derogatory information concerning him buried in the vaults of the FBI and has not taken the trouble to determine whether this unevaluated information is true or false? It is only in the rare instances when FBI reports are actually disclosed, as in the Coplon case, that subjects can discover, and perhaps repair, the injury done to them. The undisclosed files may be more dangerous than those brought into the open.

Anyone who achieves any degree of prominence is liable to be the subject of an FBI report, or the subject of an incidental reference, especially if he is engaged in political activity. The possibility is disquieting. When a man fears that his words are being taken down, that his associations and movements are under scrutiny, that neighbors and associates may be babbling about him to the police, he does not speak or act with the freedom and candor that Americans are accustomed to regard as part of their birthright.

Mr. Hoover's insistence that the FBI makes no evaluation of the material it gathers deserves examination. In answer to one of the questions submitted to him by Bert Andrews of the *New York Herald Tribune,* Mr. Hoover said, "The FBI does not make policy, recommendations, conclusions, or rulings based upon our investigations. The FBI, since I became its director in 1924, has adhered strictly to the premise that it is a fact-finding agency." This is certainly an admirable position. It would be grossly improper for the FBI to make judgments respecting the guilt or innocence of the persons it investigates. Mr. Hoover has shown much more awareness of this essential distinction between the law-enforcement and judicial functions than many members of Congress. He has repeatedly resisted congressional attempts to saddle the FBI with responsibility for determining eligibility for government employment. FBI investigation has been made by law a prerequisite to the hiring of personnel in the Atomic Energy Commission and the Economic Cooperation Administration. In March 1950 the House of Representatives went even beyond this. In legislation creating a National Science Foundation, it stipulated that no one should be awarded one of its scholarships—which entailed no access to classified information—without a definite certification by the FBI that he was loyal to the United States. Displaying far greater understanding of American principles than the legislators, Mr. Hoover promptly begged to be excused from a function so foreign to the proper duties of his agency. To give a police bureau statutory authority to pass judgment on its own investigative findings would be to merge the roles of the policeman and the judge. Fortunately, Mr. Hoover's plea prevailed, and the offensive provision was eliminated in conference with the Senate.

But despite its renunciation of judicial responsibility, the FBI inevitably engages in a large measure of the evaluation that Mr. Hoover disclaims. Indeed, if it did not evaluate as reliable and significant the material included in its reports, it is hard to see how the reports would be of any use to anybody.

An article on "Loyalty among Government Employees" by Thomas I. Emerson and David M. Helfeld in the *Yale Law Journal* of December 1948 drew an angry rebuttal from Mr. Hoover. Among the statements to which he took vehement exception was this: "The truth is, of course, that in deciding what facts to report the FBI makes constant judgments of relevancy." Mr. Hoover replied to this in part: "The facts are that FBI special agents are under instructions to report all information conveyed to them." [7] Louis B. Nichols, assistant director of the FBI, made the same point on another occasion but in a somewhat more expanded and illuminating form. "Our rule provides," said Mr. Nichols, "that when an agent interviews a citizen, he must report what a citizen tells him *that is pertinent to the investigation.* Obviously, if the citizen talks about the coming of autumn, and the grandeur of the leaves, and the like, that is not a legitimate part of the investigation. But if he says that John Doe is a Left-winger, the agent reports that John Doe is a Left-winger, and then he goes a step further, because he will not accept that. He will insist that the witness furnish him with the facts upon which he bases his conclusion. And if he has no facts, the agent will so state in his report." [8] This would certainly seem to entail a "judgment of relevancy."

Mr. Hoover objected also to an assertion by Emerson and Helfeld that "the collection of gossip, rumor, and data on private affairs becomes an inevitable part of the process"—no more, really, than Attorney General Jackson and Mr. Hoover himself acknowledged in the statements quoted above. But this drew from Mr. Hoover the rejoinder: "This statement is untrue. In

[7] "Comment" by Mr. Hoover, op. cit., p. 401.

[8] Forum on the FBI, Yale Law School, New Haven, Connecticut, October 24, 1949. (Italics the author's.)

each instance agents inquire of persons interviewed, when they express conclusions, for the facts upon which they base their conclusions. If a matter is reported as rumor or gossip, the agents try to ascertain the source of the statements so that their truth or falsity can be established. Of course, the authors should know that the first defense in such cases is a denial, and if that fails, then an attempt is made to label the information as rumor or gossip."

What this seems to come down to is an acknowledgment that gossip and rumor do in fact enter into the report, but that FBI agents endeavor to label them as such when they recognize them. But if this is not in itself an act of evaluation—and evaluation of the most subtle and significant sort—then the term has been robbed of all meaning. Indeed, evaluation seems an inescapable element of almost every step in the investigative process. It enters into the selection of subjects for investigation. It enters into the selection of sources of information—and into determination of whether they are reliable or unreliable, whether they are biased or disinterested, whether what they have said is an opinion or a fact. It enters into the determination of what facts to include in the report. For, patently, every piece of reporting entails some judgment as to relevancy. An FBI agent who came back with information as to what kind of breakfast food his subject enjoyed, as to what brand of toothpaste he favored, as to whether he preferred Proust or Joyce, would certainly be instructed to confine his inquiries to more pertinent matters. The very questions asked by an investigator entail evaluation of a most important kind.

One of the most shocking documents that came to light in the course of the Coplon trial was an FBI report that an informant, unidentified, was "satisfied" that a number of Hollywood actors or writers were members of the Communist Party. A seven-page single-spaced report on Fredric March and his wife Florence Eldridge March was read to the jury and a jammed courtroom after the prosecutor had pleaded with Judge Reeves not to divulge the top secret FBI files lest the nation's security be imperiled. It is difficult to understand how this particular report could have imperiled anything but the FBI's own reputation. A few excerpts should serve to show its character:

Confidential Informant T-6 advised in December 1947 that Fredric March and Canada Lee were two outstanding Communist Party fellow-travelers connected with the Institute for Democratic Education, Inc., 415 Lexington Avenue, New York City, along with Daniel L. Marsh, president of Boston University; Clyde R. Miller, a professor in the Teachers College at Columbia University; and Norman Corwin of the Columbia Broadcasting System. . . .

On November 27, 1945, Confidential Informant ED-324 advised that he had observed a throw-away advertising a meeting to be held in Madison Square Garden on December 4, 1945 at 8 p.m. This circular was headed "Crisis Coming, Atom Bomb—for Peace or War?" The program was set forth and listed Fredric March thereunder as a speaker, along with Dr. Harlow Shapley, chairman; Julian Huxley, F.R.S.; Senator Charles W. Tobey; R. J. Thomas; Colonel Evans Carlson; Dr. Harold C. Urey; Helen Keller; Danny Kaye; Jo Davidson; and Henry A. Wallace. . . .

Confidential Informant ND-305 advised December 25, 1945, that the subject partook in the entertainment program at a meeting sponsored by the American Society for Russian Relief held at Madison Square Garden, New York City, December 8, 1945. The informant, who was one of about 13,000 attending the meeting, stated that Helen Hayes, noted actress, and the subject portrayed a Russian schoolteacher and a Soviet soldier, respectively, in a skit, whereby they described the devastation of Russia by the Nazis at the battles of Stalingrad and Leningrad. . . .

Confidential Informant T-7 advised on February 25, 1946, that the name of Florence Eldridge March was mentioned in a conversation between Lionel Berman and Bella V. Dodd, both of the Communist Party. This conversation concerned the names of those people whom Bella Dodd had secured for a new front organization, the nature of which was not known.[9]

The question that springs most immediately to mind in connection with these "unevaluated facts" is why the FBI was spending the energy of its agents and the money provided by taxpayers

[9] *Washington Post,* June 9, 1949.

to uncover the private lives of a famous actor and actress. Neither Fredric March nor Florence Eldridge was an applicant for a government job. There is not the slightest indication in the material collected by the FBI that either of them was engaged in any violation of a federal law. There is no activity in the reports quoted above which was not candid and lawful and readily ascertainable from public records—except the evaluation by Confidential Informant T-6 that the subject was "an outstanding Communist Party fellow-traveler." It is difficult to imagine, incidentally, how Confidential Informant T-7 learned that Mrs. March was mentioned in a conversation between Lionel Berman and Bella V. Dodd unless he did so by tapping a telephone wire. The second question that springs to mind in connection with this report is why the FBI should have considered the information supplied by its agents of sufficient value to file anywhere save in a garbage can. It must have attached some value—a form of evaluation—to these facts. An outside observer can scarcely avoid evaluating them as sheer nonsense.

Prior to the disclosure of this FBI file Mr. and Mrs. March had been the targets of abusive stories in *Counterattack*. The publication had stated or plainly implied that they were Communists, apparently on the basis of information strikingly similar to that contained in the FBI file. As a result of the allegations film studios closed their doors to the Marches. They brought a libel suit against *Counterattack* for half a million dollars. The suit was settled out of court, and the newsletter published a statement that it "withdraws and retracts its previously published statements that Fredric March and Florence Eldridge are Communists." Mr. and Mrs. March cannot, of course, get any such satisfaction from the FBI.

The second trial of Judith Coplon, as a co-defendant with Valentin Gubitchev, shed an even more disturbing light upon the FBI's activities. Miss Coplon's counsel had made a charge in the first trial that the government's case was based upon evidence secured through wiretapping—evidence not admissible in a federal court. This charge had been indignantly denounced by the

United States Attorney prosecuting the case as a "fishing expedition"; and Judge Reeves, accepting the government's word, had declined to hold a pre-trial hearing to determine whether wiretapping had played any substantial part in the preparation of the government's case.

Judge Sylvester Ryan, who presided over the second trial in New York, did hold such a hearing. The testimony made it clear that the FBI had tapped the telephones of Miss Coplon and Mr. Gubitchev extensively, and the Judge granted a request on the part of defense counsel to compel the government to produce in court thirty FBI agents who had monitored tapped wires leading to the home of Miss Coplon's parents and ten agents who had tapped the wires in Gubitchev's residence. He required the government to produce also about a hundred and fifty double-faced discs on which were recorded conversations intercepted by tapping the wires of Miss Coplon's apartment in Washington and by planting a microphone in her desk in the Department of Justice. Additional records of monitored conversations which the defense sought to have brought into court could not be produced by the FBI because they had been destroyed.

The conduct of the FBI in respect to the missing wiretap records appears to have been extremely disingenuous. Several agents testified under oath that these records had been destroyed "as a matter of routine." Subsequently it was disclosed that they had been ordered to destroy the records "in view of the imminency of her trial." Throughout the investigation of Miss Coplon and the preparation of the case against her, there was a systematic effort by the FBI to conceal its resort to wiretapping. The following memorandum from Howard B. Fletcher, FBI inspector, to D. M. Ladd, assistant FBI director, was read into the court record:

The above-named informant [Tiger, the code name of the tap] has been furnishing information concerning the activities of Coplon since her conviction [for espionage, last June 30 in Washington]. In view of the imminency of her trial it is recommended that this informant be discontinued immediately and that all administrative records in the New York office covering the operations of this informant be destroyed.

Pertinent data furnished by the informant has already been furnished in letter form, and having in mind security, now and in the future, it is believed desirable that the indicated records be destroyed.

At the bottom of the memorandum was this notation:

This memorandum is for administrative purposes. To be destroyed after action is taken and not sent to files.[10]

What the FBI agents had done in the course of the Washington trial amounted to nothing less than a deliberate hoodwinking of Judge Reeves. They had sat silent while the prosecutor expressed indignation at the defense suggestion that wiretapping had been employed; several agents had said they "had no knowledge of wiretapping." Judge Ryan characterized these statements as evasions.

One agent even asserted that he had had "no personal knowledge" of wiretapping in the Coplon case, although it was subsequently established that summaries of wiretaps had been routed to him for months before the Washington trial and that he, personally, by his own admission, had destroyed "quite a number" of them. In short, the FBI had resorted to wiretapping, which Judge Ryan said was illegal, in the surveillance of Miss Coplon, and had resorted to something very like perjury in an attempt to conceal this illegality from a United States court.

All this was done, it may be readily acknowledged, with a sincere intent to protect the national security. But the government has an imperative obligation to observe restraints imposed upon it by law, and an affirmative duty when it prosecutes its citizens, to lay before a court all the relevant and significant facts. The government has vast resources and tremendous power, against which individuals may be helpless and the courts impotent to protect them unless the government itself considers the protection of individual rights as much its responsibility as the protection of national security. It is, after all, precisely against the threat of totalitarian rule that we seek to be secure.

No one, perhaps, has expressed this obligation better than Mr.

[10] *New York Herald Tribune,* January 13, 1950.

Hoover himself. Writing on "Law Enforcement and the Democratic Tradition" in the bulletin "Confidential—from Washington," issued by the George Washington University, December 1949, Mr. Hoover said:

The law-enforcement agency in a democracy has limited powers, powers specifically defined by the Constitution, judicial decisions and acts passed by legislative bodies. Totalitarian law enforcement, on the other hand, has unlimited power. The secret police, responsive only to the will of the ruling elite, creates, defines, interprets, and reviews its own activities.

The individual citizen, in a democratic state, is protected by the high standards set by good law enforcement itself. The well-trained peace officer, schooled in the democratic tradition, respects the civil rights of the accused and observes the rules of fair play and decency. He attempts to solve the criminal case by hard work, intelligent investigation, and locating the evidence which may later be used in a court trial. Brutality, third degree torture, threats to terrorize relatives, familiar weapons of totalitarian law enforcement, are shunned by good law enforcement. The accused is innocent until proved guilty by law.

This is a thoroughly admirable statement. It reflects a full recognition of the principle that efficiency in law enforcement is subordinate to the preservation of personal liberty. It acknowledges, to go back again to the words of Mr. Justice Holmes, that it is "a less evil that some criminals should escape than that the government should play an ignoble part." This is a traditional American view embedded in the Constitution itself. The whole thrust of the Fourth, Fifth, and Sixth Amendments is to restrain the police. The Fourth Amendment in particular, with its prohibition of unreasonable searches and seizures and its insistence upon warrants "particularly describing the place to be searched, and the persons or things to be seized," is a constant obstacle to quick and efficient action by officers of the law. Sometimes it frustrates the true interests of justice. But this kind of self-denial on the part of the government is an essential characteristic of any free society.

The record of the Department of Justice in regard to wiretapping has been a devious and equivocal one. It needs to be reviewed because this modern police technique has a peculiarly destructive implication for the ends to which law enforcement is but a means. In the Olmstead case in 1928 [11] the Supreme Court decided five to four—Justices Holmes, Brandeis, Butler, and Stone dissenting—that wiretapping was not an unlawful search and seizure within the prohibition of the Fourth Amendment. It was in his dissent in this case that Mr. Justice Holmes referred to wiretapping as "dirty business." In 1934 Congress adopted the Federal Communications Act with a section, 605, providing that

. . . no person not being authorized by the sender shall intercept any communication and divulge or publish the existence, contents, substance, purport, effect, or meaning of such intercepted communication to any person . . . and no person having received such intercepted communication . . . shall . . . use the same or any information therein contained for his own benefit or for the benefit of another. . . .

The Department of Justice interpreted this statute to apply only to private persons, not to government officers. In 1937, however, in the first Nardone case, the Supreme Court said the words "no person" meant no person, and that Section 605 was designed "to include within its sweep federal officers as well as others."

The plain words of 605 forbid anyone, unless authorized by the sender, to intercept a telephone message, and direct in equally clear language that *"no person"* shall divulge or publish the message or its substance to *"any person."* . . . Congress may have thought it less important that some offenders should go unwhipped of justice than that officers should resort to methods deemed inconsistent with ethical standards and destructive of personal liberty.[12]

The Department of Justice prosecuted Nardone again, using the wiretap information this time merely to secure leads for obtaining more acceptable evidence. But the Supreme Court, after hearing the second case in 1939, ruled that wiretaps could not be used even indirectly, that no "fruit of the poisonous tree" could

[11] 277 U.S. 438 (1928).
[12] 302 U.S. 379 (1937). Italics in the Court opinion.

be presented in a court of the United States.[13] Still unchastened, the Department of Justice devised the ingenious view that the words "intercept . . . and divulge" put no restraint on interception alone but merely forbade divulging the product of the interception. From this, it was easy for the Department to rationalize that divulging meant only telling the world at large but had nothing to do with an FBI agent's reporting what he heard on a tapped wire to his associates and superiors inside the government.

There is a triple incongruity in the Justice Department's position. In the first place, the notion that official colleagues are not "persons" seems a transparent fiction. In the second place, the Department has repeatedly asked Congress for legislation to authorize what it persists in pretending that it already has authority to do. And Congress has repeatedly declined to enact such legislation. In the third place, it is forced to pretend (as in the Coplon case) that its resort to wiretapping yields it no information of any value in the prosecution of criminals. If the information gleaned through wiretapping is really not used, the practice had much better be discontinued.

In nothing is the Justice Department's sense of guilt about wiretapping so clearly revealed as in the curious justification its spokesmen have contrived for their resort to the practice. Lacking any legislative authorization to tap telephone conversations, they have based their employment of this technique on a few sentences, wrested from their context, in a letter written by President Roosevelt in 1941. Attorney General McGrath, in an announcement January 8, 1950, that he saw "no reason at the present time for any change," said that Justice Department and FBI policies condoning "limited" use of wiretapping were laid down by the late President Roosevelt. Mr. Hoover offered the following defense of wiretapping:

I have never attempted to keep my views on this subject a secret, nor have I ever lacked the support of the highest levels of authority in the Executive Branch of the government. The late President of the United States, Franklin D. Roosevelt, in a letter dated February 25,

[13] 308 U.S. 338 (1939).

1941, which was widely publicized, stated the policies followed by the Bureau when he said:

"I do not believe it should be used to prevent domestic crimes, with possibly one exception—kidnaping and extortion in the federal sense.

"There is, however, one field in which, given the conditions in the world today, wiretapping is very much in the public interest. This nation is arming for national defense. It is the duty of our people to take every single step to protect themselves. I have no compunction in saying that wiretapping should be used against those persons, not citizens of the United States, and those few citizens who are traitors to their country, who today are engaged in espionage or sabotage against the United States." [14]

This excerpt from Mr. Roosevelt's letter makes it appear that he was laying down a policy on wiretapping. He was doing nothing of the sort. His letter was written to Thomas H. Eliot, then a member of Congress, in response to a request from Mr. Eliot for an expression of the President's views respecting a pending bill to legalize wiretapping. In the same letter the President said:

I have read the bill and I have no hesitation in saying that it goes entirely too far and that its provisions are unnecessarily broad. . . . The use of wiretapping to aid law-enforcement officers raises squarely the most delicate problem in the field of democratic statesmanship. It is more than desirable, it is necessary that criminals be detected and prosecuted as vigilantly as possible. It is more necessary that the citizens of a democracy be protected in their rights of privacy from unwarranted snooping. As an instrument for oppression of free citizens, I can think of none worse than indiscriminate wiretapping.[15]

It was from this foundation that the President proceeded to his conclusion that he would favor congressional enactment of a bill permitting wiretapping in limited situations and with the requirement "that the Attorney General be acquainted with the necessity for wiretapping in every single case, and that he himself sign a certificate indicating such necessity." This endorsement of

[14] "Rejoinder by Mr. Hoover," op. cit., pp. 422-23.
[15] The letter appears in full in the published *Hearings of House Judiciary Subcommittee No. 1 on Wiretapping*, February 3, 10, 12, 17, 19, 24, and 26, 1941, p. 257.

a bill to legalize limited wiretapping suggests pretty plainly that the President did not consider it legal in the absence of permissive legislation. Congress did not adopt his proposal. His advocacy of it cannot reasonably be construed as an authorization to the Department of Justice to disregard Congress. And, of course, he would have had no legitimate power to issue such an authorization in any case.[16]

No doubt the Attorneys General who subsequently permitted the FBI to tap wires did so in good faith, believing that the law did not absolutely forbid it. No doubt Mr. Hoover was entirely warranted in acting on this authorization of his superiors and did so in the sincere belief that such action was necessary to the defense of the nation. But manifestly the situation ought to be clarified by an express declaration of policy on the part of Congress.

Beneath the question whether wiretapping is legal in the absence of congressional authorization lies the deeper question whether it ought to be legalized. The real issue is obscured by the easy assumption that it can be limited, as Mr. Roosevelt put it, to "those persons, not citizens of the United States, and those few citizens who are traitors to their country, who are today engaged in espionage or sabotage against the United States." A wiretap is no respecter of citizenship or of loyalty. The only rational reason for employing it is to determine whether a person is, in fact, engaged in espionage or sabotage. This means employing it in connection with persons not necessarily guilty but suspected of these crimes. And if suspicion is so general as to include such persons as Fredric March and Helen Hayes and anyone whose neighbors report that he walks around his home unclothed, the list may be a very long one. It accords short shrift to the

---

[16] Both Attorney General McGrath and Mr. Hoover referred additionally to a memorandum from President Roosevelt dated May 21, 1940, which "authorized the Attorney General to approve wiretapping when necessary in situations involving the defense of the nation." This memorandum has never been made public, and attempts to obtain it from the Department of Justice have been of no avail.

rights of privacy to provide for their protection merely that the police must secure prior permission to tap wires in specific cases from an Attorney General or, as has been alternatively suggested, from a federal judge. When the police assert that the national security is at stake, permission is likely to be accorded automatically. Privacy cannot so readily be breached under a government of laws.

When a telephone is monitored, all who use it are overheard. These may include persons who are not under suspicion at all—guests and servants in the home of the suspect as well as anyone who happens to be on the other end of the line. They may include conversations which have nothing whatever to do with the alleged crime under investigation. They may entail the breach of confidential relations which the law has always regarded as privileged. In monitoring telephones in the Coplon case, the FBI recorded talks between the defendant and her mother, a quarrel between a husband and wife who had no connection with the case, and even conferences between the defendant and her lawyer. It learned, incidentally, about an affair, altogether unrelated to espionage, between Miss Coplon and a Justice Department attorney. There is nothing fastidious about wiretapping. It provides a fertile source for blackmail; its utility for law enforcement is less apparent.

But even if it be admitted that eavesdropping on supposedly private telephone conversations gives the police an important means of uncovering espionage, it may still be argued that the social costs of this invasion of privacy outweigh its benefits. There are, as Mr. Hoover pointed out, many means of catching spies or other criminals, which, though "familiar weapons of totalitarian law enforcement, are shunned by good law enforcement." The third degree—to take one of the weapons specifically banned by Mr. Hoover from the arsenal of a democratic police force—is certainly not without its uses in combating crime. A judicious use of the thumbscrew, a discreet resort to the rubber hose, might elicit a good deal of information—applied of course only to "those persons, not citizens of the United States, and those few citizens who are traitors to their country, who today are engaged in espionage or sabotage against the United States."

If wiretapping is an aid to the police in frustrating foreign agents, so is rifling the mails, so is unrestricted search of private homes, so is summary arrest on suspicion—the ominous knock on the door by night that came to be the symbol of the Gestapo's terror. A great deal could be learned about crime by putting recording devices in confessionals and in physicians' consulting rooms, by compelling wives to testify against their husbands, by encouraging children to report the dangerous thoughts uttered by their parents. The trouble with these techniques, whatever their utility in safeguarding national security, is that a nation which countenances them ceases to be free.

"Writs of assistance and general warrants," said Mr. Justice Brandeis, "are but puny instruments of tyranny and oppression when compared with wiretapping." This was a valid estimate when it was made more than twenty years ago; it was prophetic in view of the ease and secrecy with which telephone lines can be tapped today. The dragnet character of wiretapping, the injury done by it to the rights of the wholly innocent as well as of the guilty, the absolute irresponsibility of tappers, who cannot be detected and called to account for their acts, all make it a peculiarly dangerous police technique.

Perhaps the greatest danger involved in wiretapping is the pervasive fear inspired by a knowledge that it is practiced by the FBI on a "limited" scale. This fear may be in large part unfounded but it is nonetheless real, demoralizing, and extremely widespread; in the capital of the United States it has become endemic. It finds expression in the standard, ritualized jest that the fellow on the other end of the line had better be careful of what he says; and whenever a telephone conversation is interrupted by the static that probably denotes no more than a faulty connection, it is standard procedure to remark lightly, "Oh, that's just J. Edgar horning in." But the jest is a mirthless one. If few take it altogether seriously, even fewer find it funny. It masks anxiety of a sort which Americans have been wont, with a sense of superiority, to associate with life in the Third Reich or in the USSR.

It is this anxiety, now experienced in respect of the FBI by considerable numbers of loyal and law-abiding Americans, that constitutes one of the most alarming symptoms in the contemporary quest for national security. The FBI has developed from an agency which used to be the scourge of kidnapers and other evildoers to an agency which is now, in some degree, the scourge of liberals and nonconformists. When men fear that they may be under surveillance because of opinions or associations which a police agency considers subversive, they cease to be wholly free. In tolerating such incursions upon individual freedom, the people of the United States place in jeopardy the vital sources of their security.

The FBI is not a Gestapo and J. Edgar Hoover is no Heinrich Himmler. It is a foolish misconception of the problem they present to picture either the agency or its director as malevolent in purpose. The FBI, confined to its proper business of law enforcement, is an admirable police force. Mr. Hoover is undoubtedly a patriotic public servant, concerned to keep the FBI within democratic traditions as he understands them. But vested with too much power, he and his elite corps can become gravely dangerous. In no area is the influence of power so corrupting as in the work of the police. It is not work that attracts sensitive men; nor does it cultivate the sensibilities of those it does attract. They can be kept useful to society only as they are kept firmly under control. There ought to be periodic congressional audits of the activities of the FBI; such an audit is certainly now long overdue. The American people ought to know how many of their fellow-citizens are the subjects of FBI investigation, what standards are applied in the selection of subjects and in the accumulation of data, what techniques are employed in surveillance, what use is made of the material gathered by the FBI. It is beside the point that Mr. Hoover is well intentioned, that he has no wish to direct a secret police operation. A secret police is a police that operates in secret, that maintains secret dossiers, that uses secret agents and informers. The FBI has come too close to this description.

The eternal vigilance so commonly said to be the price of liberty was meant to be vigilance against duly constituted authority. The complacency with which we have regarded the growth of police power in the United States is more ominous to the traditions of liberty—and to the national security dependent on those traditions—than any threat from the outside. We can, if we remain free, cope with our enemies. But the greatest dangers to liberty, as Mr. Justice Brandeis warned, "lurk in insidious encroachment by men of zeal, well meaning but without understanding."

CHAPTER VIII

SCIENCE AND SECRECY

. . . Terror of the atomic bomb is natural and understandable—perhaps even healthy—but terror at the loss of the "secret" is a tribal and superstitious fear that, once gaining ascendancy in our minds, must inevitably weaken rather than strengthen our defensive power as a nation. Preoccupation with the "secret," instead of with the thing itself, will stifle the scientific research from which our real strength is derived, will strengthen the pernicious misconception that we have a monopoly of knowledge in the science of atomic energy, and will beguile us into embracing the fatal fallacy that we can achieve security for ourselves by keeping our knowledge from others.[1]

THE PARADOX of security frustrated in the name of security is most apparent in relation to scientific inquiry. Science has long been a vital element of national defense; it played a decisive part in the two world wars of the twentieth century, and with the release of atomic energy it became a principal armorer of military power. When men possess weapons that can obliterate whole communities in the flash of an explosion, pre-eminence in science is an indispensable condition of national security. At the same time, freedom is an indispensable condition of scientific pre-eminence. The contemporary cult of loyalty, with its atmosphere of universal distrust and its exaggerated emphasis on se-

[1] James R. Newman and Byron S. Miller, *The Control of Atomic Energy* (New York: Whittlesey House, McGraw-Hill Book Company, Inc., 1948), pp. 223-24.

crecy, operates to limit the freedom of scientists and thus to block their contribution to the country's strength.

A real dilemma lies behind this paradox. Secrecy is certainly a factor in security. Every nation has military plans, weapons, and techniques which it strives to conceal from other nations. But secrecy of a new order of magnitude—indeed, of a new kind —attended the development of nuclear fission. The aim of this secrecy was to retain for the United States a monopoly of knowledge not only concerning particular military applications of the tremendous new force, but also of the fundamental scientific ideas which produced it. This could be accomplished—to the extent that it was possible at all—only by imposing rigid restraints on communication among scientists and keeping a large area of their activity under strict government control. But unembarrassed communication is necessary to the fertilization of scientific thought. In whatever measure scientists are restrained in the exchange of information with each other, they are restrained also in their productivity. Science does not flourish under control.

This dilemma was recognized and stated with admirable clarity in a report of the Joint Committee on Atomic Energy, following its investigation in 1949 of charges by Senator Bourke B. Hickenlooper of "incredible mismanagement" on the part of the Atomic Energy Commission:

. . . the [Atomic Energy] law's "paramount objective" of "assuring the common defense and security" has always placed greatest emphasis upon an affirmative task: protecting our country by keeping it far ahead of rivals in the sciences, in nuclear reactors, and in quality and quantity of bomb output. This over-all task may appropriately be called "security by achievement," in recognition of the positive character of the activities which, from the outset, contributed most to our atomic defenses. . . .
. . . The correct use of secrecy as a technique of "assuring the common defense and security" furnishes us a measure of negative protection, in the sense that we avoid helping rival nations to manufacture the bomb, and hence contrasts with the positive protection afforded us through our own continuing progress. Guard posts, barbed-wire fences, investigations of personnel, materials accountability, documents control, and

all the apparatus mobilized to suppress information leaks that might benefit a foreign power may conveniently be considered under the heading "security by concealment."

It requires no argument to show that both broad types of security— "by achievement" and "by concealment"—are indispensable. . . .[2]

Recognition that both types of security are, as the Joint Committee on Atomic Energy says, indispensable requires the striking of a rational balance between them, since, to a considerable degree, they are mutually exclusive. The beginning of such a balance must be a definition of what is to be concealed. And on this score there has been—and appears still to be, despite the atomic explosion in Russia—widespread misunderstanding on the part of the American people.

Until the latter part of 1949 this nation had—or supposed it had—for the first time in its history a national secret. It was not only a secret unsettling and bewildering because of its magnitude and its crucial importance, but it was an inevitably corrupting secret because of the illusion of absolute power it conveyed. And it was also, in certain respects, a guilty secret.

No matter how we strive to rationalize and justify the dropping of an atomic bomb on Hiroshima, a residue of guilt remains with us. The action was not more destructive than the dropping of a thousand TNT blockbusters on Essen or Berlin. It may well have been warranted by the ruthlessness of the enemy against whom it was employed. Perhaps it did indeed shorten the war and thus spare many times the number of lives it cost. But the unleashing upon the world of this new and terrible force had implications beyond the reach of reason. Men are not freed from guilt just because what they have done is right or rational.

If an armed marauder enters a house and threatens to kill its occupants, the head of the house may shoot him down and remain quite innocent in the eyes of the law. But if he is a sensitive man, he is likely to be troubled by what he has done nonetheless. He may ask himself if it might have been possible to disarm and capture the intruder without killing him. He may reflect that the

[2] *Report of the Joint Committee on Atomic Energy,* October 1949, p. 7.

fellow would probably have done nothing worse, if left alone, than steal some silver. He may wonder what desperation drove his victim to burglary. And when he has dismissed all these fantasies as sentimental, he will still at times see before him with punishing clarity the crumpled body and be seized again with the enormity of having taken a human life.

It is the enormity of what was done at Hiroshima that we cannot entirely forget. And it is the recognition that human beings are capable of this enormity in relation to one another that leaves us chilled and fearful. A new frontier of inhumanity has been discovered; and we, of all people, were the discoverers. How lucky we were—yet how responsible! And this sense of responsibility, if not of actual guilt, has produced a profound anxiety, to be washed away, perhaps, only by some species of atonement.

Having created so terrible a weapon, we were naturally at great pains to keep it to ourselves, believing that no others could be counted upon to employ it with such restraint. So we contrived the myth that atomic energy was a kind of genie that could be forced back into the bottle from which we had released it and kept there until we should choose to uncork it upon the world again.

The myth had almost a greater power for evil than the reality. It inspired the notion that we were irresistible and that we could, if we chose, force our will upon any other people. How much corruption can be conveyed by such a sense of absolute power was nakedly disclosed in the talk about "preventive" war indulged in by a good many otherwise moral and responsible people. The idea of preventive war in this context encompassed the bland strategy of atomizing Soviet cities—a measure of the degree to which human sensibilities have decayed through familiarity with limitless powers of destruction. Until President Truman's dramatic disclosure in September 1949 that an atomic explosion had taken place inside the Soviet Union, proposals were more or less soberly put forward here that we should insist upon a showdown with the Russians, requiring them either to accept our plan for international control of atomic energy or be subjected to atomic war. Some of the same kind of talk began to be heard again after the announcement that hydrogen fusion—also supposed to be attainable solely by the United States—might produce a bomb one thousand times more destructive than the product of uranium fission.

The myth of monopoly also immeasurably aggravated our sense of vulnerability and insecurity. It created something much worse than a "Maginot Line" complex. It made us feel somewhat as though we were a community hidden away in some remote mountain fastness approachable only through a secret pass, and thus immune to attack so long as the location of the pass could be kept hidden from strangers. As a result, all strangers seemed to be dangerous enemies. Even members of the community were potential enemies, those who knew the location of the pass, the scientists, most of all, since through treason or indiscretion they might reveal the secret.

Out of this fantasy grew a new form of isolationism. Security came to be identified with secrecy, and therefore all communication with the outside world was suspect. The possession of a national secret did not create the cult of loyalty, which had earlier origins; but it did greatly foster the growth of the cult.

The report of the Joint Committee on Atomic Energy is illuminating as to the real nature of "the secret":

. . . much confusion has surrounded the nature of atomic secrets, notwithstanding the conscientious efforts of the nation's scientists to clarify this aspect of public thinking. There existed, for instance, an unfortunate notion that one marvelous "formula" explains how to make bombs and that it belonged exclusively to the United States. Actually, the basic knowledge underlying the explosive release of atomic energy—and it would fill a library—never has been the property of one nation. On the contrary, nuclear physicists throughout the world (including those who live behind the iron curtain) were thoroughly familiar with the theoretical advances which paved the way for practical development of an atomic bomb. Such towering scientific figures as Niels Bohr of Denmark and Sir James Chadwick of Great Britain, together with dozens of associates from almost all countries except Russia, came to the United

States during the war, participated intimately in the Manhattan District project, rendered priceless service, and returned to their native lands when hostilities ended. Equally notable figures from abroad—Enrico Fermi of Italy and Hungarian-born Leo Szilard, for example—shared in our atomic effort and established permanent American residence following the war. The Soviet Union, for its part, possesses some of the world's most gifted scientists, as well as technical experts imported from Germany—men whose abilities and whose understanding of the fundamental physics behind the bomb only the unrealistic were prone to underestimate. Russian success in breaking our monopoly dramatically exposes the fallacy that atomic secrets relate principally to pure science.

But if the notion of *an* atomic secret is a fallacy, if the basic knowledge "never has been the property of one nation," then concealment must be concerned with the techniques for utilizing atomic energy rather than with the facts of nuclear physics. "So the question," as Newman and Miller observe, "becomes not 'Shall we keep the secrets of atomic energy?'—that is impossible—but rather, 'Will the control of atomic information in the United States delay other nations enough to warrant the resulting impairment of our own research and of international comity?' " [3]

Production of the radical new weapon first used in warfare at Hiroshima represented not only a great scientific discovery but also a tremendous engineering achievement. A vast number of stubborn technical problems had to be overcome; undoubtedly a great deal was learned in the course of this enterprise, and is being learned every day in the course of continuing experimentation, which it would be folly to disclose. This is not to say that others cannot eventually gain the same knowledge through patience and ingenuity; it is to say simply that there is no sense in helping them to acquire weapons that may one day be turned against us.

But this is not a novel problem. It must have presented itself in its essentials to the earliest users of the catapult and the crossbow. It is not basically different from the problem of protecting classified information about aircraft design or submarines or the

[3] Newman and Miller, op. cit., p. 212.

uses of radar. Although we try to keep concealed a large variety of adaptations and innovations we have perfected in connection with these weapons, we do not pretend that the weapons themselves are known only to us.

The task of concealment in respect of atomic bombs may be somewhat simplified by the very complexity of the subject. The extremely esoteric nature of the data, incomprehensible to any but highly trained specialists, makes their transmission peculiarly difficult; the ordinary spy would not know what to look for or how to interpret what he found. Moreover, the diversity and diffusion of the data, the numerous interlocking yet nevertheless compartmentalized spheres of specialization within the general subject of atomic energy, operate to prevent disclosure of more than isolated facets, which may well be meaningless in the absence of related information.[4] And finally, as in any large industrial project, the real "secret" may be an open one—may lie, this is to say, in techniques which can be learned only by long practice and experience.

In all probability there are no longer any mysteries about the internal combustion engine. American pre-eminence in the production of such engines was not the product of any exclusive scientific knowledge. On the contrary, it was much more a product of general familiarity with machinery of all kinds, a developed aptitude that became a source of immense strength. "Suppose," Dr. Karl T. Compton, former chairman of the Research and Development Board of the National Military Establishment, suggested to the Senate Military Affairs Committee,

[4] Writing about wartime scientific espionage, Dr. Samuel Goudsmit, an outstanding scientific intelligence officer and analyst, observed: "There were always fantastic rumors floating around about terrifying secret weapons and atom bombs which were duly reported by the OSS and British agents, but invariably the technical details were hopelessly nonsensical. The reason was obvious. No ordinary spy could get us the information we wanted for the simple reason that he lacked the scientific training to know what was essential. Only scientifically qualified personnel could get us that, and a Mata Hari with a Ph.D. in physics is rare, even in detective fiction." Quoted in *Report of the Special Committee on the Civil Liberties of Scientists to The Executive Committee, American Association for the Advancement of Science*, December 18, 1948.

about the time when we were boys, and the automotive engine was relatively in its infancy, some agency like the War Department had conceived the idea that this might be very useful as a future military development and had clamped down the imposition of secrecy in the further studies of high-octane fuels, metallurgy, thermodynamics, and engine design, and all other features which have to go to build the most efficient possible engine. These conditions of secrecy might have involved a prohibition against doing work in this field without a license and against any discussion with other workers in the same field except by federal permission, and no right of publication of results unless this commission thought that they would be of no aid to any foreign government. We can easily see what the results of such a policy would have been. Our own development of the automotive engine and the great automobile and aircraft business would have been greatly retarded in this country. Other countries operating without such prohibitions would have forged far ahead of us. . . . In a similar way, with any development of an important new field of science which may have important practical application for either peace or war, it seems to me that our first consideration for national economy and national security must be to handle this development with a minimum of inhibitions and a maximum of assistance and inducement. . . .[5]

Perhaps the real secret of American military might in the two world wars of the century was that machinery held no secrets for Americans. Almost every nation was capable of producing a gasoline motor. But what made the United States so formidable was the fact that it was capable of producing in a single year motors for a hundred thousand airplanes and five million or more for cars, tanks, and trucks. And it was capable of manning these machines with men who knew how to operate and repair them.

The McMahon-Douglas Atomic Energy Act of 1946 declares it "to be the policy of the people of the United States that, subject at all times to the paramount objective of assuring the common defense and security, the development and utilization of atomic energy shall, so far as practicable, be directed toward improving the public welfare, increasing the standard of living, strengthen-

[5] Quoted in AAAS *Report*.

ing free competition in private enterprise, and promoting world peace." The paramountcy of defense is apparent in every section of the act and nowhere more so than in connection with the control of information. Here the conflict between concealment and achievement is quite frankly revealed. Section 10 (a) of the act reads as follows:

Sec. 10. (a) *Policy.*—It shall be the policy of the Commission to control the dissemination of restricted data in such a manner as to assure the common defense and security. Consistent with such policy, the Commission shall be guided by the following principles:

(1) That until Congress declares by joint resolution that effective and enforceable international safeguards against the use of atomic energy for destructive purposes have been established, there shall be no exchange of information with other nations with respect to the use of atomic energy for industrial purposes; and

(2) That the dissemination of scientific and technical information relating to atomic energy should be permitted and encouraged so as to provide that free interchange of ideas and criticisms which is essential to scientific progress.

The Act places in a "restricted" category "all data concerning the manufacture or utilization of atomic weapons, the production of fissionable material, or the use of fissionable material in the production of power, but it does not include any data which the commission from time to time determines may be published without adversely affecting the common defense and security." This is an all-embracive definition which puts under control everything relating to atomic energy whether of a military or nonmilitary nature, save what the Atomic Energy Commission may choose specifically to declassify. With this definition as a base, the Act goes on to provide extremely severe penalties for communication, transmission, or disclosure of "restricted data."

The severity of these penalties indicates the peculiar gravity that Congress already attached in 1946 to any unauthorized disclosure of atomic information. The Espionage Act might have been held adequate to cover any aspect of atomic energy directly related to the national defense; it could not, however, be applied to the "secrets" of theoretical and applied nuclear physics. Besides, in 1946, the Espionage Act provided a death penalty only in time of war; otherwise its maximum punishment was twenty years in prison and a twenty-thousand-dollar fine. The Atomic Energy Act provides even in peacetime a death penalty or imprisonment for life on the recommendation of a jury in cases where the offense was committed with intent to injure the United States. Apparently Congress considered it worse to try to injure the country by transmitting restricted atomic data than by transmitting the details of a bomb sight—a reflection of the special reverence accorded atomic "secrets."

The sweep of the Atomic Energy Act is even more significant than the stringency of its punishments. These punishments are applicable not alone to officials of the government and to scientists working in government laboratories, but to all persons lawfully or unlawfully in possession of restricted data—including even scientists in private laboratories whose independent research may lead to the discovery of classified knowledge. The Atomic Energy Commission itself employs only a small number of scientific workers; and for the most part their jobs are concerned with administration rather than with research. Most scientists whose work involves access to restricted data are employed in university or industrial laboratories performing contract assignments for the Atomic Energy Commission.

The Act punishes carelessness or indiscretion as well as malevolence. There may be justification for this severity in the case of a public servant entrusted with official knowledge of a most delicate kind. If, however, an independent scientist publishes restricted information gleaned from his own researches, without any intention of injuring this country or aiding another, but with reason, in the opinion of a jury, to believe that the publication would have such results, he may be sent to prison for ten years and fined ten thousand dollars. Indeed, he may suffer these penalties for merely confiding what he has learned to an untrustworthy colleague. "A scientist who communicates restricted data to his colleagues must be certain," as Newman and Miller observe, "that they are loyal, trustworthy, and non-subversive; that they are fully acquainted with the control of information section of the Atomic Energy Act and with regulations relating to restricted data issued by the Commission; and that, in addition to being loyal and versed in the law, they are also discreet and keep good company."

The effect of this is to make perilous the very interchange of ideas and information indispensable to scientific progress. If men can communicate with their colleagues only at the risk of being held responsible for an indiscretion which a jury of non-scientists might conclude they should have avoided, the consequence may be to make hermits of them all. Whatever the dividends of such a policy in terms of keeping useful information from enemies, the price is exceedingly high in terms of keeping needed knowledge from friends.

Dr. J. Robert Oppenheimer, wartime director of the Los Alamos project and now head of the Institute for Advanced Study at Princeton University, once said that "the gossip of scientists who get together is the lifeblood of physics, and I think it must be in all other branches of science." The term "gossip" is an apt one in this context; it suggests talk that is uninhibited, easy, and informal. Out of such talk comes the mutual criticism, the fresh insight, the testing of preconceptions, that are the propelling elements of the experimental method and that produce a cross-fertilization of ideas. Scientists no less than writers, teachers, lawyers, and other men need this kind of communication. Formal publications—especially if they are rigorously expurgated—can never fill this need. If there is an element of risk to security in permitting scientists to work ungagged, there is also a heavy cost entailed in an insistence upon sterile isolation.

Isolated scientists are bound to be frustrated in ways that impair not only their individual work but the whole body of scientific knowledge. Teaching becomes difficult when certain areas of inquiry are taboo. The forbidden fields are likely to be neglected if only because trespass upon them is so risky; yet these are the very fields in which cultivation is most important to security.

Younger scientists, moreover, naturally prefer research fields in which they can publish their findings. In connection with atomic energy, their work may be stillborn; it may even, without their knowing it, merely duplicate work already done by others. The net effect of putting such boundaries upon research is at once to fence in what is already known, instead of expanding the range of discovery, and at the same time to discourage the development of talent for expansion in the future.

The problem is one of balance. The promotion of security by achievement cannot wholly rule out security by concealment. But it does demand that concealment be confined within the narrowest practicable limits. The report on the civil liberties of scientists prepared for the American Association for the Advancement of Science put the matter in perspective:

As in most matters worth discussing, we deal here not with absolute choices but with questions of degree and of emphasis. Our conclusion is that the information as to which secrecy should be enforced should, in the main, be limited to immediate military applications of scientific findings, rather than the findings themselves. Data useful for further research which is not purely developmental ought as a rule be made available to the scientific world rather than reserved for the military. Inquiries which have distinct and valuable civilian implications ought not to be inhibited because, at the same time, they have a military aspect. The major line we suggest drawing is between scientific knowledge, that is, recorded observations of natural phenomena, on the one hand, and military plans, programs, physical locations, designs, and mechanisms, on the other.

Professor Henry De W. Smyth, prior to becoming a member of the Atomic Energy Commission, stated the issue dramatically in testimony before the Senate Military Affairs Committee. "Secrecy in nuclear physics," he said, "will smother the hope of progress not only in that science but in all other sciences, both fundamental and applied. In my opinion, continued secrecy means national scientific suicide. . . ." [6] This is what the country can least afford from the point of view of its security. Whatever tem-

[6] Quoted in AAAS *Report*.

porary advantages concealment may afford, an indispensable attribute of military strength today is supremacy in atomic development.

There is another respect in which secrecy poses a serious threat to security. In keeping information about atomic energy from potential enemies, we keep at the same time from the American people the knowledge necessary to democratic determination of their own future. Secrecy undercuts the basis of government by the consent of the governed and thus exposes the nation to the risk of capricious or mistaken decisions by irresponsible authorities.

It can by no means be said that the administration alone is responsible for the emphasis on concealment. The Atomic Energy Commission—its former chairman, David Lilienthal, in particular —has repeatedly exhorted the public to take more interest in the non-military aspects of atomic energy; moreover, it has made efforts to declassify technical data as liberally as a suspicious, secrecy-conscious Congress would permit. Indeed, in deciding in 1947 to permit the export of radioactive isotopes for medical research abroad, the AEC drew upon itself a storm of protest from Senator Hickenlooper and other secrecy zealots. Concealment has been forced upon the AEC much more than it has been fostered by that agency. Congress, the general public, and even the press have shown an enthusiasm for secrecy that must be reckoned altogether remarkable in a country where executive authority has usually been subject to jealous scrutiny. So far from resenting or protesting against the unavailability of atomic information, the American people, generally speaking, have tended to avoid asking questions even about the most innocent aspects of the subject.

In part, this shyness has been due, no doubt, to the abstruseness of the subject. There is a widespread notion that it must remain incomprehensible to laymen because it involves esoteric scientific mysteries. But this is as though the public were to say it can understand nothing about radio because the science of electronics is beyond its grasp. It is no more necessary to be a nuclear physicist in order to form intelligent opinions about the utilization or application of atomic energy than it is necessary to be an electronics engineer in order to form intelligent opinions about the social impact of broadcasting. The policies adopted in developing atomic energy cannot fail to have immensely important effects upon the culture, the economy, and the political future of the American people. If these policies are to be democratically determined, there must be a great deal more public information and discussion of the subject than is possible at present.

The press, not usually notable for its diffidence, has been conspicuously reticent in this area. Newspapermen who unblinkingly question the President of the United States or members of his cabinet about the most delicate diplomatic issues, who are accustomed to inquire very searchingly into details of military and naval strategy, fall into a deferential and docile silence when told that any piece of information they may seek about atomic energy is in a restricted category. The newspapers deal sensationally with tidbits of scandal concerning atomic energy—the news that a milligram of U-235 has been misplaced, or that the Atomic Energy Commission is guilty of "incredible mismanagement." But they do very little probing as to the utilization of atomic resources or the policies of the commission in letting contracts and fostering research, or the facts about the size of the atomic stockpile or the rate of production of atomic bombs or the progress in nonmilitary aspects of atomic energy. They do not even question very vigorously the wisdom of the government's refusal to make such facts available.

Yet in the absence of such facts the public is excluded from participation in the shaping of vastly important public policies. It is impossible to form an intelligent judgment as to the desirability of, say, building battleships or of universal military training or of an air force devoted to the idea of strategic bombing, without knowledge about the number and potency of atomic bombs. Censorship concerning the development of hydrogen bombs is as rigid as it could possibly be in Russia, and it is accepted almost as meekly. In March 1950 the Atomic Energy Com-

mission issued by telegram a ukase to all its consultants, its
employees, and the employees of its contractors, "requesting"
them "to avoid the release of technical information which even
though itself unclassified may be interpreted by virtue of the
project connection of the speaker as reflecting upon the comis-
sion's program with respect to thermo-nuclear weapons"—that
is, hydrogen bombs.

Before receiving this request, Dr. Hans A. Bethe, professor of
physics at Cornell University, an outstanding authority in the
thermo-nuclear field and a contract consultant to the AEC, had
written an article about the hydrogen-bomb project for *Scientific
American* and the *Bulletin of the Atomic Scientists*. After the
April issue of *Scientific American* had gone to press, the magazine
received a request from the AEC to delete several sentences from
the technical portion of the article. An AEC security officer came
to the magazine's printing plant and supervised destruction of the
type, the melting down of the printing plates with the deleted
material, and the burning of three thousand copies of the publication which had been printed before the presses were stopped.

The sole offensive feature of Professor Bethe's article appears
to have lain in his authoritative connection with its subject. The
information he gave had been formally declassified by the AEC
and had also been previously published either by himself or by
other physicists. But the commission evidently feared that there
would be danger in his discussion of it because readers might
construe what he said as reflective of secret data. The effect of the
commission's action was not alone to gag Professor Bethe, but at
the same time to blindfold the public.

There exist among scientists and others some realistic doubts as
to the wisdom of devoting a large part of the country's resources,
technical skills, and energy to the perfection of a hydrogen bomb.
The effectiveness of such a bomb from a military point of view
is seriously questioned. Although it is assumed that it will be a
thousand times as powerful as the Hiroshima bomb, much of its
power as a weapon might be wasted; it would have been pointless
at Hiroshima, for example, to destroy that city any more thor-

oughly than it was destroyed or to kill its inhabitants any more thoroughly than they were killed. Development of the H-bomb will consume raw materials, facilities, and technical abilities that might otherwise be devoted to enlarging the stockpile of plutonium bombs; it will also frustrate the development of atomic power for non-military uses. And it will certainly raise psychological and political problems of great consequence in our international relations.

Yet the American people have no means of expressing any views on so momentous a decision. Cut off from authoritative discussion even of information which is not restricted, they are cozened again into the comfortable delusion that they possess exclusively a decisive super-weapon that can protect the country from attack and force the submission of any enemy. The silencing of Professor Bethe is significant not so much for its infringement of his rights as an individual as for its infringement of the right of the American people to know what they need to know if they are to be self-governing.

The *Bulletin of the Atomic Scientists* spoke out on this score in a vigorous editorial in its May 1950 issue:

Americans are accustomed to hearing their military and political leaders and experts, from the President and Defense Secretary down to colonels and captains (not to speak of members of congressional committees), talk publicly about matters of military preparedness, national strategy, and tactics—although the access of these officials to secret information cannot but influence their statements. Even when they have used this information rather recklessly—as in last year's controversy over the B-36 and strategic bombing—no attempt was made to muzzle them. Some things said in the heat of this controversy would have been better left unsaid; but on the whole, public discussion of fundamental aspects of national military planning, of the Armed Forces and the weapons available to the nation, and the ways in which they are intended to be used, belongs to the democratic way of evolving national policies. Fission bombs, thermo-nuclear bombs, radio-active poisons, and bacteriological weapons cannot be excluded from this discussion without making the American people blind to some of the most important elements affecting our political and military decisions.

In this discussion, scientists who have the most complete knowledge of the facts, and the deepest understanding of the possibilities, have the right (and the duty) to participate, since they are best able to enlighten public opinion. The judgment they have shown so far does not justify apprehension that they will speak out too lightly or irresponsibly.

Some information must undoubtedly be kept from the public in order to keep it from potential enemies. But the striking of a rational balance respecting secrecy is as important in relation to the people as a whole as it is in relation to the scientists themselves if the democratic process is to be preserved.

Security by concealment and security by achievement alike must rest largely upon the selection of those who are to be entrusted with access to restricted data. The scientists are today's supermen. Their special knowledge is a prime source of military strength. It is also a prime threat to this strength. In the ominous language of the underworld, "They know too much." Thus they are at once the most valued and the most distrusted members of contemporary society.

Behind this distrust of the scientists lies an unconscious distrust of intellectuals in general—that is to say, of men with ideas. Men with ideas are liable to be unorthodox—today's euphemism for disloyal or untrustworthy. The discovery that information of military value concerning atomic energy was imparted to Russian agents by Dr. Alan Nunn May, and later by Dr. Klaus Fuchs, operated to fortify the distrust of scientists. Dr. May's defense of his perfidy was that science is supra-national in character and therefore gives all its votaries a right to communicate ideas freely to their colleagues regardless of national interests. Dr. Fuchs, on the other hand, ascribed his acts of betrayal to a peculiar form of schizophrenia in which one half of his personality was devoted to the Communist cause. Because military men, generally, are not subject to such rarefied rationalizations and divided loyalties, there has been from the beginning of the atomic energy program a persistent pressure to keep it under Army control. But military men are not apt to know much about the niceties of nuclear fission, nor are they temperamentally suited to the management of a great research project. Besides, military subordination to civilian authority is a premise of every free society.

Although the early steps in developing nuclear fission were accomplished by scientists working on their own initiative entirely outside the government—and subject only to their own self-imposed secrecy regulations—the tremendous engineering task of making the first atomic bombs was carried out under Army auspices, through the Manhattan Engineering District commanded by Brigadier General Leslie R. Groves. There were many who felt that because the most obvious potentiality of atomic energy lay in the production of war weapons, control should remain with the Army. The May-Johnson bill, nearly enacted into law in 1946, was designed to fix responsibility in this way. But a clamor arose at once, led in large part by the scientists, to transfer the task of developing atomic energy to a civilian commission. The scientists, who had suffered under the rigid security controls and compartmentalization of knowledge imposed by General Groves, argued that military dominance would frustrate research and therefore impede the maintenance of American supremacy in atomic armament. In their battle for subordination of the Army to civilian authority, they displayed more political insight and more awareness of American traditions than many legislators. The McMahon-Douglas Act was adopted at last, although only after the addition to it of a provision establishing a military liaison committee with semi-autonomous powers. Suggestions that control ought to be returned to the military continue to be made from time to time.

The basic security provision of the McMahon-Douglas Act is its requirement of loyalty clearance for all persons having access to restricted data. An attempt was made—and fortunately defeated—to require FBI approval of all AEC personnel. As finally adopted, the Act declares that, except as authorized by the AEC in case of emergency, "no individual shall be employed by the Commission until the Federal Bureau of Investigation shall have made an investigation and report to the Commission on the character, associations, and loyalty of such individual." And in addition to this, business concerns acting under contract or license by the AEC must agree in writing "not to permit any individual to have access to restricted data until the Federal Bureau of Investigation shall have made an investigation and report to the Commission on the character, associations, and loyalty of such individual and the Commission shall have determined that permitting such person to have access to restricted data will not injure the common defense or security."

There are three related provisions of law not contained in the Atomic Energy Act which should nevertheless be considered in this connection, since they profoundly affect the conditions under which men of science are obliged or permitted to work. The National Military Establishment requires "clearance" of great numbers of persons engaged in the planning or production of articles for military use. This applies not only to scientists employed directly in laboratories operated by one or another of the Armed Services, but also to scientists serving in other agencies of the government—the Bureau of Standards or the Public Health Service, for example—who may work at times on projects which have been given a classified status; and it applies also to scientists employed by business corporations and academic institutions performing classified work under contract. In addition, two other statutes provide for clearance of science students. Under the terms of the National Science Foundation Act, all beneficiaries of its funds are subject to FBI investigation; and this is true also of students who are awarded Atomic Energy Fellowships, although their studies afford them no access whatever to restricted data.

Obviously these last stipulations are punitive, not protective. They are based on congressional frenzy over discovery that the AEC had unwittingly awarded a fellowship to a single Communist and on the theory that "disloyal" persons ought not to be given the advantages of scientific education at public expense. But to forestall the possibility that a few Communist sympathizers might qualify for these federal benefits, all applicants for science scholarships or Atomic Energy Fellowships are subjected to a humiliating oath and an FBI investigation that may uncover innocent but embarrassing facets of their pasts. Senator Claude D. Pepper pointed out in the course of debate on the stipulation in the Atomic Energy Appropriation bill that "there is no right of appeal given in the amendment to a young man who wins this honor but is denied it because the FBI says something against him that may cause the Commission to think that he is not a fit subject. He is condemned without a hearing. . . ." And Senator McMahon said, "I should like to point out that what we are doing is imposing a test upon students . . . which we do not impose on any grant we give to students in any other field or in any university." If the idea of denying education on account of "disloyalty" were to be extended to all beneficiaries under the GI Bill of Rights, or to carry it to its logical conclusion, to all public school pupils, we should end by having an FBI dossier on every young man and woman in the United States.

There can be no question as to the imperative need for great caution in qualifying persons for access to restricted data. What may reasonably be questioned, however, is the validity of the tests and standards used in clearance procedures. The Joint Committee on Atomic Energy had this to say on the subject in its report on the Hickenlooper charges:

Denying information to the potential enemy involves a probe into the minds and hearts of the human beings who work on our atomic energy project. If their "character, associations, and loyalty" fail to meet certain standards, they are refused access to "restricted data" as defined in the McMahon Act. Since direct contact with the complete inner workings of a man's brain cannot be established by any means, even through hypnosis or the use of drugs, reliance is placed upon his spoken utterances, the company he keeps, the organizations he joins, the reputation he enjoys, and similar matters—as developed through an FBI investigation. This phase of guarding secrets is known as personnel security. It transcends all other phases in importance; for a person who is cunningly disloyal or addicted to alcohol or merely indiscreet might betray confidences despite all additional checks designed to keep information inviolate.

The principal defect in this formulation is that, as in the loyalty program, the tendency is to trust orthodoxy—an attribute more likely to be a liability than an asset in scientific research. In judging the future dependability of a scientist from the point of view of security, reliance on "his spoken utterances, the company he keeps, the organizations he joins" may be even more misleading than in the case of a lawyer, an economist or a foreign service officer. This is particularly true when reliance is placed on these considerations as disclosed in an FBI report; for the FBI naturally seeks unconventional utterances and associations, presenting these as "derogatory information." It may well be that a mind capable of grappling with theoretical physics would seem perplexing or peculiar—and therefore untrustworthy—to the mind of an FBI agent.

Moreover, brilliant scientists are sometimes politically naive. The best of them are likely to be men of genius; and it should not be surprising if they exhibit certain eccentricities of genius. They may have uttered the "wrong" political opinions or associated with the "wrong" people and still be valuable assets to the national defense, thoroughly dependable in situations where the need for secrecy has been made clear to them. A good many of the individuals who contributed most to American primacy in developing atomic energy belong, perhaps, in this category. Indeed, it is exceedingly doubtful whether, if they were now young and unknown men, without the prestige of their tremendous wartime work behind them, they could pass the security standards currently enforced by the Atomic Energy Commission.

Dr. J. Robert Oppenheimer, for example, was charged by an ex-Communist testifying in May 1950 before the California State Legislature's Committee on Un-American Activities with having attended a Communist party meeting in California in 1941. He has categorically denied this allegation. But in the early days of the Manhattan District Project he candidly disclosed to its military director, General Groves, that he had belonged to several Left-wing organizations, that he had once entertained a Communist Party organizer at his home, and that he had even on one occasion been approached for atomic information by an agent acting at the behest of an official of the Soviet consulate in San Francisco. No contemporary security board would dare to qualify an obscure scientist with such "derogatory" information in his record, no matter what his professional competence and promise. Yet General Groves, to his credit, took what must have seemed to him a calculated risk on Dr. Oppenheimer and placed him in charge of the Los Alamos laboratory, where the first uranium bomb was actually perfected and detonated. It is generally agreed among his colleagues that Dr. Oppenheimer contributed at least as much as any individual to this result. He continues to serve the AEC as chairman of its General Advisory Committee and ranks as one of the country's most distinguished physicists. The loss of Dr. Oppenheimer's services would be a high price to pay in terms of security by achievement for the sake of security by concealment.

One of the lamentable aspects of personnel security is its tendency to spread beyond rational security requirements. In projects where only a few scientists need or are granted access to restricted data, the clearance mechanism is sometimes extended to associates who have no connection with classified work. At the Brookhaven National Laboratory, according to the report of the AAAS Committee on the Civil Liberties of Scientists, about ninety per cent of the work is concerned with fundamental nuclear and radiological research and is wholly unrestricted. The remaining work, having to do with a uranium-graphite reactor, is, of course, highly classified. But all the scientific personnel at Brookhaven have to be cleared on the ground that those who have access to restricted data mingle socially with those who do not. The same policy has been enforced in some of the industrial laboratories where classified research occupies only a fraction of the personnel. One effect of this, says the AAAS special committee, is that "Scientists who have no desire to work in classified fields or to use restricted data are being barred from important non-secret research because of clearance difficulties."

FBI investigation poses certain formidable hazards. It involves awkward questioning of relatives and professional associates. It may involve a long, costly, and nerve-wracking period of uncertainty and idleness pending clearance. It may involve in the end a rejection that could mean the ruin of a career. These hazards sometimes keep young men of "liberal" or "Leftist" backgrounds from volunteering for or accepting appointments to classified jobs which they are well qualified to fill and for which they could probably be cleared if they were willing to put their reputations to the test. But the by-ways are safer and pleasanter.

The injuries suffered by individual scientists in consequence of the prevailing concealment obsession could perhaps be considered negligible if they contributed genuinely to national security. But the country's pressing need for scientific supremacy is scarcely served by a profligate waste of scientific talent.

More damaging and dangerous than the formal clearance procedures required by law is the systematic harassment of scientists by the House Committee on Un-American Activities and other inquisitorial bodies. Spy scares are their staff of life. And although they have not yet succeeded in producing a single instance in which an American scientist has been shown to have divulged confidential information about atomic energy to any foreign agent or other unauthorized person, this has not reflected any want of effort or imagination on their part. Through unremitting hospitality to professional ex-Communists and self-styled former FBI undercover agents, they have managed to besmirch the reputations—and destroy the usefulness—of a number of scientists who might otherwise have advanced the country's atomic-energy program. They have managed also to maintain a feverish state of popular anxiety over the safety of the national secrets.

The ordeal to which Dr. Edward U. Condon, director of the National Bureau of Standards, was subjected by the Un-American Activities Committee is only the most celebrated case in point. Dr. Condon is recognized among scientists as one of the foremost living authorities on quantum mechanics, microwave electronics, and radioactivity. He played an important part in the development of both radar and atomic energy. He was one of the first men summoned in 1940 to serve on the National Defense Research Committee and became a pioneer member in 1941 of the Roosevelt Committee on Uranium Research. Throughout the congressional consideration of atomic-control legislation, he served as scientific adviser to the Special Committee on Atomic Energy.

Nevertheless on March 1, 1948, a subcommittee of the House Committee on Un-American Activities released to the press a formal report which asserted that "from the evidence at hand, it appears that Dr. Condon is one of the weakest links in our atomic security." The "evidence at hand" as presented in the subcommittee's press release consisted of some generalizations about Soviet espionage aims, including the dubious observation that "the Bureau of Standards, because of its importance to the national defense, has become a focal point for espionage agents attached to foreign governments," the unsupported charge that "Dr. Condon, knowingly or unknowingly, entertained and associated with persons who are alleged Soviet espionage agents," and a portion of a confidential FBI loyalty report which stated that "the files of the bureau reflect that Dr. Edward U. Condon has been in contact as late as 1947 with an individual alleged by a self-confessed Soviet espionage agent [presumably Elizabeth Bentley] to have engaged in espionage activities with the Russians in Washington, D. C., from 1941 to 1944."

The "evidence at hand," as presented, did not include that portion of the FBI report which declared: "There is no evidence to show that contacts between this individual and Dr. Condon were related to this individual's espionage activities." This not irrelevant sentence was "inadvertently" omitted according to the subcommittee chairman, Representative J. Parnell Thomas. Nor did "the evidence at hand" include any testimony on the part of Dr. Condon himself, who was given no opportunity to testify in response to these charges either before they were made public or during the subsequent ten months of Mr. Thomas's tenure as chairman, although he asked repeatedly to be heard in his own defense.

Dr. Condon's vindication had to come from the Atomic Energy Commission, which asked the FBI to search the minutiae of his past, checked the files of Army Intelligence, and after studying the voluminous record reached the conclusion that there is "no question whatever concerning Dr. Condon's loyalty to the United States."

The effect of this assault on a distinguished scientist's integrity —and of the numerous assaults on less distinguished scientists— cannot be quantitatively reckoned. The open-house invitation extended by legislative investigators to every renegade Communist and stool pigeon, and the eager credence given their sensational allegations, operate as a powerful deterrent to security by achievement.

One way in which a foreign power might seek to cripple the American atomic energy program would be to single out a few of the country's foremost nuclear physicists—there are not so very many—and dispose of them by assassination. A knife-thrust in the dark, a bullet fired from ambush, a drop or two of poison— these could effectively take out of action the men who have done the most to create American supremacy in atomic weapons, such men as, say, Bacher, Rabi, Fermi, Bethe, Condon, Oppenheimer. These men carry about in their minds secrets—and the skill to discover new secrets—more valuable than any that could possibly be uncovered by espionage.

But murder is a messy, awkward business. The assassins might be caught and executed; the plot might be discerned before it could be completed. Moreover, it is quite unnecessary. How much more simply the same results can be achieved by a few words craftily spoken before some legislative committee or whispered anonymously to an FBI investigator! Character assassination is at once easier and surer than physical assault; and it involves far less risk for the assassin. It leaves him free to commit the same deed over and over again, and may, indeed, win him the honors of a hero even in the country of his victims.

As President Truman observed in an address to the AAAS in 1948, "We cannot drive scientists into our laboratories, but, if we tolerate reckless or unfair attacks, we can certainly drive them out."

CHAPTER IX

UNIVERSITIES
AND INTELLECTUAL FREEDOM

This institution will be based on the illimitable freedom of the human mind. For here we are not afraid to follow truth wherever it may lead, nor to tolerate error so long as reason is left free to combat it.[1]

IN MID-MAY of 1950, President Dwight D. Eisenhower of Columbia University sent to some seven hundred and fifty institutions of higher learning in all parts of the world an invitation to join in celebrating Columbia's two hundredth anniversary in 1954. The invitation read, in part:

In considering what would be the most appropriate theme for Columbia to emphasize in its celebration, the trustees, aided by a committee representing the faculties, students, and alumni, have agreed that there is one principle which all free universities unfailingly must defend. This is the ideal of full freedom of scholarly inquiry and expression, the right of mankind to knowledge and the free use thereof.

For many centuries the civilized world has held that this privilege is essential to human liberty, welfare, and progress. Unhappily, it is now being subjected to serious and systematic attack in many lands. . . .

This tradition of academic freedom has ancient roots in the great universities of Europe, which, from their inception, were

[1] Thomas Jefferson, in a letter to prospective members of the faculty of the University of Virginia.

governed by their faculties. It has only recently received the recognition even of general homage in the United States. With some notable exceptions, American colleges, and especially the great number which came into being during the latter half of the nineteenth century, were conducted in considerable degree as proprietary institutions. Their faculty members were underpaid and were looked upon by the wealthy patrons who supported them as refugees from the world of competition. They were expected to observe the written and unwritten rules drawn up by regents and trustees representing these patrons. Tenure in their positions was dependent not merely on good behavior but on orthodoxy of opinion. Every period of national emergency produced academic purges in which teachers were the scapegoats of the country's anxieties and emotionalism.

The tendency to see danger in unorthodox ideas is greatest, of course, in times of tension. This is particularly true when the ideas appear to indicate disloyalty to the nation. Thus, in the excitement of the First World War, the regents of the University of Minnesota ousted a professor who had served as a member of its faculty for sixteen years, on the ground that he was "a rabid pro-German" and that "unqualified loyalty" to the United States must be a condition of employment in any American institution. In 1938, however—twenty-one years later—the action was rescinded, the resolution requiring it was expunged from the regents' records, and the teacher was made a professor emeritus.

The traditions of Harvard made it possible for that university to act quite differently in a similar situation. Professor Hugo Münsterberg was also accused of pro-Germanism during the First World War, and a rich alumnus threatened to annul a bequest of ten million dollars to the university unless Münsterberg was immediately deprived of his professorship. The "disloyal" professor promptly wrote to the Harvard Corporation, tendering his resignation if the graduate would immediately remit five million dollars to the Corporation. The response of the Corporation was a public announcement: "It is now officially stated that, at the instance of the authorities, Professor Münsterberg's resignation has been withdrawn, and that the university cannot tolerate any suggestion that it would be willing to accept money to abridge free speech, to remove a professor or to accept his resignation."

The consistency with which instances of intolerance have brought a later feeling of shame, as in the case of the University of Minnesota, should suggest that the principles of academic freedom and tenure are useful in practice as well as in theory. But this appears to be one of the lessons that each generation is obliged to learn for itself. It was not until the American Association of University Professors was established in 1915 that the right of the teaching profession to freedom and tenure won general recognition, even in theory, and that the profession itself presented anything like a coordinated front in defense of those principles. Since then, the Association's Committee A (on Academic Freedom and Academic Tenure) has had an extremely busy existence; it has investigated and tried to adjust more than a hundred cases of alleged violations annually. Its view of academic freedom was defined in 1940 in these terms:

(a) The teacher is entitled to full freedom in research and in the publication of the results, subject to the adequate performance of his other academic duties; but research for pecuniary return should be based upon an understanding with the authorities of the institution.

(b) The teacher is entitled to freedom in the classroom in discussing his subject, but he should be careful not to introduce into his teaching controversial matter which has no relation to his subject. Limitations of academic freedom because of religious or other aims of the institution should be clearly stated in writing at the time of the appointment.

(c) The college or university teacher is a citizen, a member of a learned profession, and an officer of an educational institution. When he speaks or writes as a citizen, he should be free from institutional censorship or discipline, but his special position in the community imposes special obligations. As a man of learning and an educational officer, he should remember that the public may judge his profession and his institution by his utterances. Hence he should at all times be accurate, should exercise appropriate restraint, should show respect for the opinions of others, and should make every effort to indicate that he is not an institutional spokesman.

Tenure is simply a means to the maintenance of academic freedom. "After the expiration of a probationary period," says the 1940 AAUP Statement of Principles, "teachers or investigators should have permanent or continuous tenure, and their services should be terminated only for adequate cause. . . ." The probationary period is set at a maximum of seven years. "Adequate cause," including such offenses as gross immorality, treason, neglect of duty, and incompetence, is to be judged by a group of the teacher's professional colleagues as well as by the institution's governing body, under procedures in conformity with Anglo-Saxon traditions of justice—written charges, confrontation of accusers, and a chance to be heard in his own defense. The simple, practical purpose of these principles is to enable a teacher to follow the truth as he sees it without fear of losing his job. Teachers fearful of expressing unpopular ideas are neither free men nor good teachers. They cannot command the respect of students and they cannot give society the full benefits of research. Academic freedom and tenure are not privileges extended to the teaching profession, but a form of insurance to society that the teaching profession will be able to discharge its function conscientiously.

General Eisenhower's reference to the attack upon academic freedom points plainly, and justifiably, to the countries behind the iron curtain. Education there has been made an outright instrument of the State, a form of propaganda. Only the most rigid conformity is tolerated among teachers. Even scientific doctrines which have won universal civilized acceptance are ignored or distorted for the sake of official aims. There has certainly been no comparable disregard of truth or suppression of free inquiry in the United States. We have had no Trofim Lysenko to lay down a party line on genetics and to threaten with official wrath any researcher who dares to find value in the work of Malthus or Mendel. It may be healthy, nevertheless, to look critically at the state of academic freedom in this country.

The Russians have no room in their schools for "men alien to the world outlook of the Soviet people" or "Menshevik idealists in philosophy and science" or "rotten liberals" or "propagators of the harmful, hostile myth of the international unity of science" [2]—which is to say, the unorthodox from the Communist point of view. But our own schools today are not generally hospitable to any unorthodoxy from our point of view. Communists are not much more likely to teach in American institutions than capitalists in Russia. Moreover, the attempt to purge American institutions of Communist unorthodoxy has resulted in their being purged of other forms of unorthodoxy as well. It has produced a powerful drive toward conformity.

This drive is one more expression of the pervasive personal insecurity and anxiety of our time. It does not promote the national security. The country cannot be said to be endangered by "disloyalty" among teachers in the way that it might be endangered by "disloyalty" among government employees. Institutions of learning are not, in general, profitable places for spies and saboteurs. There are no official secrets to be gleaned there, except in the laboratories devoted to special research for the government; and everyone with access to such projects is meticulously screened by the Atomic Energy Commission or the National Military Establishment. The danger apprehended in the schools is not espionage or sabotage, but heresy.

If Communists or other nonconformists are dangerous as teachers, it must be on account of their ideas. To the extent that there is a rationalization of the current anxiety about teachers, it reflects a fear that their ideas will subvert the devotion of young minds to the patterns of free enterprise and "the American way of life." But the loyalty of free men is not readily overborne. The dominant cultural bents of a society are not lightly forsaken—especially if each generation is allowed to challenge them, or hear them challenged, and is left free to accept or reject its inheritance.

Even the most skilled of Communist propagandists is unlikely

[2] Epithets applied to those who differed from Lysenko's ideas of heredity—quoted by Bertram D. Wolfe in "Science Joins the Party," *The Antioch Review*, Spring 1950.

to be effective in the face of the overwhelming forces that propel young Americans toward devotion to the United States. If students are led to question existing institutions, that is a healthy part of the educational process; they need to be made to doubt, to wonder, and to form judgments of their own, so that their loyalty, when they mature, will be something more than mere nationalism. There is no reason to fear that the ideas of a "disloyal" teacher will prevail over the ideas of "loyal" teachers and over the ideas students receive in their homes, their churches, and their voluntary associations. Why is it that the Americanists seem to take it for granted that communism, with all its repressive discipline and submergence of the individual, will prove more attractive to young minds than democracy?

The answer certainly lies, at least partly, in the sterile nature of the Americanist notion of democracy. Men who see communism in a desire to repeal poll taxes or to aid sharecroppers or to strengthen labor unions or to amend shortcomings of the free-enterprise system tend naturally to fear that it will win converts widely. Moreover, the fear of freedom, the hostility to change, the distrust of ideas that characterize the Americanists make education the special target of their anxiety. Teachers, like scientists, being pre-eminently men of ideas, are peculiarly subject to suspicion. Inquiry and challenge are their business. But inquiry and challenge are precisely what the stereotyped "loyalty" of the Americanists can least tolerate. Their purge program is aimed, therefore, at all teachers who dare to question the eternal verity of established patterns. This effort to lay down standards of political purity for the schools operates as a powerful form of intimidation, limiting the freedom of teachers to express their views in the classroom or outside it—and, as a result, also limiting their ability to discharge their vital function.

The first recourse of the Americanists is to require of teachers a special oath of allegiance—an oath that can have no efficacy in restraining actual disloyalty to the United States, but serves well enough to silence criticism and independent thinking.

The proponents of special loyalty oaths for teachers commonly ask the question, "Why not?" They mean by this innocent query that they can see no reason why a patriotic American should object to swearing that he is not a member of the Communist Party or its affiliates and that he does not advocate overthrow of the United States government by force or violence. Stated in so bald a way, the requirement of a test oath may seem unexceptionable. There are few teachers who could not take such an oath in good conscience.

But a prior and more apposite question is "Why?" Why should teachers be singled out as a special class and be asked to profess their innocence of an attitude which there is no good reason to suspect them of holding? Why should the public interest demand this of teachers if it does not demand it of lawyers or physicians or certified public accountants or businessmen? Why should they be expected to swear that they are not Communists any more than they are expected to swear that they are not counterfeiters or embezzlers? Teachers are understandably sensitive to the groundless suggestion that theirs is a profession peculiarly infiltrated by the Communists and peculiarly lacking in loyalty to the United States.

Some of them are even more sensitive, however, to the suggestion that membership in their profession ought to be conditioned upon any standard of political orthodoxy—including the standard of loyalty to the State. The danger presented by an occasional teacher who might be disloyal—as Professor Münsterberg was accused of being at Harvard in 1918—does not seem nearly so great as the danger that the introduction of a political test will result in the dismissal of men for honest though misguided convictions. It can scarcely be doubted that to require a non-Communist oath of teachers is to impose a political test. And this remains true even though the Communist Party is an alien conspiracy and not a political party in the accepted American sense; it is a political conspiracy, and membership in it is a political act expressing political belief. Furthermore, it is an act which, at least until recently, has been considered entirely lawful.

Requiring a non-Communist oath of all teachers inflicts upon any teacher who belongs to the party the punishment of permanent exclusion from his profession. Many teachers who abhor the party are unwilling, nevertheless, to punish a colleague in this way for adherence to it. If they consent, themselves, to take the oath, then they force disclosure and punishment on the few who are unable to take it. There was a period in American history when anti-Catholic feeling ran very high; indeed it was widely believed that Catholics had an allegiance to the Vatican transcending their allegiance to the United States. If another "Know Nothing" movement should ever develop here, no doubt there would be Americans able truthfully to swear that they were not Catholics, but unwilling to do so because the effect of such an oath would be to expose Catholic Americans to punishment for their beliefs. Even among Americans who had no sympathy for Catholicism there would surely be some who would value tolerance enough to protect the holding of opinions they did not share. Just so, there are teachers today who value academic freedom enough to protect the holding of hated and even disloyal political views on the part of a few members of their profession whose scholarship and classroom performance are satisfactory and whose conduct violates no law.

To say that proscription from a profession is not punishment is to ignore reality. It is not only punishment of an exceedingly painful kind but it is punishment visited peculiarly on those who refuse to swear falsely. Moreover, it is in many cases an *ex post facto* punishment. It operates like the post-Civil War test oaths to penalize men for past errors. In the Missouri Test Oath cases of 1867,[3] counsel for Glover dealt with these points in memorable words:

We will not punish treason against the United States or this State, or any other offence mentioned in this long catalogue, but unless thou canst or wilt swear that thou hast done none of these acts, we will deprive thee of thy means of living, and thy places of honor and profit held by thee of the gift of private individuals—thou shall not serve at

[3] See Chapter I, p. 10, note.

the law, nor receive the profits of its profession—thou shall not minister at the altar of God, nor receive a salary from those worshipping thereat —thou shall not teach the young mind the truth, nor receive pay therefor—thou shall not direct the business of any private corporation, although its wealth be all thine own. We will not punish thee—we are merciful! But go—we proclaim thee an outlaw, disabled from following thy past calling—we forbid thee earth, fire and water, and commend thee to the charity of some other country in which we wish thee all success.

No punishment? I defy the history of the world to invent a punishment more refined and ingenious than to punish a man through his love of truth, his adherence to his word. He will not lie, he will not swear a false oath; no matter how guilty he be of offences, he has a regard for the truth and will not lay a perjury to his soul. It is indeed an ingenious punishment; it dispenses with statutes defining offences and providing penalties therefor; it dispenses with courts, with all their paraphernalia of indictments by grand juries and trial by petit juries, executing the law upon offenders; all that is needed, is, that a law be passed every year or two requiring every citizen to swear that he has never wronged or defrauded anyone; that he has never slandered his neighbor; that he has never committed murder, burglary, larceny, adultery or fornication; and if he cannot thus swear, then forbid him to follow any profession, trade or calling, for that will not be a punishment inflicted upon him, but a mere regulation of the trades, callings, and professions in the State. . . .[4]

Loyalty oaths involve two real dangers for the teaching profession; and the dangers are, in point of fact, greater for non-Communists than for Communists. The oaths are effective only to the extent that they are buttressed by the threat of prosecution for perjury. But this threat has serious implications for a teacher who does not belong to the Communist Party—and could therefore take the oath in good conscience—but who had expressed heterodox opinions or had belonged at one time or another to suspect Left-wing organizations designated as subversive by an attorney general or a legislative committee. Such a teacher would be forever in danger that, maliciously or mistakenly, he

[4] Murphy and Glover Test Oath Cases, 41 Mo. 340, pp. 360-61.

would be charged with membership in the Communist Party. He might find himself, then, subject to prosecution for perjury with all the difficulties inherent in attempting to refute an allegation which is in a real sense irrefutable. These difficulties may be peculiarly grave for ex-Communists, who outnumber present members of the party by at least five to one. Withdrawal from an organization is not easily demonstrated. In a tense time like the present, juries are not disposed to give much weight to the protestations of an accused who admits that he once belonged to the party or to an organization which seemed innocent enough when he joined it, but which has since been ruled to be subversive. Thus, loyalty oaths may well operate to penalize men for past conduct which was in no sense criminal or even disloyal.

The difficulty of determining the precise point at which a Communist becomes an ex-Communist was illustrated by the testimony of Mr. Lee Pressman before the House Committee on Un-American Activities on August 28, 1950. The transition in his case was by no means an abrupt one; indeed, it extended, apparently, over a period of about fifteen years. About 1934, Mr. Pressman told the committee, he joined a Communist group or cell consisting of himself and three other employees of the Department of Agriculture. In the latter part of 1935 he left government service to re-enter private law practice in New York and "discontinued any further participation in the group." This ended, as he put it, his *organizational* contact with the Communist Party.

But Mr. Pressman, by his own admission, did not come to a final ideological break with the party until 1950. His status in the intervening years is not easily defined. If his testimony is accepted, he was not, to use the conventional cliché, a "card-carrying member" of the Communist Party. Does it follow from this, however, that he was not a Communist? The question illuminates a real difficulty inherent in non-Communist oath requirements. The difficulty is revealed also in a news story in the *Daily Worker* of the same day that "Ben Gold, president of the International Fur and Leather Workers Union, yesterday announced his resignation from the Communist Party in order to comply with the Taft-Hartley law. . . . Gold at the same time made it clear that he did not abandon the convictions gained in nearly thirty years of membership in the Communist Party." Affiliation with the Communist Party may take different forms. It is, to a certain extent at least, subjective, and it is often not easy to prove or disprove. But independent opinions which parallel those voiced by the party may easily be misconstrued as indicative of affiliation.

The second serious danger of the loyalty oaths is that they are likely to lead universities into a pattern of investigation like that now pursued by the federal government. Communists do not necessarily wear any identifying insignia and may subscribe to a non-Communist affidavit falsely. To enforce the proscription against them effectively means, therefore, inquiry into the private beliefs, activities, and associations of all teachers. Institutions of learning would be obliged to undertake secret investigations of the members of their faculties; these in turn would require star-chamber hearings and judgments of guilt by association on the basis of testimony from anonymous accusers. The procedure is one that opens the door to a wholesale harassment of teachers who deviate in any way from strict orthodoxy. It is a cure that seems a great deal more painful and malignant than the disease.

There is an old story from Russia that seems pertinent enough to bear repeating in this connection. A large number of rabbits came streaming westward across the Polish border about 1930. "Why are you running?" the Poles asked them. "Because Stalin passed a law making camels illegal." "But you aren't camels." "No," said the rabbits, "but try telling that to the Gaypayoo."

Early in 1949 when California State Senator Jack B. Tenney introduced seventeen bills designed to combat subversive activities in his state, he included lawyers and doctors as well as teachers among those who were to be required to take a loyalty oath. The lawyers and doctors protested at once with a vigor that put an end to this nonsense as regarded their own professions. But a kind of palsy apparently overcame Robert Gordon Sproul, president of the nation's largest institution of higher learning; he was persuaded to suggest to the regents of the University of California that they require a loyalty oath of all members of the university's faculty in order to forestall the same requirement by the legislature. The board of regents complied with alacrity. It stipulated that all of the university's nine thousand employees should subscribe to an addition to the standard oath that had previously been taken by them along with all other public servants in the state. No member of the faculty had any objection to the long-honored oath of allegiance to the federal and state Constitutions: "I do solemnly swear that I will support the Constitution of the United States and the Constitution of the State of California, and that I will faithfully discharge the duties of my office according to the best of my ability." No Communist can subscribe to the aims of his party and at the same time conscientiously support the Constitution. But the regents insisted that these words should be added to the oath: ". . . and that I am not a member of the Communist Party or under any oath or a party to any agreement or under any commitment that is in conflict with my obligations under this oath."

It was an established policy at the University of California, endorsed by the faculty, that Communists should not be employed as teachers. Thus, presumably, all members of the faculty could have signed the oath without hesitation. Most of them did so. But a number of the university's most distinguished professors, many of them staunch conservatives and as vigorously anti-Communist as any member of the board of regents, accompanied their subscription to the oath with an assertion that they would resign if it should be enforced against employees unwilling to subscribe to it.

There lay behind this seemingly subtle distinction an issue of very great importance—whether the determination of teaching fitness should be made by the board of regents or by the university's professional personnel in accordance with the tradition of academic freedom. After bitter conflict and recrimination between the regents and a committee of the Academic Senate representing the faculty—President Sproul belatedly came over to the faculty side—it was agreed that the oath demanded by the regents should not be made an absolute condition of employment. Instead, the university's employees were required to sign a letter including the statement that "I am not a member of the Communist Party or any other organization which advocates the overthrow of the Government by force and violence." An employee unwilling to sign this statement could petition the president for a review of his case by a committee of the Academic Senate. This committee was to report to the president, who was in turn to report to the regents.

In July 1950 the Faculty Committee on Privilege and Tenure, supported by the president, recommended that six members of the faculty, one of them a full professor, be dismissed—they had refused to cooperate with the committee—but that forty others who had declined to sign the required statement be retained in their positions. The regents at first accepted this recommendation by a narrow vote of ten to nine, then at their next meeting in September reversed themselves and decided that all non-signers must forfeit their jobs. A few of the forty have since consented to sign; a few others resigned; eighteen have joined in taking the issue to the California courts, pleading that the stand of the regents involved a breach of contract and that the affidavit requirement violated the Constitution of California. The Academic Senate adopted an angry resolution condemning the regents for bad faith in dealing with the faculty and for "gross violation" of the university's tenure principles.

The effect of the conflict and of the partial victory of the regents upon the prestige of the University of California is not subject to easy assessment. It can scarcely be questioned, however, that the university's status as an exemplar of the tradition of academic freedom has been gravely injured. Some able members of its faculty have already resigned. Scholars at other institutions have been showing reluctance to accept invitations to teach at California; particularly among the most promising younger men, it is predictable that there will be a preference for appointments at institutions where political orthodoxy is not a condition of tenure. Jack H. Hildebrand, dean of the College of Chemistry and a member of the Academic Senate, said of the long controversy: "No conceivable damage to the university at the hands of the hypothetical Communists among us could have equaled the damage resulting from the unrest, ill-will, and suspicion engendered by this series of events."

There are good reasons why a faculty should be unwilling to admit a Communist into its fellowship. In the light of what we have learned during the last twenty years, anyone so emotionally unstable and lacking in judgment as to be willing to submit to the party's discipline would seem to lack the qualifications for university tenure. A university, like any other employer, is quite justified, therefore, in exercising care to avoid granting tenure to a Communist. The position that Communist Party membership of itself disqualifies an individual as a teacher seems perfectly valid with respect to recruitment. A different question arises, however, when this position is applied to a member of the faculty whose performance as a teacher has won him permanent status and whose discharge of his academic duties has been thoroughly satisfactory.

At this point we might consider the somewhat analogous situation that exists in the different treatment accorded under the law to aliens and naturalized citizens. Aliens seeking admission to the United States enjoy no legal rights; admission is a privilege to be granted or withheld at the sovereign's discretion. An alien may be excluded by administrative fiat without so much as a hearing or a specification of reasons—as the unhappy case of Ellen Knauff revealed in 1950. Once an alien has lawfully entered the country, however, certain procedural requirements protect him from arbitrary deportation; and once he has been admitted to full membership in the American society through naturalization, his citizenship can be revoked only after a full trial and proof acceptable to a court of law that it was acquired fraudulently.

The definition of academic freedom formulated by the American Association of University Professors and quoted above affords ample ground for the dismissal of any teacher whose affiliation with the Communist Party corrupts his teaching. If he uses his lecture platform as a propagandist or if he distorts his subject, he may be dismissed for incompetence. If he abuses his position as a member of the faculty by conducting himself intemperately and improperly outside the university, he may be dismissed for immorality or neglect of duty. These are judgments which should, of course, be made by his professional colleagues. But if he fulfills his classroom obligations competently and faithfully, confining his political views to lawful extra-curricular activities, the worst that can be said is that he is an embarrassment to the university in its public relations. If he keeps his party affiliation entirely to himself, avoiding political activity on and off the campus, then it is, and ought to remain, a private matter of no more concern to his colleagues than his religion. The practical question that presents itself, therefore, is whether it is wise, for the sake of ridding the university of an embarrassment, to imperil the principle of tenure so vital to academic freedom.

It can scarcely be doubted that dismissal of a teacher who has permanent status, who has performed his teaching duties satisfactorily, and who has not been guilty of any immoral conduct, impairs the principle of tenure in a very serious way. Membership in the Communist Party is foolish and indicative of disloyalty to the United States; but it is a folly and an expression of political opinion which must be allowed teachers to the same extent that it is allowed other members of the community—that is, so long as it takes lawful forms. A university can rationally tolerate this particular vagary in one of its teachers just as it can tolerate an individual teacher's belief in pacifism or in Ptolemaic astronomy or in the Biblical view of the origin of species, provided such opinions do not impair the quality of his teaching. The best colleges do put up with eccentricities on the part of men who have earned respect for their scholarship in a particular area; indeed, in a number of cases they put up with disappointing inadequacies on the part of teachers who failed to fulfill youthful promise. They do this for the sake of a principle which they recognize as more important than the occasional mistakes that seem to call its validity into question—the principle of tenure. Tenure has been so long fought for and so dearly won by teachers in the United States that it ought not to be sacrificed lightly.

Tenure does not, of course, give teachers any special immunity. Like all other citizens, they are subject to prosecution by the government if they violate any law. If mere membership in the Communist Party should be made criminal, or if, in case of war, Communist Party members should be interned as participants in a hostile conspiracy, Communist teachers would be dealt with like Communist lawyers, doctors, or factory workers. Tenure means only that so long as they remain within the law they shall not be deprived of their professional positions on account of their political beliefs and affiliations, whatever these may be. In the long run it is a great deal better for a university to run the risks involved in tolerating even odious errors of opinion than to run the risks involved in suppressing or punishing them.

The principle of academic tenure as applied to Communists was brought sharply into issue in cases which developed at the University of Washington in 1948. The university had been vaguely accused for a number of years of being a "hotbed of communism" and a "nest of Communist professors." In 1947 the legislature of Washington established a Joint Legislative Fact-Finding Committee on Un-American Activities under the chairmanship of State Senator Albert F. Canwell. The Canwell Committee undertook a study of alleged Communist activities on the University of Washington campus. In the course of its hearings ten members of the faculty who enjoyed tenure under university rules were named as being or having been members of the Communist Party. Two of the ten flatly denied any association with the party. Five admitted past membership but asserted that they had withdrawn. The three others refused to testify as to membership, past or present. It seems significant to note how few were involved when the roll of some seven hundred full-time faculty members was actually called in this university denounced as a "hotbed of communism." It seems probable that Communist Party members were more numerous on university faculties in the 1930s. But very few remain today.

Following the legislative hearings, the dean of the College of Arts and Sciences filed complaints with the University's Faculty Committee on Tenure and Academic Freedom against six members of the faculty—the three who had refused to testify and three of those who had admitted past membership. Tenure is defined in the administrative code of the University of Washington as "the right of a person to hold his position during good behavior and efficient and competent service, and not to be removed therefrom except for cause. . . ."

The faculty committee was unanimous in recommending retention of the three professors who acknowledged past membership in the party but denied that they any longer belonged to it. This recommendation was accepted by the board of regents, subject to the condition that the men file affidavits declaring that they "have not been members of the Communist Party since the respective dates cited in their testimony before the Faculty Tenure Committee" and that "they be placed on probation for two years."

The faculty committee divided respecting the remaining three. A majority argued that there was no basis under the administrative code of the University for removal of two of them, Professors Butterworth and Phillips. These men had told the faculty committee frankly that they had been members of the Communist Party since 1935, and that they continued to belong to it as a matter of conviction. Prior to the hearings, however, they had kept their party membership secret. Their general scholarship and teaching ability were not challenged. "It is impossible," said the report of the committee majority,

to conceive how the mere fact of membership in the Communist Party could, in any way, affect the competency of respondent Butterworth as a teacher of Old English Literature. As to respondent Phillips, there is potentially a greater question. As a teacher of philosophy, it might be suggested that, without specific proof, his objectivity as a teacher would necessarily be impaired by his strong bias in favor of a doctrinaire political philosophy. However, the testimony of his colleagues and students is directly to the contrary. Although he does have occasion to discuss Marxian philosophy in his teaching, it appears that his practice is to warn his students of his bias and to request that they evaluate his lectures in light of that fact.

A majority of the committee declined to find the accused men incompetent or guilty of neglect of duty. A minority of the committee dissented strongly from this position, holding that "active present membership in the Communist Party USA is an overt act of such reckless, uncritical and intemperate partisanship as to be inimical to, and incompatible with, the highest traditions of academic freedom and responsible scholarship, and that such active present membership should be declared sufficient grounds for dismissal of any faculty member so committed."

The remaining case, that of Ralph H. Gundlach, an associate professor in the Department of Psychology, presented a somewhat different problem. He had refused to testify before the legislative committee and indeed, in a conference with the president of the university prior to the legislative hearing, he had been evasive and equivocal as to whether or not he had ever joined the Communist Party. To the faculty committee, however, he stated definitely that he was not and never had been a party member, but accompanied this denial with so much evasiveness as to leave the committee with doubts about his veracity. The committee divided in its recommendations. A majority decided that "the simple fact of membership in the Communist Party does not subject the member to removal under the administrative code as presently constituted and interpreted." Four members felt, however, that Professor Gundlach's evasiveness to the president of the university constituted a substantial neglect of duty on his part, warranting dismissal. One committee member felt that dismissal was warranted on the ground of incompetence as well. Two members felt that his ambiguous relationship with the Communist Party constituted a ground for dismissal in itself. Four members concluded that the charges against Professor Gundlach did not warrant his removal from the faculty.

Dr. Raymond B. Allen, president of the university, transmitted the committee's report to the board of regents, together with a recommendation on his part that Professors Butterworth, Phillips, and Gundlach should be dismissed—a recommendation which the regents accepted. The effect of this was to break the principle of tenure by overriding the faculty judgment. The chief reason given by President Allen is one which has now become the most familiar and formidable argument against the retention of known Communists on the staff of a university. He stated the case in these words:

I would point out that the teacher and the scholar have special obligations with respect to the sincerity of their convictions which involve questions of intellectual honesty and integrity. Men in academic life—teachers, scholars, and scientists—are engaged in a vocation which is concerned with the finding of truth and its dissemination, with the pursuit of truth wherever it may lead. Is it possible for an individual, however sincere, to embrace both this unhampered pursuit of truth and, at the same time, the doctrines and dogmas of a political party which admits of no criticism of its fundamental principles and programs? Put in another way, a teacher may be ever so sincere in his belief in communism, but can he at the same time be a sincere seeker after truth, which is the first obligation and duty of the teacher? My answer to these questions is, "He cannot." Therefore, I believe these men, by reason of their admitted membership in the Communist Party described in the above findings, to be incompetent, intellectually dishonest, and derelict in their duty to find and teach the truth.

The gist of this argument, which has been stated in various forms by other able and sincere academic leaders, is that Communists do not deserve the privileges of freedom because they are not themselves free men. It is a persuasive but dangerous argument. No one is compelled to become a Communist; and it is clear from the great number of ex-Communists that one may leave the party at will—that is, whenever one ceases to subscribe to its doctrines. Membership in the party must be presumed, therefore, to be as much a free choice, however benighted, as any other affiliation. For a university to preclude this choice—or to punish a professor for making it—is to set an arbitrary limit upon freedom. If it be acknowledged that a university may properly preclude this choice, then it will become easy to justify the precluding of other choices. Freedom necessarily includes the right to be wrong.

Communists, it is true, embrace "the dogmas of a political party which admits of no criticism of its fundamental principles and programs." It cannot be presumed, however, that all Communists embrace equally all dogmas promulgated from Moscow. To the extent that they do embrace them, their minds are captive. But few men are altogether free; most of us are prisoners in some degree of our prejudices, anxieties, obsessions, and loyalties. Communists are rigid doctrinarians. But so are many men strongly convinced of ideas to which most of the rest of mankind does not adhere. Every strong conviction precludes its opposite. And every conviction that runs counter to prevailing opinion is liable to be looked upon as evidence of intellectual enslavement. Anti-communism is in danger of becoming as doctrinaire as communism—and of embracing its root evil, intolerance. To deny men freedom in any form on the pretext that they themselves are not free is to put freedom into the strait jacket of orthodoxy.

The question is not whether Communists are desirable teachers; they are not. The real question is whether, as a practical matter, universities should involve themselves in the investigation of political belief and breach the principle of academic tenure by ousting Communists as such—that is, solely on account of adherence to the party in the absence of any unlawful conduct, specific dereliction of duty, or evidence of incompetence. It is safer to test teachers on the basis of their performance in their jobs than on the basis of private beliefs which may be thought to enslave their minds. Professor Butterworth, retained in his position as a teacher of Old English Literature, could have injured the University of Washington no more than Professor Münsterberg injured Harvard in 1918; but Professor Butterworth, dismissed on account of adherence to obnoxious political dogmas, leaves the tenure of all his former colleagues in jeopardy. In a university, if nowhere else, Jefferson's ideal ought to be respected; for the toleration of error is an inescapable condition of the pursuit of truth.

Academic freedom is threatened even more seriously by random harassment than by the formal restraints designed to keep Communist teachers out of the schools. The Americanists aim to smother, rather than to expose and rebut, ideas they consider dangerous. The effect of their zeal is the effect of blackmail. Over every teacher's head they hold the threat of denunciation. The threat serves effectively to keep the teachers in line, to curb their work in the classroom and to silence them outside it.

The threat affects many who are admittedly not Communists but who are disposed to support some program or movement which is called communistic or which has the backing of the Communist Party. Especially in some of the smaller American colleges, a number of teachers have been disciplined and even dismissed for mere affiliation with unpopular minority groups. George F. Parker, assistant professor of religion and philosophy at Evansville College, Evansville, Indiana, was dismissed from the faculty in 1948 because he served as chairman of the Vanderburgh County Citizens for Wallace Committee and presided at a Wallace for President meeting held in Evansville. The Committee on Academic Freedom and Tenure of the American Association of University Professors investigated the case exhaustively and came to the conclusion that Professor Parker's dismissal "resulted . . . from the exercise, off the campus, of political functions which are the privilege and duty of citizens in general."

Teachers have as much right as any other member of the community to take an active, responsible part in public life. Indeed, they have a special obligation to do so. The community which has enabled them to carry on research and study is entitled to expect of them in return honest criticism and illumination of issues about which they are informed. But it is precisely in this area that the fear of ignorant, bigoted "investigation," the fear of McCarthyism, operates most repressively to thwart their performance of essential functions.

Professor Owen Lattimore of Johns Hopkins University has spent a lifetime in the study of the Far East. He has lectured and written extensively about that area, presenting strong views on American policy respecting it. These views, openly offered for criticism, deserve such weight as the knowledge and reasoning behind them may seem to warrant. Senator McCarthy's attack on Dr. Lattimore early in 1950 was, however, strictly *ad hominem*. Taking advantage of the immunity from legal redress afforded him by the United States Senate, the Senator called Dr. Lattimore at various times "the top Russian espionage agent in the United States," "one of the top Communist agents in this country," the "chief architect" of American Far Eastern policy, and finally, if somewhat anticlimactically, "a bad policy risk" for employment in the State Department—where, of course, he was never employed. Not even the ex-Communist and the ex-FBI undercover agents called by Senator McCarthy as witnesses presented any corroboration of these charges; on the other hand, virtually every American scholar and writer who enjoyed a reputation as an authority on the Far East submitted letters or affidavits testifying to Dr. Lattimore's scholarship and integrity.

In the second of his courageous appearances before the Foreign Relations subcommittee investigating the McCarthy charges, Dr. Lattimore pointed out the implications of the assault on his character for the academic profession in general:

Gentlemen, you cannot, you must not, permit a psychology of fear to paralyze the scholars and writers of this nation. In a remarkable letter to me, the great Professor Zechariah Chafee of Harvard—an expert on this sort of suppression of freedom—speaks of this McCarthy attack as a "barbarian invasion." It is just that; and it is at least as un-American as the evil to which it is so ineptly addressed.

The danger of suppressing freedom of scholarship and opinion is, of course, not merely a threat to the scholars. It is a direct and immediate danger to the national interest. Attacks of this sort which have the effect of intimidating scholars and researchers are bound to affect the quality of their work, to circumscribe their sources of information, and to inhibit the freedom with which they state their facts and conclusions.

Dr. Lattimore's ordeal was, of course, only the most spectacular instance of legislative punishment of teachers for expressing their opinions. Professor Melvin Rader of the University of Washington, to cite one more example, had a narrow escape from lynching at the hands of the Canwell Committee because it disapproved of his opinions and of some of the organizations he had joined. The committee did not scruple to use what was later shown to be perjured evidence in Professor Rader's case and even to withhold documentary material in its possession indicating that he was innocent of the principal allegations made against him.

Professor Rader was accused by a former Communist and FBI informer named George Hewitt of having attended a secret Communist school in New York during the summer of 1938. Hewitt testified before the Canwell Committee under oath that he, personally, had been Rader's instructor in the school. Some patient work by Rader and by a reporter for the *Seattle Times,* Ed Guthman, who was awarded a Pulitzer Prize in 1950 for his series of articles on the case, uncovered conclusive evidence that the professor had taught at the University of Washington's summer session until July 20, 1938, and had spent the month of August at Canyon Creek Lodge, a resort in the northern part of the State of Washington. A subsequent investigation by the Attorney General of Washington confirmed the validity of this evidence and resulted in a report which declared: "The only reasonable conclusion that can be reached . . . is that George Hewitt did not tell the truth."

In what is perhaps a unique case of its kind, the informer rather than his victim was indicted for perjury. But Hewitt fled to New York; and when the State of Washington sought to extradite him for prosecution, the Canwell Committee persuaded a New York judge to set him free by giving testimony which, according to the Attorney General of Washington, "was an obvious distortion, whether by mistake, inadvertence, or otherwise." Hewitt had been used as a government witness in previous prosecutions and derived such status as he enjoyed from this fact alone. There is no way to reckon how many men were punished unjustly as a consequence of his babblings.

Professor Rader was vindicated and retained his position on the faculty. His experience could scarcely have failed, however, to raise in the minds of other teachers precisely the kind of apprehension the Canwell Committee desired it to raise. Academic freedom can be destroyed by political intimidation of the colleges as well as by frontal assault.

The University of Chicago faced a similar sort of political pressure in 1949 through an investigation by the Subversive Activities Commission of the Illinois legislature, popularly known as the Broyles Commission. The fear of communism on the campus seems to have stemmed in this instance as much from student activities as from alleged "Communist front" associations of members of the faculty. University students had demonstrated, apparently in a somewhat indecorous fashion, against certain bills introduced in the state legislature by the chairman of the Subversive Activities Commission, Senator Paul Broyles himself. Chancellor Robert Maynard Hutchins of the University of Chicago appeared before the commission and told it uncompromisingly that "the policy of the University is to admit law-abiding students who have the qualifications to do the University's work. It would not be in the public interest to exclude students of communistic leanings. If we did, how would they ever learn better?" Then he went on to give the Broyles Commission an elementary lecture on the nature of the educative process:

The policy of repression of ideas cannot work and never has worked. The alternative to it is the long, difficult road of education. To this the American people have been committed. It requires patience and tolerance, even in the face of intense provocation. It requires faith in the principles and practices of democracy, faith that when the citizen understands all forms of government he will prefer democracy and that he will be a better citizen if he is convinced than he would be if he were coerced.[5]

Wherever university officials have, like Chancellor Hutchins, courageously and toughly resisted political encroachment on their domain, they have managed thus far to preserve academic freedom in the United States. Harvard University dealt with the threat to academic freedom through the publication of a notable exchange of letters among President James B. Conant, Grenville Clark, senior member of the Harvard Corporation, and Frank B. Ober, a member of the Maryland State legislature and an alumnus of the Harvard Law School. Mr. Ober initiated the correspondence with a letter to President Conant explaining why he had decided not to subscribe to the Harvard Law School Fund. His decision was based, he said, on "the apparent attitude of Harvard toward extra-curricular activities of professors giving aid and comfort to Communism." He objected specifically to an appeal made by an assistant professor of English, John Ciardi, at a rally of the Progressive Party in Maryland to raise funds to fight anti-Communist laws sponsored by a Maryland legislative commission of which Mr. Ober himself was chairman; he objected also to the participation of Professor Harlow Shapley, director of the Harvard Observatory, in the Cultural and Scientific Conference for World Peace, held in New York in 1949 and widely considered to be under Communist auspices. "The test of a professor's actions," wrote Mr. Ober, "ought not to be whether he can be actually proved guilty of a crime. Reasonable grounds to doubt his loyalty to our government should disqualify him, for the position is one of trust, and the government has, if it chooses to exercise it, regulatory power over education."

Dr. Conant referred the Ober letter to Mr. Clark, asking him to reply to it, and Mr. Clark did so, in part as follows:

5 Robert Maynard Hutchins, "Statement to the Subversive Activities Commission of the Illinois State Legislature, 1949," quoted in *Primer of Intellectual Freedom,* edited by Howard Mumford Jones (Cambridge: Harvard University Press, 1949).

I cannot help wondering whether you have thought through the implications of what you propose.

Since you wish to discipline professors for taking active part in meetings such as those at which Professors Ciardi and Shapley spoke, would it not be fair to pass in advance on the kind of meetings professors could safely attend? Would this not call for a university licensing board? And would not such a board have an obnoxious and virtually impossible task? . . .

Moreover, I think you will agree that there would be little sense in censoring attendance at meetings and leaving free from censorship speeches on the radio or writings in the press, magazines, pamphlets, and books. Would not your proposals call for a censorship of all these? . . .

Beyond that, however, how could an effective "closer watch" on "extra-curricular activities" be maintained unless the watch extended to conversations and correspondence? And how could that be done without a system of student and other informers—the classic and necessary method of watching for "subversive" utterances? . . .

What I have just said applies to the professors. But how about the students? Would it be sensible to have the teachers censored and watched while the students remain at liberty freely to speak and write and to attend such meetings as they choose, subject only to the laws of the land? On your philosophy are you not driven on to restrict, censor, and discipline the students also?

What sort of a place would Harvard be if it went down this road? It would, I think, not require six months to destroy the morale of both our teachers and students, and thereby our usefulness to the country. I think one need do no more than state the necessary implications of what you ask to demonstrate that nothing could be more alien to the principle of free expression that Harvard stands for.

Yet this is precisely the road down which the Americanists, whether they are aware of the destination or not, want to take American education. They want conformity, although they label it patriotism. And they will have their way, as their counterparts had it in Germany and Italy before the war and have it today behind the iron curtain, unless the academic profession closes ranks, recognizes the peril to its independence, and fights resolutely for its dignity and its inheritance.

The situation in public elementary and high schools may be said to differ somewhat from that in colleges and universities. A Communist teacher may exert a more baleful influence at the grade-school level; and any attempt to indoctrinate young pupils with alien propaganda—or any propaganda at all—should be strictly prohibited and vigorously counteracted. But tenure is important in the grade schools too. If teachers do their teaching competently—which means without propagandizing—it is safer to allow them political as well as religious vagaries than to undertake the dangerous course of judging them on the basis of imputed political beliefs. The excesses into which the latter undertaking inevitably leads are illustrated by the system of surveillance set up in the New York City public schools. There, school principals are required to report on the loyalty of the teachers under them, assistant superintendents on the loyalty of principals, and so on up to the apex of the city's Board of Education. The impact of such an arrangement on the morale of teachers, the atmosphere of general distrust bred by it, the possibilities of unjust accusations grounded in ignorance, bigotry, or malice, outweigh the danger that a few teachers may abuse the positions of trust they hold. It is surely preferable to confine punishment to actual, provable instances of abuse.

The "serious and systematic attack" to which, as General Eisenhower observed, scholarly inquiry and expression are now being subjected in many lands exists here too. It is the age-old attack of intolerance upon learning. If the freedom of the human mind is really, as Jefferson considered it, illimitable, we had better resist all attempts to limit it. If we really mean to follow truth wherever it may lead, we had better tolerate error so long as reason is left free to combat it.

CHAPTER X

THE UTILITY OF FREEDOM

Liberty is to faction what air is to fire, an aliment without which it instantly expires. But it could not be less folly to abolish liberty, which is essential to political life, because it nourishes faction, than it would be to wish the annihilation of air, which is essential to animal life, because it imparts to fire its destructive agency.[1]

INDIVIDUAL freedom, as the term has been used in this book, presupposes a tolerance of ideas which are thought to be mistaken, disloyal, and even dangerous. Tolerance of opinions which are thought to be innocuous is as easy as acts of charity that entail no sacrifice. But the test of a free society is its tolerance of what is deplored or despised by a majority of its members. The argument for such tolerance must be made on the ground that it is useful to the society.

The proposition to be proved, in short, is that free societies are better fitted to survive than closed societies. This is a proposition peculiarly relevant to the present struggle between the United States and the Soviet Union. Here the struggle is between a nation committed to the idea of individual freedom, and therefore to the principle of tolerance, and another nation which, in effect, denies the significance of the individual personality and the value of freedom.

Tolerance of diversity of opinion gives rise, undoubtedly, to

[1] James Madison, in the tenth essay of *The Federalist*.

what Madison called the spirit of faction. As long as men are permitted to express diverse opinions they will do so. As long as they are permitted to join in voluntary associations for the advancement of purposes they hold in common, there will be jostling for group advantage, pressure for special interests. Such conflicts are in greater or less degree disruptive. The resolution of them is the business of the democratic process. It is a process that has worked effectively for the American people in the past and can be counted upon to work in the future, so long as there is general acceptance of certain fundamental values and an underlying mutual trust among members of the society.

It is true that opinions challenging fundamental values and corroding mutual trust present a threat to social stability. To tolerate an organization like the Communist Party, which operates outside the democratic process and would destroy that process if it ever came to power, is to tolerate what must seem a seed of destruction. Similarly, to countenance the nihilism of a Senator McCarthy is to countenance methods that ignore standards of decency and poison the springs of confidence. Undoubtedly national unity—and therefore national security—suffers from such attacks on either side. But, paradoxically, loyalty in a free society depends upon the toleration of disloyalty. The loyalty of free men must be freely given—which is to say, that those who give it must be genuinely free to withhold it. Nothing is more fundamental to freedom than that this choice be a real one. The premise on which every free society rests, the American society more explicitly than any other, is that only through such freedom can loyalty be evoked and counted on to endure.

Moreover, to forbid disloyalty is to let it triumph. At bottom, the Communists and the Americanists are frighteningly similar: they are believers in the suppression and punishment of dissent. That they would suppress and punish different sorts of opinion is less significant than that, alike, they would suppress and punish. At bottom, they are alike also in being sick men: they are men who would relish a chance to use whip and club. It is necessary, therefore, to keep whips and clubs out of their hands—that is, to enforce the laws forbidding acts of violence, whether by them or against them. It is, however, equally necessary to enforce the laws which guarantee them the right to speak as they please. To suppress and punish their opinions is to embrace their opinions; it is to practice what they preach; and the end of that practice is the destruction of all diversity.

If tolerance of diversity involves an admitted element of risk to national unity, intolerance involves a certainty that unity will be destroyed. Unity does not grow out of uniformity; it grows out of resolved conflict. "Like the course of the heavenly bodies," Mr. Justice Brandeis once observed, "harmony in national life is a resultant of the struggle between contending forces. In frank expression of conflicting opinion lies the greatest promise of wisdom in governmental action; and in suppression lies ordinarily the greatest peril." [2]

While speech can be silenced by authority, and silence may give the appearance of assent, thought cannot be wholly controlled by any instrument of suppression yet devised. Thought that is silenced is always rebellious. It can be won to an acceptance of contrary opinion only if it has been accorded a chance to be heard and assured of a future chance to win acceptance for itself. Majorities, of course, are often mistaken. This is why the silencing of minorities is necessarily dangerous. Criticism and dissent are the indispensable antidote to majority delusions. Afforded free expression, they serve as the self-regulating mechanism of a democratic community.

There is a persistent and prevalent myth that totalitarian societies are somehow more efficient than free societies. A dictatorship can move more swiftly, it is true, than a government which depends upon the voluntary consent of the governed. This is merely to say that the policies of irresponsible leaders are more speedily translated into action—which may be disastrously mistaken—than the policies of democratic leaders. Leadership is as necessary in a democratic as in a totalitarian state; and when leader-

[2] *Gilbert* v. *Minnesota*, 254 U.S. 325 (1920).

ship is lacking or inept or misguided, the consequences may be very costly. But free men have a means of correcting mistakes by a change of leadership. The incorrigible defect of dictatorship lies in the absence of any remedy for error on the part of the dictator.

This defect was revealed in numerous ways in the course of the war. For all its vaunted efficiency in the techniques of total war, Germany never fully mobilized its resources or its people. There was nothing like the all-out effort of Britain. Neither the industrial capacity nor the manpower of the country was ever wholly integrated. Unnecessary consumer goods were produced in plants that might have been converted to war production; the luxury of domestic servants was widely enjoyed throughout the war, especially by Nazi Party officials. The United States Strategic Bombing Survey, which conducted an intensive study in 1945 of the impact of the air war on the German economy and German morale, made these significant findings:

... Measured by the standards of other belligerents, there was no "total mobilization" and no long-term planning to bring the war effort to its attainable maximum. The production of civilian goods was only restricted to a moderate extent; there was no further mobilization of women and no great transfer of labor from the nonessential to the essential industries. Even in the face of reverses, the German leaders were still hypnotized by their belief in their own infallibility. . . . German armament industries with few exceptions worked only single shifts throughout the war, and the great capacity reserve that would have been available from double- or triple-shift operations was never completely utilized. . . . While Britain, in the course of the war, increased the proportion of women in whole- or part-time work (outside agriculture) from 40 to 56 per cent, the number of German women mobilized remained practically unchanged throughout the war. The number of German women in domestic service fell only slightly—from 1.5 to 1.3 millions between May 1939 and May 1944. In Britain, over the same period, the number of domestic servants was cut from 1.2 to 0.5 million. . . . Whether mobilization of women, movement of labor into the war industries, or the length of the working week be taken as the test, it is clear that Germany did not mobilize its labor force as fully as she might have, not even after the much advertised manpower drives in 1943 and in the summer of 1944.

These fatal inefficiencies in German mobilization grew directly out of the nature of totalitarian rule. There was no one to tell the Führer that the war effort was not being administered satisfactorily. To have questioned his wisdom would have been tantamount to treason. The mistakes therefore went uncorrected and in the end proved disastrous to the German people. The Strategic Bombing Survey reached the conclusion that these mistakes were rooted in a fundamental miscalculation about the strength of the nations ranged against Germany:

. . . The conclusion is inescapable that Germany's war production was not limited by its war potential—by the resources at its disposal—but by demand; in other words, by the notions of the German war leaders of what was required to win. The Germans did not plan, nor were they prepared for, a long war. . . . After the occupation of France, England, though not invaded or brought to heel through aerial bombardment, was no longer considered an immediate threat. Possible intervention by the United States was not taken seriously. The attack on Russia was started in the confident expectation that the experience of the earlier campaigns was to be repeated; Russia was to be completely subjugated in three to four months.

Faulty intelligence produced faulty planning all along the line in Germany. The belief that victory could be achieved quickly and cheaply produced an emphasis, in the composition of the German air force, on fighters and bombers of a type suitable to close cooperation with ground armies; Germany lacked, in consequence, the long-range bombers necessary to win the Battle of Britain. The development of jet planes, in which German technicians pioneered, was "much hindered," according to the Strategic Bombing Survey, "by Hitler's insistence that the aircraft be used as a fighter bomber." The assumption that Britain and the United States could mount only a limited air attack—"Allied production figures were disbelieved"—resulted in totally inadequate civilian-defense precautions. And when the mass air raids struck

Germany, their psychological impact was compounded by Nazi propaganda which had stressed the infallibility of the Führer. A government based on coerced consent and the suppression of diversity lacked the capacity of a government based on voluntary consent to call for all-out effort and sacrifice on the part of the governed. It could command no comparable loyalty. It could achieve no comparable unity. It possessed no resiliency in disaster, comparable to that of the British after Dunkerque or the Americans after Pearl Harbor, to correct errors and restore confidence.

The validity of what has been said here is not lessened by the fact that totalitarian Russia was among the victors and democratic France among the vanquished in the war. The Soviet dictator demanded, and received, heroic sacrifices from the Russian people; no nation waged war so totally. Russia mobilized tremendous strength, although wastefully in many respects; and her soldiers and civilians alike stood with magnificent fortitude at Stalingrad and Moscow, rallying after losses that, to the world outside, seemed catastrophic. But this qualification should be noted: the Russians were invaded, and by an enemy so stupidly ruthless as to leave them no alternative to resistance save extermination; even so, great numbers in the Ukraine and elsewhere showed themselves willing to join the Germans in fighting against their own government. In the vast unconquered land mass of the Soviet Union, however, the Nazi attack solidified devotion to leaders whom the people had no choice but to follow; and no doubt this attack from the outside forged a loyalty, beyond anything the Communist propagandists had been able to create, to a political system which with all its faults was their own.

France collapsed for a variety of reasons, perhaps the most fundamental of which was that she lacked in the 1930s the acceptance of common values and the underlying mutual trust which have been suggested as prerequisites to the working of the democratic process. The French people were united only in devotion to France as a geographical entity. They were rent by a political factionalism that went beyond mere rivalry for public office or mere conflict as to policy; the Cagoulards and the Croix de Feu and the Monarchists and the Catholics and the Socialists and the Communists reflected deep cleavages respecting the nature of French society and the role of the State. There was no agreement among them as to first principles; agreement had to be forged, at last, through the anguish of defeat and regeneration. There is a profound warning for Americans in the French experience.

It has not been intended to suggest here that free societies are necessarily and invariably stronger than totalitarian societies. The point is simply that freedom is a source of strength if it is used wisely. It cannot provide a guarantee against ruinous mistakes; but it can provide a means of correcting mistakes, a means denied to those who live in a society where dissent is silenced.

There were many blunders, of course, in both British and American planning of the war effort. They were subject, however, to unremitting and caustic criticism. Gradually, as a result, they were overcome. The harnessing of American industry was begun under the National Defense Advisory Council; when that agency proved unsatisfactory, it was replaced by the Office of Production Management, which in turn gave way to the Supply Priorities and Allocation Board. The bludgeoning of critics, who, in Germany, would have been considered traitors, forced this to yield at last to the War Production Board, which measured up to the gigantic job pretty well. The process commonly called "trial and error" is peculiarly democratic; it can work successfully only where opposition parties and the press and individuals are free to expose error, and where trial is always open to protest. Criticism is liable to seem captious or crackpot or disloyal to those in authority, and often, no doubt, they are quite right about it; but it is an invaluable goad and tonic all the same. For all its excesses and inconveniences, societies that tolerate criticism unconditionally tend to be stronger and more stable than those that do not.

The contrast between the German and American experiences in the development of atomic energy affords perhaps the most dramatic illustration of the pragmatic uses of tolerance. Some of the most brilliant German scientists, driven from their homeland because they were Jewish or because they were politically unorthodox, found asylum in the United States and in Britain and made important contributions to our primacy in perfecting an atomic bomb. German science, once pre-eminent, was crippled even more by the tendency to entrust authority over research to politically "reliable" scientists—to scientists who were more political than scientific. Doctrinaire insistence on Nazi fetishes of race supremacy accelerated the deterioration. The outcome, in strictly practical terms, was to impair German national security.

A similar process seems to be taking place today in the Soviet Union. In a number of fields, science is being cramped by orthodoxy. There is no reason to think that purges will promote efficiency there any more than they did in Germany. Moreover, the Russians, like the Germans, appear to be victims of their own doctrinaire assumptions. It is a part of Russian doctrine—as it was so mistakenly a part of German doctrine a decade ago—that the United States is hopelessly divided and decadent. No one who reports on conditions in this country dares, therefore, to call the doctrine into question. Intelligence is bound to be faulty when the bearer of bad tidings fears that he will fall into disfavor; and faulty intelligence is likely to produce mistaken policy.

There is a lesson for us in this too. We are in danger of allowing prejudice to distort our estimates of Soviet strength—as we did in 1941 when our military experts took it for granted that the Wehrmacht would destroy the Red Army in a matter of weeks. If we allow men like Owen Lattimore and John Service to be slurred and silenced because they say what we do not wish to hear, we shall end by formulating policy on the basis of fancies instead of facts. Nothing could be more perilous to national security. There is no sense in emulating the errors of our enemies.

Democracies may unconsciously embrace their own peculiar form of totalitarianism through extra-legal pressures for conformity. If their members all talk alike and think alike, they run the serious risk of being plunged alike into disaster. The Gadarene swine had their own species of democracy when they rushed down the hillside together into the sea—acting with perfect unanimity, all agreeing, none contradicting.

From the point of view of national security, tolerance of diversity has proved itself to be a powerful asset. It has been the real "secret" of American strength. It has welded the diverse elements of the American people into a union in the genuine sense of the term; and, more than any other single factor, it has kept that union invulnerable to outside attack. The whole of the American experience refutes the notion that tolerance is a luxury to be enjoyed only in untroubled times. It is the genius of American growth. It is needed most, and most urgently, precisely in times like the present when the nation is subject to extraordinary stress. It may well be that for a long time to come we shall find ourselves ranged against the Soviet Union in a conflict of endurance which is not war in the conventional sense but which involves, nevertheless, a test of the survival value of the two societies. Those who hold that time is against us and therefore urge an immediate attack on Russia—preventive war is the phrase in fashion—betray a loss of faith in our own institutions. The American society—if it remains free—possesses a greater capacity for growth, a greater resourcefulness in meeting new problems and changing situations, than any closed society. Time is not against us; it is on our side. In the long run, the free have triumphed over the enslaved. We shall grow in strength as we exploit our freedom.

The principal purpose of this book has been to show that tolerance of diversity is now being vitiated in ways dangerous to national security. Fear—and a diminution of faith in our own institutions—has led us into a condition of panic threatening self-destruction. The condition is depicted in Shelley's terrifying image:

> 'Tis we who, lost in stormy visions, keep
> With phantoms an unprofitable strife,
> And in mad trance strike with the spirit's knife
> Invulnerable nothings. . . .

Certainly there are real dangers to be faced. Espionage and sabotage are not imaginary threats to national security. They need to be countered by careful, realistic screening of government personnel, by systematic controls over classified communications and data, by watchful police or military protection of all vital installations. There are disloyal men, especially among the Communists. But to see disloyalty everywhere, to suppose that the Communist Party in the United States is a powerful octopus with tentacles reaching into every avenue of American life, is to strike at invulnerable nothings. Communist propaganda is undoubtedly aimed at the subversion of American values. But the antidote is not repression: it is free and unlimited discussion.

Let us face the real dangers with the techniques of freedom. These techniques have kept us safe and made us strong. To forsake them now is to forsake the most vital element of national defense.

The discussion of freedom in this book has been in utilitarian terms—in terms of its value for the security of the United States. But there is no disposition here to ignore its significance from the point of view of the individual. If, as we profess to believe in the United States, the nation exists only as an instrument to promote the welfare of its citizens, tolerance of diversity is imperative, because without it, without the personal liberty and individualism that flow from it, life would lose its savor. Progress in the arts, in the sciences, in the patterns of social adjustment springs from diversity and depends upon a tolerance of individual deviations from conventional ways and attitudes. The totalitarian society is not only less efficient than the free society in terms of its own survival; it is also stultifying and degrading to the human beings who live in it. Freedom gives a release to the human spirit, provides the indispensable condition for the realization of its limitless potentialities.

Individual freedom is, then, a means, an invaluable means, toward national security and survival. But it is an end as well—the supreme end which the government of the United States was instituted to secure. Faith in freedom as a means and as an end must be the ultimate touchstone of American loyalty, of the loyalty of all free men.

INDEX

INDEX

243

Date Due